MAXINE

MAXINE

BY

DIANA FORBES-ROBERTSON

Illustrated

HAMISH HAMILTON
LONDON

First published in Great Britain, 1964
by Hamish Hamilton Ltd
90 Great Russell Street London WC1

Copyright © 1964 by Diana Forbes-Robertson

Acknowledgement is made to the following sources which supplied background material and from which, in some instances, brief passages are quoted:

Beerbohm, Max. "Nat Goodwin—and Another" from *The Listener* (published by The British Broadcasting Corporation).

Eaton, Cyrus. *A History of Thomaston, South Thomaston and Rockland* (Hallowell: Masters, Smith and Co., 1865).

Forbes-Robertson, Johnston. *A Player under Three Reigns* (London: Fisher Unwin 1925).

Goodwin, Nat C. *Nat Goodwin's Book* (Boston: Richard G. Badger, The Gorham Press, 1914).

Moses, Montrose J., and Gerson, Virginia. *Clyde Fitch and His Letters* (Boston: Little, Brown and Co., 1924).

Myers, A. Wallis. *Captain Anthony Wilding* (London: Hodder and Stoughton, 1916).

Printed in Great Britain
by Ebenezer Baylis and Son, Limited
The Trinity Press, Worcester, and London

ACKNOWLEDGEMENTS

IT WOULD be impossible to list everyone who has helped in the preparation of this book. I can say that almost anyone mentioned in the text has had a friend or relative with whom I have talked, and if alive has talked to me personally.

My family has enthusiastically given me access to all papers still in our possession. In particular I would like to mention the usefulness of the diaries kept by my sister Blossom (Mrs. F. G. Miles). In Rockland I was helped by the family Bible and many pictures in the possession of my cousin Bob Brewer; by the diary of Captain Hiram Hall II in possession of a remoter cousin, Snow Hall; and by the diary of my great-uncle Fred J. Hall, in possession of his grandson and my cousin, David Keating of Walnut Creek, California. Letters have been lent me from many kind correspondents—many of them strangers—and I had numerous ones of my own.

I would like to acknowledge my gratitude to the whole town of Rockland, Maine. Many of the friends and relatives who helped me there are mentioned in the text of Chapter 2: I owe an equal debt to those who are not mentioned, but feel I must give my special thanks to Sydney Cullen, editor of the Rockland *Courier-Gazette*, who allowed me to study the back copies of the newspaper; Mrs. Doris M. Scarlott of the Public Library; Eaton Simmons for his invaluable map of old Rockland; and also my friends Mrs. Arthur Lamb, and Woodbury Snow, who patiently gave me hours of their time.

Without the help of the museums and libraries and drama departments in universities the book could not have been written at all. My debt of gratitude to George Freedley of the Theatre Collection of the New York Public Library, and to his whole staff, cannot be measured. I would also like to acknowledge especially, among all the other kind experts who helped me, the assistance of Miss Helen D. Willard of the

Theatre Collection, Houghton Library, Harvard; Mrs. Henry McAneny of the William Seymour Collection, Princeton; Mrs. Dorothy Crawford of the Jack Crawford Collection; Miss May Davenport Seymour and Sam Pearce of the Museum of the City of New York; James de T. Abajian of the California Historical Society; Mrs. Helen H. Brentnor of Bancroft Library of the University of California, Berkeley; Robert Applebee of the Searsport (Maine) Maritime Museum; Karl Kortum of the San Francisco Maritime Museum; Herschel Bricker of the Drama Department, University of Maine; Pat Quinby, Drama Department of Bowdoin College; and, in London, Raymond Mander and Joe Mitchenson, and Mrs. Joan Saunders of the Writers and Speakers Research Bureau.

I would like to give special thanks to Kathleen, Countess of Drogheda, for allowing me to see the diary she kept on the barge *Julia*, and to Miss Phyllis Wilbourn for the use of Constance Collier's unpublished papers.

Friends on newspapers have helped greatly, notably Howard Cail of the Portland (Maine) *Express Herald*, Mrs. Millie Robbins of the San Francisco *Chronicle*, and Leonard Verbarg of the Oakland *Tribune*.

I have benefited by the magnificent expert help of Samuel Stark of San Francisco, who has checked all names, theatres, and dates from his own knowledge and his great theatre collection, now donated to Stanford University, and who helped to compile the index.

I bow down in wonder at the faultless memory of Johnson Briscoe, who cannot be defeated by a theatrical fact and whose initial gift to me of cast lists and tour itineraries made it possible to begin the book.

In all the worlds in which Maxine Elliott moved I have found people ready to help, and the period of research has been made a joy by kindnesses encountered and friendships made.

Finally I would like to thank Marshall Best of The Viking Press, who has nursed me through from start to finish; Edwin Kennebeck, also of Viking, who patiently struggled through the final stages; and Hamish Hamilton.

D.F.-R.

CONTENTS

TO
HAROLD K. GUINZBURG

ILLUSTRATIONS

1

THE LEGEND

MAXINE ELLIOTT—the name had mystery, and a strange, foreign sound, but it was pleasing, too. I noted it and tried it, and the grown-ups round me went on talking about how beautiful she was. This seemed entirely suitable, and I decided she must be a princess, and I would like to meet her. I was staying at the time in Hartsbourne Manor, the house of my Auntie Dettie outside London, and tea always went on a long time, under the trees, and everyone talked and talked, but it was rude to go away.

I don't remember who revealed to me that Maxine Elliott was the name of Auntie Dettie herself. When I found out, I lost interest. She was quite nice, on the whole, and seemed to find me funny, which was usually flattering but sometimes embarrassing; but for me the romance had gone from the name because she was simply an aunt, a grown-up, and not beautiful at all. My mother was beautiful, and my sister Blossom, but nobody else was.

The impact of her personality hit me at another time as I sat at the same tea table, under the same tree, trying not to fidget. I was beside my mother on a broad hammock seat. Everyone was talking as usual, and this time I wasn't even listening. Mother's big white garden hat was on the grass at my feet, and I picked it up and tried it on. Nobody noticed. I turned to look at Mother sitting beside me. She was leaning forward, laughing a little, black-haired and beautiful and dressed in a white tennis dress with my favourite 'wasp' over it—a black and yellow striped jacket. Suddenly I decided I would put the hat on Mother's head, and did so firmly with both hands. She gave a little scream and pulled away and tossed the hat on to the other side of the hammock seat, anxiously patting her hair, and as she did so she shot a look that frightened me toward where Auntie Dettie was sitting near the silver teapot. I had no idea what it meant. Mother laughed nervously and, seeing my scared face, patted me and said it was all right. I sat in dumb agony. And the agony persisted; it came over me sometimes in bed at night when I'd remember and suddenly throw myself over on the pillow and mutter into it, 'Oh, I wish I hadn't done it, I wish I hadn't done it.'

What on earth was all this drama about?

As I have slowly put Auntie Dettie and Maxine Elliott into one person—the older sister of my mother—I believe what I felt at that moment was the power she held over Mother. If Mother was afraid, I was too. Hers was the fear of the little sister who always tried to please, who looked upon Maxine Elliott as both father and mother. Little May Gertrude's done something silly again, she's got her hair all mussed; her gloriously beautiful sister with the great, dark, brooding eyes—a figure of male authority—would be angry. Or the woman in Maxine—a young, petulant woman who cried easily over trifles and stamped her foot—would be upset. Gertrude had been doing so well, sitting there among the titled people who were Maxine's world, looking just as if she were at ease, and then one of her children had behaved like a child, and perhaps 'Dettie' would be annoyed.

If Gertrude Elliott feared her sister (though Gertrude was a distinguished actress in her own right, and, furthermore, a woman of title, as wife of the actor Sir Johnston Forbes-Robertson—whom we called 'Dad' or 'Dadsy'), she also worshipped and loved her. Thus the incongruous nickname 'Dettie' survived from childhood days when Maxine Elliott had been Jessie Dermot and Gertrude had been May Dermot, and the best that little May could make out of the name Jessie was an infant distortion, 'Dettie'. This name persisted within her family through all the grandeurs of Maxine Elliott, used by her sister and her sister's children: 'Jessie' survived a shorter time, used only by her brothers when they wrote to borrow money. 'Maxine Elliott' became hers entirely, her own invention; it was not only a stage name taken to express an exotic personality and to conceal herself from a disapproving

New England family and an angry husband, but her social identity as well. It was all the more hers for the fact that before her the first name did not exist; any girl today who bears the name 'Maxine' has her to thank for putting it into circulation.

*

Many years before the time when I was first becoming aware of Auntie Dettie, Maxine Elliott had been one of the most beautiful women of her era. It was, however, the personality allied to beauty that put her into the legendary class. Many a perfect, classic face has been admired at first sight and then forgotten, dull after closer examination. The relationship between beauty and magic is not necessarily close at all. 'It is the defects of my love's face that make my heart turn,' Stendhal said in his *De l'Amour*. A beautiful woman is often a static picture; inertia and her own self-absorption can make of her a bland diet. Maxine Elliott astonished people at first sight—brilliant black hair, ivory skin, enormous eyes of a strange dark colour that seemed to change from blue to brown to purple, described as 'midnight eyes', and features of even proportion that made her look like a head on a Greek coin; then she further astonished by the power of her driving ambition, her clear financial brain, a disconcerting matter-of-factness. She was one of the timely ones who catch the imagination of a period, the woman who was the ideal of all women, the archetype. She mystified people, so the legends began. She was seen in places where she had never been, her name coupled with people she did not know; she became public property.

The whispers of her day connected her with one man after another. She had been called the most beautiful woman in the world; therefore, there must be a man somewhere. The names of her admirers got bigger and grander; it seemed a man only had to reach the top in his field for his name to be linked with Maxine Elliott's. J. Pierpont Morgan was mentioned again and again ("He built a theatre for her"). King Edward VII occurs in the legend too ("He built her villa in the south of France"—a remarkable feat twenty years after his death). There are a Widener, an Astor, a Rothschild, a Gould who crop up; an ex-Prime Minister of England and an ex-Viceroy of India who expected to be Prime Minister, who both proposed marriage; also any handsome actor from 1890 to 1910. Frequently I have heard it said, 'She never married' —odd indeed, for she married twice, and one husband was a famous comedian. Marriage evidently does not suit the popular conception of Maxine Elliott. Men were supposed to be lined up waiting to offer her jewels, furs, houses, advice on the stock market. She loathed publicity and fled from it, so the stories burgeoned.

These public legends that included admiring men were natural for such a romantically beautiful woman. What is contradictory, however, is the quality of the stories about Maxine from sources that were actually close to her. Her legal counsel, Thomas L. Chadbourne, was asked if he had advised Maxine on her investments, the popular idea being that no one as beautiful as Maxine could possibly bother her lovely head with business. Tom Chadbourne laughed and replied, 'If Maxine had been a man, Schiff would have been her secretary and Carnegie her office boy.' Mr. George Bernard Shaw's comment, when he heard she was staying in Palm Beach in the direct line of an approaching hurricane, was, 'Oh, that won't worry Maxine at all. She's a tornado herself.' One of her husbands declared that he was quite incapable of stopping her from doing what she wanted: 'I couldn't hold in a locomotive'; the other described her as 'a Roman senator'. This forceful, practical character hardly seemed suitable. The romantic picture of a dangerous siren was continually destroyed—the Helen of Troy, the Cleopatra aspect refused to cling. Rather than destroy people, she made them over; she acquired male admirers and then annexed their wives as devoted friends. Her own words repudiate the idea of splendid men rushing to her protection or easing life for her. To a woman friend she said, 'Men? The best thing I know about a man is his back, going out of the door.'

It was difficult for me, growing up as her niece, to see the vision that she had of herself which had driven her to create her life. My sisters and I saw the result of her efforts, and it seemed anything but romantic, a rich woman interested in card playing, house building, the stock market, food, and the activities of her friends. My childish impression of her was an enormous looming woman of mink, turbans, and jewellery, easily bored, whose most familiar form of expression was the short, debunking comment. It seemed entirely unsuitable that such a presence should be called 'little Dettie' by her sister (my mother), who was a good head shorter, or even 'the little thing', or sometimes 'poor little Dettie'. She seemed neither poor nor little. She was extremely rich, with houses, cars, expensive clothes, many presents for us; she was rich in friends, who all addressed her as 'darling'; she was anything but physically little, having grown fat in her old age. Her whole aspect—body, clothes, and pattern of living—was opulent. As to the 'poor', meaning someone to be pitied and cherished, this seemed equally out of character; she was someone of authority, who commanded her pleasures, and never in front of us showed any emotion stronger than irritation over material things, such as delays in a building project or trouble with a dressmaker.

The most unromantic fact of all for us was that she was a social snob. Of this we were certain because our charitable father, who seldom said a malicious word, remarked, 'Your aunt dearly loves a lord.' As if opening the door of a magic castle she introduced us to the world she admired, and we were amazed at its dreariness. The people had titles and good clothes, but they never seemed to talk about anything but houses, money, and servants. So this was Lord X; he was just a pleasant enough man playing backgammon with Auntie Dettie. The fact that he was Lord X seemed satisfaction enough for Maxine, but we found her pleasure in his title merely funny. My sister Jean returned from a trip to New York and reported that an unattractive young man with pimples had pursued her round the decks of the liner and she had complained to Auntie Dettie. 'But, my dear, he's Lord Y,' said her aunt. 'But I don't like him,' said Jean. 'Always remember, dear,' said Auntie Dettie, 'that a lord is just that much better than anyone else.' A great 'Ha!' shot out of Dad when he heard the story.

My sister Blossom told us how angry Auntie Dettie had been when Dad refused to be lured by the offer of a peerage to do propaganda work during World War I. 'Why should a title matter to Dad?' asked Blossom. 'He's been knighted as

an actor, which is honour enough.' 'It's selfish of Forbie,' said
Auntie Dettie. 'It would have made you all honourables.' My
sister Chloe and I, when we learned this story, spent days
bowing low and asking, 'How's my dishonourable sister today?' Another time, when I was quite small, Auntie Dettie
called me to be introduced to Tom Bridges and the Duke of
Rutland, 'The two tallest men in London' (she loved super-
latives). I gave the duke an appraising look after I'd made
my bob and said to myself as I turned to go, 'I'm glad I've
met one of those.' It was perfectly clear to me what I meant;
it was interesting as it would be to meet a tinker or a poacher.
Over the years Auntie Dettie embarrassed me by repeating
this story, apparently delighting in it because it included a
duke.

Her social snobbery developed only after she had con-
quered many other worlds. She always liked the people at
the top, no matter what level she had reached, and perhaps
her queenly beauty made it seem proper for her to belong
among those who ruled their worlds. She had already shown
in which direction her interests lay one night, as a very young
girl in New York, when she was taken to a theatre with Jenny
Willey, a friend from her home town, Rockland, Maine. When
the audience was assembled, there was a sudden rustle of
excitement, and into the stage box came the newly elected
President of the United States, Grover Cleveland. The audience rose in a body. President Cleveland acknowledged the
ovation while his party stood grouped behind him; in their
midst was a pretty, beautifully dressed young woman, only a
few years older than Maxine (at that time 'Jessie'), who gazed
at her avidly from her place in the audience. It was the
President's ward, Frances Folsom, and already rumour was
spreading that she would become his wife. Jessie leaned over
and whispered in Jenny's ear, 'I'd give half my life to be in
her shoes'. In the end the life of Miss Maxine Elliott contained
far more variety than Mrs. Grover Cleveland's.

Her nieces had no idea where Maxine's snobbery had its
origins and felt it very alien. Our lords and ladies wore suits
of armour and floating veils and existed in books or our own
drawings; we drew knights riding up winding roads to im-
pregnable castles in which a lady in distress was incarcerated.

We did not realize that Maxine knew the knights, had been the lady, and sometimes had played the role of knight errant herself. She had a true feeling of romance about her own life, and succeeded in making all things she wanted come true because she had the gift to overstep the limitations of reality, practically and clearly living out a Cinderella story of her own, making herself the Fairy Godmother who held the magic wand that turned pumpkins to coaches and frogs to footmen. Someone only had to say to Maxine, 'It can't be done,' and she did it.

She lived out fantasies similar to ours in reality itself, and her characters were real people. Being human, these people were often disappointing, but she went on hoping that the next might be a knight in armour who would ride round the corner into her life. Once one did—and he behaved precisely as knights should; he was modest, pure, and beyond reproach, and went out to seek the Holy Grail dressed in khaki in the First World War. In her later life it seemed as if Maxine also recognized another knight who had been her friend—a rotund statesman, out of office, armed with cigar, paint brush, and pen. Maxine dreamed her dreams, and did not let them fade away as most pretty daydreams do.

*

Her life, which began in Rockland, Maine, a few years after the American Civil War was over, ended in the south of France in the early months of World War II. Her monument remains a large villa on the sea, facing across the Bay of Cannes toward the Iles de Lerin and the promontory of Cap d'Antibes; it is now owned by the Aga Khan, and the remains of his father, Aly Khan, were buried in the garden beneath the windows of rooms that were once called 'the Forbes-Robertson suite'. The builder and châtelaine of the Château de l'Horizon gave no suggestions of New England origins, not even of a career of some thirty years in the theatre, and was more royal in behaviour than her princely successors. Aly Khan's wife, Rita Hayworth, when trying to run the Château, was thoroughly browbeaten by Maxine's own maid, Fanny Vandystaedt, who took pains to tell her, 'Miss Elliott wouldn't have done it that way.'

That aura of grandeur which Maxine left behind her had

been acquired in the years between Rockland and Cannes, in the New York theatre and Edwardian London. Her theatrical career seemed dim indeed when I knew her, marked only by two full-length portraits which hung on her staircase, one of Maxine as Zuleika in *Joseph and His Brethren*, the other of her in *Lord and Lady Algy*. They were both by fashionable painters and could have been protraits of a society woman dressed for a costume ball. She gave her nieces no impression of an actress. Had we been anything but the children of actors, this might not have been strange, but we had no illusions that actresses were 'actressy' or part of some odd breed different from others. I never had doubts of my father's calling, although he had retired before I could see him in anything but a few performances for charitable purposes or on the lecture platform; but I could name his roles and identify them by photograph. I was equally clear about Mother's theatrical carer; it continued after Dad's retirement to my thirteenth year, so I was able to see her several times; later if I went to plays with her she judged performances and productions with a professional's eye. Finally, my sister Jean, ten years older than I, started in the theatre at sixteen, so from the age of six on, the theatre was part of my life. Beyond these members of the immediate family were three uncles and four cousins on the stage. I was quite used to it and passionately interested. But Auntie Dettie seemed to look at the theatre from the outside, as her society friends did. (Only if someone spoke disparagingly of actors did Maxine rise at once; when Winston Churchill came in distress to say his daughter Sarah had married 'an out-of-work actor', Maxine hit right back— 'Is that so different from an out-of-work politician?') We found it impossible to imagine Auntie Dettie as a working actress like others in the family. She had no enthusiasm for it, and no memories to impart.

My own parents were full of fascinating reminiscences about appalling stage disasters; we took a particular pleasure in tales of a melodrama called *Zillah, or the Scar on the Wrist*, a pretentious production that Dad suffered through in his youth, which was full of mishaps: a misplaced bridge tipped and slapped the actors on the behind as they crossed it; the flats failed to reach a trick sofa from which the leading lady was supposed to be spirited away to make a sudden startling reappearance as a twin sister, and she was seen by the audience crawling off stage on all fours. We loved the story of the play scene in *Hamlet*; Dad instructed the company to invent their own words to make a confused babble at the cry, 'Lights, lights,' and our cousin Maud Buchanan, one of the ladies of the Court of Denmark, was heard leading the girls in the chant, 'Votes for women, votes for women . . .' We were fascinated to learn that Mother managed her many quick changes in *Eyes of Youth* by wearing the stockings that went with each change one on top of another and peeling them scene by scene. There were a thousand more. We loved to hear them; Mother and Dad loved to tell them. Maxine had no anecdotes. She seemed to look upon her theatre career, if it was mentioned at all, as a weary penance she had been through, best forgotten.

Some of her public utterances about her life on the stage bore out the attitude we observed at home. Lee Shubert, trying to persuade her to put off retirement, had suggested she would miss the glamour. 'I'll miss it about as much as the early Christian martyrs missed the man-eating lions in the arena,' she said. I read the interviews she gave to the press when she visited New York in 1933. 'There's no good talking to me. I never really liked the theatre. I just happened to be in it. Night after night I have played in successes and they became drearier and drearier.' No names of plays she performed sprang to mind. Her photographs, though beautiful, had a posed sameness. We had little to go on because her career had been chiefly in the United States and we grew up in England; Dad contributed the negative information that he considered Mother a much better actress than her sister. I came on the interesting words of Alexander Woolcott in *While Rome Burns* that she could not be counted a bad actress, but was rather 'a non-actress'. She had been immensely successful, however, and in New York there was a theatre she owned called Maxine Elliott's Theatre. Dad was considered one of the leaders of his profession in London, but there was no Forbes-Robertson Theatre.

It seemed a mystery indeed that Auntie Dettie should have been in the theatre at all. In her private life she was thoroughly

impatient and entirely practical. The audiences that imagined
her a lovely, delicate spirit easily bruised might have been
startled had they witnessed an incident at Hartsbourne Manor
when the plumbers had been called to fix a defective lavatory.
Her brother-in-law, Forbes-Robertson, chivalrously hurried
to the scene in the belief that a lady would be embarrassed to
discuss such a subject. He arrived to find two plumbers standing outside the door, and Maxine already there, demonstrating
the trouble. She reached for the overhead chain and gave it a
hearty yank which was followed by a feeble trickle of water
inside the bowl. 'Look at that,' she said, pointing. 'That's no
good to me.' They might have been equally startled at her
unromantic comments on love and marriage. 'Infidelity is a
flea bite compared to drunkenness,' she told a woman whose
husband was giving trouble. To another woman complaining
of her married life, Maxine said, 'I wouldn't leave him, you've
made all your friends through him and people may not be so
kind if you do.' 'Oh, fair-weather friends,' cried the lady, 'who
wants them? I'd always have the real ones. I'd always have
you.' 'Oh, no you wouldn't,' said Maxine. 'I'd be the first to
go. I can't stand fools.'

In the theatre she was presented romping with children, and
the audiences cooed with pleasure. She never romped with
us. Our nurse, 'Nonny', Miss E. M. Biller, witnessed the
nursery scene in *Her Own Way* and gave an audible snort.
Auntie Dettie adored us, planned for us, built nurseries for us
wherever she lived (whether the Forbes-Robertsons wanted
them or not); she lavished presents on us, and when she died
endowed us for life. She was not at ease with us, however,
and was inclined to stage-manage rather than communicate
with us. In her house we underwent frequent changes of
costume for our presentation to the visitors—drawers, petti-
coats, and a hat for the garden for Blossom, Jean, and Chloe,
much of which I escaped as a wartime baby who was permitted
curious one-piece frilly rompers (called my 'Carusos') or
woollen suits. We were awed by her swooping invasions when
she flung open a door to usher in a group and show them 'the
nurseries I've made for Gertrude and Forbie's children'. This
was nerve-racking indeed for Nonny, who felt as if she were
asked to be constantly on stage, keeping the rooms orderly, the

children neat and clean. Auntie Dettie had little idea of what a child is like, and was incapable of understanding our sudden shynesses or rapid retreats when she asked us to perform parlour tricks before strangers. She was indulgent without thought. Once she gave a shiny sixpence each to Blossom and Jean; Blossom was old enough to throw hers up and catch it; when Jean tried to do the same, her sixpence disappeared in a flower bed. A howl went up, and from her ground-floor bedroom Auntie Dettie called to learn what the trouble was. 'Oh, my poor darling,' she said to Jean, who was choking in sobs, as the two children came in and stood beside her dressing table, where she was arranging her hair. She emptied a gold mesh bag of its contents, but found no other sixpence, so she scooped up twelve shiny pennies and poured them into Jean's hands. Now Blossom was in despair; she could count, and saw that Jean had a much better bargain. Auntie Dettie sailed on, leaving conflict in her wake.

Maxine's plans for her nieces were constantly frustrated by a surprising Fifth Column within the bosom of her family. Her brother-in-law, Johnston Forbes-Robertson, eleven years older, a Victorian, was a modern spirit, far in advance of his times. Her little sister, Gertrude, who seemed entirely under her thumb, had the same quality. It is curious that while few of Forbes-Robertson's and Gertrude Elliott's photographs seem dated, all of Maxine's do. The four Forbes-Robertson nieces were raised in the atmosphere of 22 Bedford Square, a house with a pungent flavour of its own, beautiful architecturally (by the brothers Adam), furnished with Forbes-Robertson's taste for the simplest in Georgian elegance upon which were piled the comfortable additions of family living and furnishings from theatrical productions. The point of view of the household was high-minded, frugal, orderly, idealistic, an outgrowth of Forbes-Robertson's own upbringing as the son of a Scottish art historian and his beautiful, austere wife. Earlier, the elder Forbes-Robertsons lived in Islington in a house swarming with their children, often dangerously short of money, but ready to entertain (with a cheap bottle of wine and some sandwiches) such characters as Swinburne, Whistler, Oscar Wilde, and many of the Pre-Raphaelite painters. My own growing-up was in the years of

Johnston Forbes-Robertson's retirement, and still there flowed to his house men and women of intellectual and artistic bent. We had Sir James Barrie sticking stamps on the ceiling of the nursery by flipping them there, lodged on a penny; we saw Mother studiously working out vegetarian menus from Mr. George Bernard Shaw. We breathed in with the air of the house the belief that the best was created for itself alone, and not for money; that beauty was more important than fashion, that a quiet conscience was to be preferred to success. We all drew and painted and wrote stories together: we considered a trip to the British Museum or the National Gallery a rare treat; we dreamed through childhood in a happy mist of romanticism, and two of us, Jean and Chloe, became realized as artists, respectively an actress and a painter. The social world had no interest for us at all; we were aware that it bored Dad and terrified Mother.

Into this entrenched household swept Maxine Elliott, with hands outstretched, ready to offer us high society, but we shied away. We learned that the passion in Auntie Dettie which seemed so lacking for anything artistic came out strongly on the subject of appearance—the passport, it seemed, to the social world. We dreaded the joke language that came when we were out with her and something was wanting in our make-up: 'A ittle-lay ore-may olor-kay on the eeks-chay.' After seeing a play, Maxine called the costumes a disgrace, and said that whoever made them deserved 'six months hard labour twice a year'. This we could understand, because it was applied to 'costume'; when she applied the same fervour to clothes for ourselves we found it disturbing and physically exhausting. Maxine, aged and heavy, was able to endure longer hours of fittings than any of her young nieces could. When we made feeble efforts of our own to take trouble we were greeted with dismay: 'What on earth have you got on?' 'Why don't you put on your pink? It's the prettiest little thing you ever had.' This was usually something we loathed, a dressmaker creation that had belonged to a friend of Auntie Dettie's and had been refitted for us, loaded with the memory of standing while pins were stuck in—something that felt as if it never quite belonged.

I, as the youngest of the quartet, inherited the diminished

drive of her last decade, but nevertheless Fanny, her maid, always fetched me for an inspection before dinner when I was staying at her house in France. My newly wed husband 'Jimmy', Vincent Sheean, was alarmed by the violence of my reaction when I returned from one of these trips up the grand white staircase to Auntie Dettie's bedroom, where I had gone confident that I would be passed without comment for the first time. Jimmy had given me a beautiful dress from Paquin, dark blue taffeta with a soft pale blue taffeta off-the-shoulder fichu ending in a bow in front. 'I haven't time now before dinner,' said Auntie Dettie, 'but tomorrow morning you bring that dress up. I want to alter the bow.' I raged and wept—not in her presence—and the pearl from the pearl-and-diamond ring Auntie Dettie had given me as a wedding present went scudding across the floor.

My sisters and I fell short of her inner vision of us. We were projections of herself, and she imagined us triumphant beauties, as she had been. We were always a disappointment. She passed over what was all right (the nearest to a compliment I ever got from Auntie Dettie was her brief remark about a plain white dress I had on: 'You must always wear white'), and she pounced on what was wrong; thus we always had a feeling of hopelessness. When we talked to her friends we felt her listening and watching, determined that we, her nieces, should shine more than anyone in the room, so we became awkward and mute—a family of girls who never stopped talking at home. Although she never felt that a party was complete without a member of her tribe, we pleased her more, I believe, when we were not present, because she could tell others of our doings. Blossom gave her infinite joy when she and her second husband, F. G. Miles, the aircraft designer, took all first five places with Miles models in the King's Cup Race for small civilian aeroplanes (the fourth was designed by Blossom herself). She gloried in the fine reviews that Jean got for every performance she gave. She seized Chloe's portrait of me and hung it above her bedroom mantelpiece, a trophy acquired rather than an act of appreciation for art (for which she did not care at all). I never dared tell Chloe that Auntie Dettie asked her architect, Barry Dierks, to redden the lips where Chloe had painted a highlight.

Maxine swept Blossom's first wedding out of the hands of
her parents (Blossom married 'Nigs' Freeman-Thomas, who
later became Marquess of Willingdon). My father wrote of
this event to a friend, Mollie Tompkins, 'It is to be a very
splendid affair, which vexes me, as it is all out of proportion
with my views on life, and very much against the young
people's wishes.' I wonder if Maxine, whose weddings had
taken place without fanfare, was realizing her own romantic
dream of a shimmering bride, a great congregation, with
police holding back the populace. She tried to rush me into
marriage with a man I'd never met, telling me to cancel my
plans to go to Salzburg—'Nobody goes to Salzburg; everybody comes to Cannes'—and only the friendly intervention of
a friend, Charlotte Boissevain (who had been Charlotte Ives
in the theatre), one of the few who did not fear her, prevented
me from being forced to stay and ignominiously be looked
over. At a later date, after the man's subsequent marriage had
caused society to buzz with gossip of its incompatibility, I
dared to ask her if she really thought this would have been a
fortunate alliance for me. She said impatiently, 'It could work
perfectly with discretion. There's lots of money and an enormous house. Each can go a separate way and conserve appearances.' 'But, Auntie Dettie,' I protested, 'I couldn't have
coped with that. I want a real marriage.' Her expression was
one of weary disgust; she had heard this before. She gave a
long deep sigh. 'Oh, all you Forbes-Robertsons are so sentimental.'

When I did marry, however, Maxine showed her mag-
nificence. She did not want me to be a writer's wife ('an
insecure life'), but when I married Vincent Sheean she
promptly declared him the best writer since Shakespeare and
forced his books on her friends. Worried over our nomadic
life, she presented me outright with the gift of her Paris
flat, complete down to the last monogrammed linen table nap-
kin. It would give us a 'good address'. To make still more
sure that our life would acquire a more formal pattern, she
sent us visiting cards from Cartier's—slim, small ones for
the gentleman, larger ones for the lady. We could not see
ourselves making the rounds of society in the afternoons,
dropping cards with correctly bent edges. It was touching, over-

whelming too, but quite unsuitable for the world we inhabited.

Resistance to her management endured in her nieces for a long time, long after her death. Mine had to be overcome before I could attempt to write about her. I recognized that she was a towering character, and it seemed unfair that her biography should be written by one who, it must be confessed, in childhood and youth often did not like her at all. In our struggles to find our own feet, we of the younger generation found it difficult to submit. The change in manners that took place after World War I contributed to the lack of understanding. Maxine had been a pioneer who fought her way to the top in the Edwardian era; the troubled, conscience-stricken young of the generation that followed wanted only to discard the world she valued. Recently I found a letter in response to one of mine which must have been a howl of anguish from her Riviera house. My correspondent was Alexander Scotty-Gatty, an actor friend of the family; 'Jack' to us, and 'Funniman' especially to me, he had been a beloved confidant from earliest childhood. He wrote: 'Poor darling. I read between the lines. . . . The Dominant Personality and all that. Your mother was always a sort of daughter to Maxine. I am so old, however, I see things in the big proportion if I can so explain myself, and I am frankly a devoted admirer of your aunt. She has the strong hallmark of her period and of the great practical result she has achieved . . . don't mistake it, my Dinahkins, your aunt is a *great* woman.' With more brevity Winston Churchill told his daughter Sarah the same thing on her return from the Château, where Maxine had evidently tried to manage her too: 'My child, you're too young as yet to understand the rich and mellow vintage.'

Her equals understood her and admired her, and when she tried to manage them were strong enough to let her do so, because she had rare good sense. She was pronounced the most staunch of friends, equally beloved of men and women— an important tribute to a woman of such beauty. People came to her for advice on emotional affairs, finances, practical questions of arrangements of their houses; with a few succinct comments she could toss out a clear course of action for the first two, and as for her friends' houses, she was liable to move in and re-do them entirely. The great, ailing ex-Prime

Minister, Lord Rosebery, found himself berated by her for the poor quarters he had prepared for his daughter-in-law, Lady Dalmeny, about to give birth to his grandchild; finally, he requested Maxine herself to effect the changes she thought proper: 'And that'll cost him a pretty penny,' said Maxine with satisfaction. She enjoyed choosing scripts and casting plays for others, and is credited with having suggested Jeanne Eagels for Sadie Thompson in *Rain*. She pointed out to Brandon Tynan, the Irish-American actor and playwright, that he could write a sure-fire hit if he combined New York Jewish and Irish people and made a Romeo and Juliet romance with a happy ending. He did not do it, but Anne Nichols, who followed that formula in *Abie's Irish Rose*, broke theatre records for the length of the play's run. Maxine browbeat Constance Collier into forgetting her own past as a romantic beauty when she emerged into public again after a long illness, and persuaded her to take the part of the elderly, wicked duchess in *Our Betters* (in the London production), with which she stole the show.

In the theatre Maxine's casting for herself was out of character although thoroughly successful. In life, however, the casting she gave herself through the years was ideal. She was the haughty, Junoesque beauty of the turn of the century, an embodiment of the spirit of the times. The last phase that I saw, the old lady on the Riviera, was superb; she had simply become a member of the ruling classes, as magnificently rude as any duchess, as perfect in her knowledge of court protocol as a monarch. No wonder she was bored by acting in the theatre, where she played beneath the capacity of her own intelligence, being sweet and namby-pamby when her own character was made of granite as hard as the rock quarried in her own New England. She used tact, graciousness, and perfect manners as she set out to conquer London society, and, once in, she set aside those qualities (except when they became necessary) to be an outspoken aristocrat, determinedly Philistine. We chuckled over her bookplates—'My books and friends—and this is happiness'; it sounded gently blue-stocking, a phase she had passed through years before. Her reading during her late years, devoid of literary pretension, was chosen to distract herself. Charlotte Boissevain brought about the meeting of Maxine Elliott and H. G. Wells, and in her introductions said, 'And, H. G., Miss Elliott is a great admirer of yours.' 'I was,' said Maxine, 'until I discovered Edgar Wallace.' She arranged her books and pictures as adjuncts of her social life: the pictures had been bought largely according to size and colour by one of her attorneys, Louis Levy, or were gifts; her books had been ordered in collected editions with the same attention to their physical outsides, not to their content. She did not, however, close her mind if something happened to hit her fancy; when she was moving into a new house in London, she came upon her copy of Alexandre Dumas's *The Three Musketeers*, sat down on top of a ladder, and began reading; within the next few weeks she went through Dumas's entire works, which had stood unread in the libraries of her former houses for twenty years. She lived her last years totally as herself, everything accomplished, nothing further needed, except the will to pass on to the next generation of her family the advantages she had fought for and won. Much of the time she was sunk in game-playing so deeply that she hardly noticed who came and went, secure in the knowledge that perfect organization in her household gave them food, drinks, swimming, and conversation with others. If sufficiently stimulated she could still rouse herself to flashes of wit and a rich, velvet charm. A newcomer could not be blamed if he thought this apparition a scion of a most ancient house with the habit of privilege bred into her bones through generations.

Although Maxine pushed theatre life out of her own conversation, her name remained a household word in the years of retirement. Her name buzzed about the theatre at the opening of Edna Ferber's and George Kaufman's *Dinner at Eight*, in which the part of Carlotta Vance, played by Constance Collier (later by Marie Dressler in the movie version) showed a rich, retired actress with a theatre in New York and important friends in the financial world. More than a decade had passed since the end of her own career, but an audience in which many were too young to have seen her said with confidence, 'It's Maxine Elliott.' Any such references to her as a personality or a woman with a past merely bored her. 'More fools know Tom Fool than Tom Fool knows,' was her favourite comment; when Jimmy Sheean passed on to her a request that she give Marcia Davenport permission to see her and write her life story for the *Saturday Evening Post*, she shook her head wearily and said, 'Let them write what they like after I'm dead. But now, just leave me in peace.'

*

One moment of tenderness of which I can be sure (felt by me, I mean, and recognized as tenderness) did occur between Auntie Dettie and myself. It was the only time when I felt able to give her something. It was at the Château de l'Horizon when she was sixty-six and I was twenty. A guest plaintively wailed that she wished Maxine had a boat because it would be such fun to go to Cannes by water, instead of along the dreary old Route Nationale by car.

'But I have a boat,' said Maxine in her beautiful, low voice, which happily contrasted with the nasal bleat of Lady C.

The handyman Jules was told to bring the *Maxine* to the jetty, and everyone scattered to change clothes. I heard an engine sputtering somewhere out of sight. Soon a steady chugging followed. I heard the voices of reassembled guests on the terrace below and ran downstairs.

'Is that the tub we're going in?' shrieked Lady C., watching the squat dory making a dignified progress toward the dock, with Jules upright at the tiller in rakish Basque beret and striped *maillot*. 'We'll never get to the Carlton Bar in time at that rate.'

There was a change of plan. Two cars would be going in, and at once. They called to me: 'Come on, Dinah.'

Auntie Dettie had not appeared. It seemed appalling to rush off and leave her. I was longing to go—we escaped rarely from the Château—and I did not want to stay alone with her, certain that I could not amuse or interest her. But I said I would stay. The others rushed off, obviously relieved to be rid of a boring young niece before whom they were supposed to edit their conversation.

Maxine appeared in dark blue jersey jacket and skirt, a dark blue peaked cap on her head. (I did not know at the time how like her sea-captain father she looked at that moment.) I was touched at the dancing light of anticipation in her eyes. There was fun afoot and she was eager for it. I told her what had happened.

She was silent a moment. Then she turned to me and smiled, her eyes suddenly changing from the light sherry colour to the dark. She took my arm.

'Gadabouts,' she said. 'Let's go anyway. It'll be much more fun, just the two of us.'

2

IN SEARCH OF JESSIE
DERMOT

———

TWENTY YEARS after the death of my aunt I found myself faced with the project of writing her life. It was an interesting idea; then came the dismay: while that formidable presence loomed in the foreground, I knew almost nothing of her early days. But I remembered that *Alice in Wonderland* advises a storyteller to begin at the beginning, go on till he comes to the end, and then stop. The beginning was in Rockland, Maine, when Maxine Elliott was a little girl called Jessie Dermot, so that was where I must start.

I don't remember hearing Auntie Dettie say much about Rockland. Mother (also now dead) had left some pictures of it in my mind; sometimes she had gone to school by sled with ice forming on her eyelashes; in summer she and her sisters had gone to visit an uncle who had a farm, where they could eat as much corn on the cob as they could stuff, then follow it with apple pie. I knew Rockland was a sea-coast town in Maine, north-east of Boston, the last state before the Canadian border. Mother said the sea fogs that rolled in over the English Channel and enveloped our country home at St. Margaret's Bay, Kent, came in just that way over the town of Rockland to make the offshore islands disappear; when I walked with her on the cliffs of Dover we would pause to listen to the gulls laughing or weeping, and she said it was one of the earliest sounds she remembered of Rockland.

There were old photographs, hung in small oval frames round the looking-glass of my mother's dressing-table at 22 Bedford Square. There was a beautiful woman (very like Mother) with intense eyes, dressed in a bonnet and ruched dolman, with neatly gloved hands; also a dimmer picture of the same intense face when she was a child, the cheeks chubby but the eyes burning. That was Maxine's and Gertrude's mother, my grandmother, who had been born Adelaide Hall. Their father, Thomas Dermot, was shown as a handsome man with boldly defined jaw and my mother's perfect small Roman nose; there was an older one of him, too, standing beside a tiny woman, his second wife, who held a dog in her arms. 'He was such an ugly little dog,' Mother said, 'but "little Mother" adored him. He was called Kobe because your grandfather brought him back from a voyage to Japan.' There were other pictures of assorted uncles and aunts, and a very sad-looking old pair, the man frilled with beard, the woman drooping in peak-faced melancholy—my mother's grandparents, Isaac Hall and his wife Sarah Hahn. An awkward moment occurred when I found a photograph lying loose in a drawer, and said, 'Who's this hideous man?' 'It's my brother Sam,' said Mother tartly, 'and he was considered very good-looking.' I hurriedly dropped the saturnine, black-browed face with a big moustache and murmured, 'I only thought he looked fierce.'

None of these ageing pictures adorned the dressing table of Auntie Dettie's bedroom. There was only a little flat gold case marked 'M.E.G.' which lay on the table, and inside it was her intense-eyed, chubby-cheeked mother as a child.

*

The Dermot family left Rockland so long ago that I doubted if I could find much. Who could still be alive who would remember the sixties, seventies, eighties? Some dates at least I knew. Auntie Dettie, whom I must learn to think of as 'Jessie', had left for an early marriage in 1884; by 1888, the mother, Adelaide Dermot, was dead, and Captain Thomas Dermot had sold his house and furniture and gone to Oakland, California. There might be Perry or Brewer or Hall cousins still around, but they would be of a generation too young to remember those distant events.

I heard the gulls crying when I looked out across Rockland Harbour. It is a fine enclosure of water, with a breakwater forming its north-east arm and a point of land, Owl's Head, to the south-west. Beyond lie North Haven and Vinalhaven Islands, and much farther out, I knew, lay an island called Matinicus, a spot in the Atlantic where early Hall ancestors had lived.

Memories came dimly back; Mother had told us of an ancestor called Ebenezer Hall who claimed that island, held it against the Indians, finally succumbed, and was scalped. It seemed strange to me then, looking across Penobscot Bay in search of Maxine Elliott's past, that we English children, growing up in a London nursery, had not had more curiosity about a romantic tale of pioneers and Indians actually connected with us. Why had we not bombarded Mother with questions? Were knights and ladies, cavaliers and round-heads, our only fantasies? The answer lay deeper than that. Most of the Forbes-Robertson relatives had looked upon Gertrude Elliott as an American interloper when she married their Johnston, and theirs remained the prevailing influence in the Forbes-Robertson nursery. Maxine Elliott saw no romance in her American past, so she added nothing. I remember that when I asked her what it was like to sail on her father's barque, she indicated it was something too dull to report and spoke of the yacht of Kaiser Wilhelm II in the Kiel Canal. Now, as I looked at the harbour from which Jessie Dermot had sailed, its wharves long in disuse, launching slips vanished in grass, railroad tracks leading to a once teeming dockside, I saw a busy port spring to life. Long ago, in the early eighties, a small vessel, the *Will H. Case*, sailed from here, with Captain Thomas Dermot on the quarter-deck expertly navigating his way through crowded shipping. The daughter at his side, about fourteen years old, had grown to be Auntie Dettie who spoke of royal yachts.

On Rockland's Main Street I found the local newspaper office, the Rockland *Courier Gazette*. Immediately I heard Mother's voice telling of the old 'Currier', and unbidden came to mind the name of the editor of their day, Will O. Fuller. It occurred to me I knew more than I thought if I could so promptly recall that Mr. Fuller had pince-nez and moustaches that drooped, and was much in demand as a witty after-dinner speaker. Snatches of detail about Rockland must have penetrated as I sat drawing at 22 Bedford Square. . . . Indeed, as I

turned the pages of back copies of the *Courier* a great-uncle
jumped out at me with ease—Captain Hiram Hall, who liked
to write verse, much of it printed there, and I knew he was the
one who nuzzled scratching whiskers against my mother's face
as a tiny child and recited:

> *'May is a darling. May is a dear,*
> *But she hasn't kissed her uncle,*
> *And I find this very queer.'*

The change in size of the *Courier* over the years told much
of Rockland's history. In mid-nineteenth century, when it
carried serialized stories, important editorials, and discursive
articles on famine distress in Ireland, Southern unrest, or
religious persecution in Central Europe, it was a newspaper
as fat as today's *New York Times*. Then Rockland was at
the height of its prosperity, an important shipbuilding centre
and the major lime-producing area of the country. Rockland,
with the rest of New England, sprang to answer the call of
the West and its gold, with fleet clipper ships that dashed
down the lips ready for the run round the Horn, or for the
race against British ships for the tea from China. The fastest
of them all, the *Red Jacket*, was launched from Rockland in
1853, and claimed the record for the Atlantic run: thirteen
days and one hour. The whole territory had world importance:
as Rockland gained a city charter in 1859 the state of Maine
in which it lay (a state only since 1820) sent a Vice-President
to Washington. Hannibal Hamlin, who came to office in 1861
with President Abraham Lincoln. International affairs, far
more important to Rockland than to inland cities, were shoved
to secondary importance by the internal struggle of the Civil
War, and Rockland's ladies bombarded the Sanitary Commission with their bandages and shirts, as the men departed
with the 2nd Maine Battery. Long, long is the list of Rockland men who fell at Manassas, or died from wounds at
Gettysburg.

I knew that Maxine's father was not Rockland born but
had come there as an immigrant boy about 1850 and married
into one of the old pioneer families, whose forebears had
already been in the territory for about two hundred years.
Tom Dermot had been befriended by a New England sea

captain named David Ames, who turned out to be 'of Thomaston', the name of the original settlement from which Rockland had developed, first as Thomaston's 'Shore Village', then East Thomaston, finally the City of Rockland. Captain Ames was one of the important men of the town, who owned lime kilns and a fleet of vessels; one of his descendants, Mrs. Jessie Mains, showed me his ornamental looking-glass and also his wife's jewellery. But it was from a lady in New York that I happened to learn the account of Captain David Ames's adoption of Tom Dermot. The lady was a Boston newspaper-woman, a descendant of Captain Ames's first wife, Lucy Frye Ames; her story was a detailed one, preserved in her family. Alas, before I could get her name she disappeared from an auditorium in New York University where we had attended the same lecture.

She told me that Mrs. Lucy Frye Ames, stepping ashore from her husband's vessel onto the Liverpool docks, saw a fight in progress between two boys, Liverpool 'dock rats', and was led by her strong Methodism and sense of seemly behaviour to break it up with her parasol. One boy fled; the one who stood and defied her was named Tom MacDermot. She admonished him to go home to his mother, and so learned that he had neither home nor mother and was sleeping in an old molasses hogshead he had lined with paper and straw for warmth. It was a time when Liverpool was jammed with diseased and starving Irish who had fled from their country when it was ravaged with the potato blight, and the dream of all was to go to America. It was well known that greedy agents were packing immigrants into 'coffin ships', taking their few last pennies for passage, careless of the fact that the ships were not fit for human beings. Mrs. Ames, faced with one Irish boy, whose story she learned, determined to make him her project. She persuaded Captain Ames to take him on as a cabin boy on their return to America. The Captain, who wished to be entirely correct, inquired of the port authorities whether he could take the boy, and the British official asked without much interest what Mrs. Ames intended to do with him when she got him on the other side. Captain Ames, usually poker-faced and forbidding on his quarter-deck, is supposed to have broken into a grin and replied, 'Wash his face, send him to school, make a good Methodist of him.'

On the voyage back, the Ames couple examined their pro-
tégé and found him a boy of exceptional vigour, his language
good, ready to recite them long poems of the Irish legends,
the sad tales of Deirdre and Cuchulainn; he was a quick
learner who took his place in the work of the vessel with
energy and intelligence. They congratulated themselves that
they had picked well. They had recently lost several children
in early childhood, so the protection of Tom may have filled
their own emotional needs. The Captain offered to stand bond
for him on arrival; he also advised him to drop the Mac off
his name, because the New York and Boston docks in particular were crammed with Macs, the very sound of the name
causing resentment among other dock workers, because the
destitution of the Irish made them work for any wage offered.
'They don't like Micks over there,' he told Tom.

They took him to their mansion at 47 Middle Street in
Rockland, the most elegant avenue in the town, lined with
elm and beech and the fine houses of prosperous sea captains
and lime-quarry owners. The house was filled with treasures
the Captain had brought from his voyages over the world;
Tom Dermot must have goggled at the great gilt looking-
glass I saw, and admired the stiff China silk in which Mrs.
Ames rustled about. They did indeed clean him up, admonished him to forget his Liverpool curse words, and sent him
to school at Thomaston Academy, where he studied under
an inspired teacher, 'Uncle' Henry Paine. He learned English
composition, Latin, algebra, geometry and penmanship.
'Uncle' Paine also conducted classes in the theory of navigation, so Tom immediately began work on his future profession, following in the steps of his patron. In the summer,
when school was out, he worked aboard Captain Ames's
coastal vessels, learning at first hand the intricacies of the
Maine coast and currents.

The Ames family must have known the details of Tom's
past, but it was not transmitted. All that is known of his
Irish beginnings is that he was born in County Galway on
December 18, 1837, a member of the big MacDermot clan
which is centred in Roscommon but spills over into Galway
and Mayo. He could have been the child of a peasant or

related to the gentry, equally impoverished and dispossessed of their ancestral home at Loch Key. Tom's childhood memories could not have been happy, because he passed none down to his children and became a militant Yankee, ready to take to fisticuffs in the shipyards of Rockland if anyone chaffed him as a Mick or a Limey. He did preserve, however, one legacy from his Irish home—his clear, good speech, which he passed on to his children. He refused to allow them a Yankee twang, and thus assisted greatly the theatrical future of his two daughters.

*

The girl Tom married, the one of the burning eyes, was easier to trace in Rockland than I might have expected. A local historian and genealogist had prepared a two-volume history of the region.* Eight generations of Halls, starting with a George Hall who had come from Taunton, Devon, in 1636 with his wife Mary, ended in Isaac T. Hall, married to Sarah Hahn—Maxine's and Gertrude's grandparents, whose faces I already knew—and their progeny included Adelaide, listed as Addie C., born in 1842. My letters flew across the Atlantic to my sister Blossom in England, who began to open old boxes. Out came an essay written by Addie C. Hall at Thomaston Academy. 'I do love to go to school. Blackboards have a fascination for me and the old clock that goes tick, tock all day long above my head. . . .' The eager girl, who also said that she 'did so admire Virgil', and that 'algebra is a fine study', became a teacher herself, the youngest and prettiest in the Maine state school system.

The shipping news of the *Courier* soon revealed Tom as a master mariner, coming and going through the 1860s in a small coastal schooner, *Petrel*, and a barque, *Charles Brewer*. In 1863, when Addie Hall must have been diligently sewing for the Sanitary Commission, aged not quite twenty-one, Tom Dermot remained in port long enough to win her in marriage. Some letters of an old schoolmate of Maxine Elliott published in the *Courier* in 1933 said his determination had managed to edge out all her local suitors, a triumph for the immigrant Irish boy who could be acceptable to a girl of exceptional

---

* *History of Thomaston, South Thomaston and Rockland*, by Cyrus Eaton (Hallowell: Masters, Smith & Co.: 1865).

delicacy of manner, high education, and beauty. He led her to the altar at the Methodist church on March 8, 1863; within eight days of the wedding Tom was at sea again, and ran aground off the coast of Delaware at Lewes in his 319-ton *Charles Brewer*. No one knows whether Addie was taken on that trip—many wives did sail with their husbands—but apparently she never went on another. Perhaps this mishap made her frightened of the sea and helped to explain her later nervousness.

I began to hear stories galore now of the Rockland Halls, Captain Tom, early Rockland days, as present-day residents who became my friends joined in the hunt. The two lines united in the parents of Maxine Elliott were sometimes complementary, sometimes in conflict.

Tom Dermot allied new blood and his own force of character to a family which had been just as vigorous as himself in past generations but had now withdrawn into a settled community no longer at war with Indians, French, British, or the primeval forest. The Halls had boasted an officer at the Battle of Louisburg and the above-mentioned Ebenezer, who settled Matinicus in 1750 accompanied only by his wife and children. A son who survived the Indian massacre—also named Ebenezer—had a sister-in-law who married Henry Wadsworth Longfellow's grandfather, which I had long known from Mother's recitations of 'Lives of great men all remind us', written, she said with a chuckle, 'by your great-granduncle Henry'. Maxine's grandfather, Isaac Hall, is listed as a peddler in Eaton's history, but entered himself as 'Captain' in the family Bible, the property of my cousin Bob Brewer of Rockland. Evidently he had gone to sea for a few years.

Tom Dermot, the Irishman who had known living in its most violent aspect, had to tone himself down to suit a girl from a community which was strictly moralistic, supported temperance, believed in frugality and avoidance of ostentation, and knew itself to have a history that pre-dated most other regions of the United States. Added to his wife's particular brand of New England dignity and reticence was the special ingredient from her own mother Sarah Hahn, a Moravian, whose people had come from Bohemia in protest against the laxity they felt existed in the Protestant Church. Sarah Hahn Hall's religion was even more exclusive and soul-searching than New England Methodism. Gradually, as I began to understand these forces in the background of Maxine Elliott, I understood how she had managed to baffle both her worshippers and the scandal-mongers. New England taught her how to hold her tongue, to act according to her own will and let her own conscience be her only mentor. She also shared the dash of the Irishman who leaped from one world to another and adapted himself perfectly, so in the end no one remembered that Captain Tom barking about upon his quarter-deck was not a Yankee like everyone else. In the end of Maxine Elliott's life, many forgot she had not been born a member of the ruling classes of Europe.

Captain Tom and Adelaide Hall moved in to a small Cape-Cod-style house on State Street where it crosses Pleasant Street. The Isaac Halls lived farther up State Street at No. 12, and Addie's older sister, Clara, who married George Perry, lived at 15. The Dermot house is gone now, removed when the station yard needed the area, and the remains of it now stand at 13 Hall Street. Up until a fire in 1960 a plaque adorned this house which said: 'Birthplace of Maxine and Gertrude Elliott (Lady Forbes-Robertson), noted actresses. Born Jessie and May Gertrude Dermot.' No date was attached; Maxine would not allow it.

The Dermots had six children. The oldest was Thomas, Jun. Second in the family came Jessie C., and one may assume that the C stands for her Aunt Clara, though it is never specified, even on the town register of births, where Maxine could not control the relentless entry of her birth date, February 5, 1868. The *Courier* reports a particularly severe winter, the harbour immobilized in ice: 'No arrivals. No clearances. Ice here, ice there, ice everywhere.' For Addie Dermot the freeze-up was a blessing because the schooner *Planet*, her husband's current command, was among the vessels unable to stir. Not till March 19 did the harbour clear, and that day saw an exodus of twenty-two vessels, the *Planet* among them. Over the years, the births of subsequent Dermot children and the comings and goings of the Captain's vessel tell a story common to many Rockland families of the time, a household dominated by women with fathers away many months at a time.

I visited Rockland first in winter and did not know till a springtime visit, when the snow had cleared to reveal a tiny grave, that another little Dermot girl, Gracie, had been born besides Jessie and May Gertrude. I knew there were three boys—Tom, Lew, and Sam. Tom shared school days with Jessie, her senior by two and a half years; Lew was four years her junior, the space between them accounted for by the nine-month life of little Gracie; my mother, May Gertrude, was born December 14, 1874, and Sam, the baby, came two years later. It is curious that reports of Tom Jun. survive—when Tom is farthest away in years, but Lew seems to have left no school friends who remember him, or elders who left letters that include him. He became a seaman and died at sea, and my guess is that he ran away at an early age; one member of such a family usually did. No such urge was in Tom Jun., who combed his hair constantly, washed his hands six times a day, was poetic and melancholic like his mother, and finally was driven from the house by Captain Tom to earn a living. He drifted to the West Coast and had a nugget of gold beaten into a little ring for his Rockland sweetheart. I saw it on the hand of Mrs. Dorothy Snow, whose mother, Jenny Willey, received it from him. Tom Jun. told Jenny her eyes were like the 'o-see-un'—some odd pronunciation of his own. He did not return, however, so Jenny married another, but through girlhood was a staunch friend of Jessie Dermot.

Jessie herself began to emerge from the shadows. One of her classmates, Mrs. Margery Ingraham Thorndike, ninety-four when I met her, remembered her constantly rushing over to her family's house, welcomed by Mrs. Ingraham, who observed that Mrs. Dermot was nervous and withdrawn and the Captain often over-strict, so she was sorry for Jessie. Other classmates, now dead, contributors to an article on Maxine Elliott in the *Courier-Gazette* in 1933, gave similar sketches of a girl big for her age, restless, tomboyish, always in a hurry. She is described as already a marked beauty by the age of ten, but not all her contemporaries agreed. Some found the opaque skin inherited from her Moravian grandmother odd and gipsy-like, her hair so black that she seemed 'foreign'; she had not the required dainty waist of the period, causing her much distress when she tried to exchange dresses with Marge Ingraham. She sewed constantly, making and remaking clothes for herself, often so impatient to wear them that she would go out held together by pins. One classmate, Elvira Wood Haley, in a letter to the *Courier*, wrote: 'She was handsome, knew it right well, and made use of it, but the knowledge never made her disagreeable or conceited in a petty way as so often is the case. Everyone liked her although at times she made them hold their breath. As a child she was daring, full of capers, not amenable to home rule and took delight in escapades.' Woodbury Snow of Rockland has told me that his older brother Will was taken aback when Jessie egged him on to smoke behind the barn and joined him with a will. Lillian Sprague Copping, aged ninety-five and living in Los Angeles, directed her son to tell me that Jessie's clothes tended to be rather loud and over-striking as a girl . . . 'at that age Jessie had no taste.'

Judge E. K. Gould contributed a letter to the *Courier* in which he told of Jessie's direct, frank ways, a strong personality, 'hard to describe, that set her apart as a unique figure.' He said, 'She was never during her school life the "best girl" of anyone . . . yet most kindly and friendly to them all . . . She was a girl who liked to please . . . she was always tactful and liked to be a "good fellow".' He said the whole classful of boys and girls in the grammar school were a bunch of 'wild jackasses' (his long and delightful account destroys the picture of demure little darlings of the seventies and shows a sort of seething New England 'blackboard jungle' with striped stockings flying, sailor hats whirling). Once, he says, their clever teacher, Mrs. Martha Leach, quelled the uproars and encouraged the completion of tasks by promising that the last period would be devoted to the reading of the romantic novels of Elijah Kellogg, which they all devoured under their desks. Mrs. Leach selected Jessie Dermot as the reader. Her choice was calculated; the Dermot children had this curious clear, unaccented speech insisted upon by the Captain; Jessie was a developing beauty and the boys could be kept quiet if allowed to stare openly. The class was all silent attention.

High spirits erupted again, and Ed Gould, nicknamed

'Happy Jack' by Jessie from the name painted on his red 'sharp-shooter', describes him tearing around the class-room, in and out of desks, in a struggle to cut off a lock of Jessie's black hair with her own sewing scissors. Finally she bargained with him to cut off a piece herself, doing it her way rather than his, to give to him. It was a dull victory, but the boy accepted, and the man in later years cursed himself for losing the black lock that had remained long in a geometry book. Jessie offered constant surprises. When some girl friends wailed at being upset in a big sled, she defended the pilot, who had yanked it over to avoid hitting an overturned single-seater. She let 'Happy Jack' walk her home, tempting him with a promise of her mother's molasses cookies, but denied him entry at the door. She demanded that he prove himself like the man in the novel she was reading, ready to perform any feat of daring for his lady-love. 'Happy Jack' caught the spirit; he declared he would invade the Dermot home by way of the rose trellis and enter through a first-floor window. Unfortunately the trellis collapsed, and, fearful of Captain Tom's well-known roars of anger, he fled.

There is a series of small glimpses that flash by and are gone—Jessie playing Portia in class with a Shylock two heads shorter than herself, the tall girl's terror . . . Jessie reciting a foolish poem invented for the school rag, 'I am sweet Jessie, the belle of the school,' kidding herself . . . Jessie, hoping to avoid further recitations by claiming she had developed the same sort of migraine headaches that were already the torture of her mother . . . Jessie, modest and sweet-mannered, coming to read to Mrs. Levi Hall Verrill, a lady of the Rockland *élite* whose sister, Augusta, was then Captain David Ames's second wife. Mrs. Verrill told her niece, Mrs. Jessie Mains of South Thomaston, that the girl's voice was beautiful and low, her manners impeccable, all the tomboyishness in abeyance. . . . There is Jessie with a hammer competently mending the step of the Perry house on State Street. . . . There is also Jessie eager for trips on her father's vessel to New York, where she could stare in shop windows and perhaps even go to the theatre . . . Jessie hungry for the big parties given at General Tillson's house or Mayor White's house, fuming to get a new dress made in time . . . Jessie, with a long black pigtail bobbing on her back, hauling her chubby-legged little sister May Gertrude to kindergarten, while a boy, Oliver Lovejoy, nearly a hundred years old when I saw him, moved the curtains aside in his family's house to peep out at her and watch the long stride and proud head . . . (Mr. Lovejoy, a tiny little man showing the years only by deafness, leaped to his feet in the room in Rockland where I visited him, and paced nobly across it to demonstrate the free-swinging walk of the girl long ago.) There is Jessie curled up on the parlour sofa, reading, all the time chewing an empty reel of cotton, knowing she would bite her nails if she did not chew on something. This is a memory that came from my mother, who remembered that the reels all grew slim waists from Jessie's vigorous gnawing and the slight indentations of her teeth disappeared. It is a gesture I recognize; I often watched Auntie Dettie reading at the Château de l'Horizon, chewing off the red nail polish that had just been expensively painted on at Antoine's.

These pictures, garnered over many visits to Rockland, suddenly stripped the mystery from the lost Jessie Dermot for me. There was Auntie Dettie in all her practicality and directness. None of the world-weariness had come—it took many years to acquire and the whole world to be won—she was still full of the morning light, a-tiptoe on the snowy slopes of Rockland, waiting for her place on the bobsled that would send her hurtling to the bottom of the hill, her eyes already on the departing ships that can be seen when you stand up at the top of Middle Street, with the town at your feet, and look across to the water and the islands beyond. The view she saw was strictly New England—a collection of white clapboard houses, some with captains' walks; church spires popping up; elms that blaze in autumn and in summer break the white, the yellow stucco, and the red brick with their luscious green; firs that give accent; and the soft mauve and white of lilac in spring, the roses, the honeysuckles, the huckleberry hedges. . . . The line of land and water, perhaps over-familiar, the home that hedged her in and that she longed to escape, is more beautiful than the combination seen from the windows of the Château de l'Horizon, but it is by no means dissimilar.

*

Missing pieces remained to be found. The jolly, slightly comic Jessie Dermot was there, a girl rather too free-wheeling for her surroundings, but the element that eluded me was the sad one, the blackness, some memory of hurt that made Auntie Dettie exclude Rockland from her conversation. I remembered that my mother said their father suffered a great loss when a vessel of his was smashed. The history of the territory teemed with stories of wrecks and sinkings, so numerous that I was baffled at first. I did not even know if Captain Tom's disaster had happened in Rockland or in some far foreign port. The kind men of Rockland, led by Woodbury Snow, now eighty-two, tracked it down for me in the end. It happened just before Jessie's tenth birthday.

Captain Tom had prospered. He had sold the State Street house in 1875, bought shore and Main Street property which would bring good rentals, and acquired a new house for the family at Park and Broad Streets. All this new real estate was signed over by him to Addie Hall Dermot, 'for one dollar and the love and affection I bear my wife.' The expansion was considerable. The new house had two parlours, a dining room, a large kitchen with a brick Dutch oven built into the wall beside the cooking range; there was ornamental stained glass in the hall windows, and the house stood three stories high. When I found this house and then entered its doors I was immensely reassured; here at last I saw a long banister— for months I had been wondering how Mother could have told me that they slid down the banisters when their house was a compact Cape Cod cottage. Here was enlarged living, separate bedrooms for the children, a good address on the same side of the railroad tracks as the moneyed class of the town. It was a shorter walk to school; the public skating rink was at the foot of the street; it was on the line of march when Barnum's circus paraded into town.

With the new house came also the answer to a shipmaster's dream. Captain Tom had put money in the construction of a brand-new barque, built to his specifications at Starrett's shipyard. Other money came from the Cases, Whites, Hitchcocks, chandleries, and shipping; thus Captain Tom was in partnership with the big money of the town. By Christmas 1877 the vessel was almost ready for her ceremonial launching

and the maiden voyage. She was 578 tons, 141.1 feet from
bow to stern, 31.8 feet in width, constructed of hard pitch
pine, with iron and copper fittings, and bark-rigged. She
would be called the *Will H. Case* in honour of Mayor John
Case's little son, since the Mayor's interest in the vessel was
the largest. Her first trip was planned for an Atlantic crossing
straight from Rockland to Liverpool.

On the night of January 10, 1878, a great storm hit Rockland. The *Will H. Case* was moored to the Railroad Wharf
with one man already sleeping aboard her. It was the ship's
cook, who was Captain Tom's own brother John, evidently
rediscovered on one of Tom's voyages abroad. Captain Tom
and his mate both dashed to their ship as they heard the rising
fury of the wind, just in time for Tom to cut her loose from
the wharf, which itself began to collapse. The vessel was swept
into the churning waters of the harbour, filled with colliding
shipping and debris from the wharves, and only Tom's expert
navigation saved her from being smashed to pieces. He managed to run her ashore at Haskell's Beach, a flat cove south of
the town. Her main topgallant mast was gone, some planks
started, timbers broken, her keel badly ripped.

The *Courier*, reporting the extent of damage to the town,
printed a special editorial on Captain Tom's rescue of his
vessel. She was towed back to the Starrett shipyard by a Coast
Guard cutter for repair. Everyone congratulated Captain
Tom, but the damage was a disaster for him. No insurance
had been carried, and Tom's share in the vessel had come
out of his own earnings. Since he refused to touch the money
he had made over to his wife, he was obliged to sell his share
back to the other owners, all men with interests which could
carry them through this extra expenditure required for
repairs.

Jessie was ten years old and a bright, mature girl. She undoubtedly heard her father's discussion of his problems and
learned for the first time the difference between men who had
money which made money, and those who earned a living by
work. Captain Tom was forced back into the position of a
paid employee, never able to realize the profits from his
trading trips that his owners could make. He was a clear-
headed, practical man who saw the trend of the times; his

future could never be what he had planned. He knew the days of sailing ships were numbered, too, and though only forty years old felt incapable of switching to a steam vessel. Already at this time Captain Tom must have had his eye upon the West Coast, which was buying up the sailing vessels of the eastern seaboard for the lumber and salmon trade with Alaska. It was impossible for him to make the move as yet; his wife needed her family and a familiar town. So he sailed away when the *Will H. Case* was seaworthy, extending his voyages further and further afield to gain all possible profit from her. When the shipping news of the *Courier-Gazette* reported his departure from Montevideo for 'foreign parts' his family knew he had picked up cargo for trade outside the continent of America and was bound for Europe, the Far East and Australia.

Financial loss to the family may not have been felt in immediate patterns of living for the Dermots. It did not mean there was less to eat, or that schooling was interrupted, or a house swept away. But Jessie had been made aware of loss of status for her father. She also bore the brunt of his long absences in their effect upon her mother. Rockland people who have helped me in this search are infinitely polite and kind. They were not willing to divulge the knowledge many of them had from their parents that Addie Hall Dermot became more and more strange. By degrees it came out; Mrs. Dermot was becoming a nervous invalid, a woman locked in a darkened room complaining of a migraine headache. She withdrew more and more from the life of the town, unwilling to join the happy bustle of church suppers, upset by noise, her great eyes showing a sudden widening in unknown terror.

Jessie took on more responsibility; she dressed May Gertrude for school, she tried to run the house, though she had little domestic interest. Her forcefulness was sometimes too much for her mother, just as Captain Tom's was also—she was described as 'a handful', and yet Mrs. Dermot was obliged to depend upon her. There was always help, of course, from the Perry cousins. Aunt Olive Clara Perry, the oldest of Addie Hall Dermot's brothers and sisters, was a woman who took family leadership easily, but she had a family of her own, and now the grandparents, Isaac and Sarah Hall,

4

were ageing and in need of care. In time the Park and Broad Street house was given up so that there remained only the two State Street houses opposite each other, Nos. 12 and 15, which facilitated division of labour. Captain Tom put his wife and children in No. 12 with the old people, with the Perrys across the street to supervise. The atmosphere at No. 12 was probably depressing, and it was then that Jessie was constantly finding solace in overnight visits to the Ingrahams and other families where life was jollier and young girls could sit up late hours combing their hair and gossiping, with a competent older woman in charge.

Every one was concerned for Mrs. Dermot, who was much loved; she was looked upon as a delicate flower, always beautiful but childish in comparison with the vigorous women who coped with their houses, their children, their men. Marge Ingraham Thorndike told me that she caught a glimpse once of Mrs. Dermot peering out of the window of her house, an Ophelia-like apparition with long black hair unpinned. The heavy coils hurt her head, she said, adding to the agony of her migraine. Captain Tom came in for a fair amount of criticism; he was considered over-vigorous, inconsiderate of his wife when he escaped to the grog shop with the men, too brusque and severe with his children. It was claimed that he handled Jessie unwisely, and their strong natures, very similar, clashed. Both Captain Tom and his daughter Jessie were too hearty and down-to-earth for the more delicate temperaments in their family.

There were small gaieties and companionships, of course, to enable family anxiety to be pushed aside. And there was one big event: Jessie was chosen with twenty-four other girls to form the team of 'Tea Tray Cadets' who would wait upon dignitaries of the Maine division of the Grand Army of the Republic when it held celebrations in Rockland for the twentieth anniversary of the outbreak of the Civil War. On February 22, 1881, when Jessie had just turned thirteen, she marched on stage at Farwell's Opera House in the line of girls all dressed alike in grey calico ('with a flowered pattern and a border' ninety-five-year-old Mrs. Copping wrote me, herself a member of the team eighty years before), their trays held at shoulder level. Then the girls sped to serve a hundred and forty guests, while patriotic recitations and sentimental ballads were performed on stage. Jessie was too self-conscious to be chosen as one of the performers, but in later life she could do some wicked imitations of 'News from the Front', or 'The Empty Sleeve'. The girls received Grand Army badges, and their captain, Addie May Crocker, was told she ought to go on the stage. No one seriously believed a Rockland girl would.

The success of the Tea Tray Cadets made them much in demand at other gatherings in the state. They were taken to Portland, to Augusta, to Lewiston, to Auburn. (Maxine Elliott loved Nat Goodwin's joke, mysterious to many, that the colour of his hair was 'next to Lewiston', i.e., auburn.) Acclaim from outsiders, a little travel, and her own burgeoning adolescence were making Jessie restless. She already had a woman's bosom; perhaps men in other towns flirted with her instead of just larking and kidding as her Rockland boy friends did. She was becoming over-ripe, and presently scandal broke.

This last incident of Jessie's brief Rockland girlhood came to the surface as slowly as her mother's nervous illness. It revolved around a young man called Arthur, or Art, Hall, no relation to Jessie but a member of a family of the *élite* set. One of his aunts was Mrs. Verrill, to whom Jessie read; another was Mrs. David Ames; his mother was a White, and all the men who held ownership in the *Will H. Case* were his relatives, Cobbs, Cases, Hitchcocks. He was ten years Jessie's senior. He was among the first of Rockland's playboys, a new class in town where fortunes were recent, made from shipping, lime, and even flour (represented by a native Rocklander, Mr. Pillsbury). Art had no intention of working as his forebears had. He bought trotters; he rode one of them back to front down the middle of Main Street; he was a menace in his fast tandem. His worldly dash and his high-jinks appealed immediately to Jessie. Meetings began, hardly approved of, so they became clandestine. Jessie, barely fourteen, had no business dashing about with a reckless young man, but her loyal girl friends, taken into her confidence, were not as censorious as her elders. Madeline Bird of Rockland, older daughter of Jenny Willey, told me that her mother was one

who used to fib for Jessie, declaring that she was staying overnight at the Willey house. Where she was, Jenny Willey never
pretended to say, but undoubtedly Jessie had found somewhere possible to meet Art Hall. Alas, one day Captain Tom
thanked Captain Willey for being hospitable so often to his
girl, and Captain Willey said he hadn't laid eyes on Jessie in a
coon's age.

Almost immediately afterward, Jessie was removed from
school for a long voyage from Rockland with her father. Reluctantly F. L. S. Morse, long superintendent of schools and
local historian, finally admitted to me that his father told him
that all Rockland believed Jessie Dermot had been 'got into
trouble'. Mrs. Elvira Wood Haley says the report given out
was that Jessie had to leave Rockland for her health and that
diabetes was feared . . . 'it was certainly true that at that time
she lost her high natural colour and her face was chalky white'.
It is possible such an early disaster did indeed poison the girlhood of Maxine—certainly she never had children, which
might mean that her own child-bearing capacity had been
fatally impaired. In future years she always showed a savage
protectiveness for women, insisting that proper care should be
given to a woman expecting a baby as if aware, as many
childless women are not, of all the physical and emotional
problems that might do damage. There is nothing but ancient
gossip to support this story, except Maxine Elliott's later
attitude, and a beautiful, headstrong girl can so easily find
herself in the position of creating this sort of speculation. At
least, it is safe to say she was humiliated. She had become
involved with the most privileged elements of the town and
undoubtedly felt herself unwelcome, with Art Hall unwilling
to limit his own future by taking responsibility for her. The
Captain whisked her away, probably furious with everybody.

The voyage on the *Will H. Case*, lasting many months and
taking her to South America and across the Atlantic to Spain,
turned into a triumphal journey for Jessie. She was admired
whenever she and her father stepped ashore, and caused a
stampede among the Spanish males. A high dignitary offered
her his hand in marriage. Annie Frost of Rockland repeated
to me tales that Jessie had told her friends of the wicked ways
of the world she had observed while on her foreign travels.

Jessie had come back wearing gold ear-rings, and carried a parrot on her shoulder. Her whole bearing suggested defiance; she thoroughly enjoyed shocking everyone. It was obvious that more trouble lay ahead if she should be put back into high school in Rockland. So Captain Tom, hearing that General Tillson's girl Minnie was being sent to a Notre-Dame Academy convent school outside Boston, in Roxbury, decided to send Jessie there too.

At home, in the long absence of both Captain Tom and Jessie, the mental condition of Addie Dermot had worsened. Sometimes she would rise in the night and wake my poor, small mother, only seven at the time, and dress her, then haul her through the dark night streets, unable to rest, unable to venture out alone, taking the little girl as companion—an experience which left a deep scar. Captain Tom temporarily abandoned the sea and took over management of the Main Street property he owned, and there helped run a jewellery store in association with Thomas Hix, an in-law of his wife's. It was not a happy situation for a seafaring man, and sometimes he broke away for short trips, once taking little May Gertrude and Sam with him. Mother calmly described to my sister Blossom being out in a rowing-boat in the harbour of Montevideo—or possibly Rio—and seeing a large steamer bearing down upon the boat, an experience she found funny, while her mother's nocturnal prowls terrified her. It was a time when the headstrong schoolgirl at Notre-Dame could be of little help in the family. Her beauty augured an early marriage; 'the earlier the better' was unquestionably the opinion of her father and her loyal Aunt Clara Perry in troubled family conference.

The last impression I had of Jessie in the Dermot home before she took flight came from Annie Frost, the contemporary of my mother. The two small girls were playing on the floor in the parlour, to the sounds of Jessie's piano in the next room. It stopped abruptly. The tall girl, a grown woman to little Annie, stood in the doorway and gazed at them abstractedly. She was home from Notre-Dame for the summer holidays, already more responsible, and had roundly scolded the little ones for stuffing themselves on raw vegetables at the Perry-Hall lot at the Head of the Bay. They looked up at

her rather timorously, but she saw they were quiet and good,
and said nothing. She seemed to be far away, said Annie Frost.

Years later, when Maxine had gained theatrical and social
success, she took an excursion back to Rockland one summer.
This seems oddly out of character for a woman who could
close a door on one phase of her life after another with such
firmness and no backward glance. She and Gertrude and their
cousin Suzanne Perry rented a summer cottage for a few weeks
at the south end of Rockland near the shore. A young Perry
cousin, Theodore, or 'Ted', told me that the women engaged
him to be odd-job boy, and he spun over on his bicycle to
bring the groceries and empty the rubbish. He was dazzled
by the stage actresses, who all smoked like chimneys and wore
beautiful clothes. 'Maxine ran everything,' he said. 'She gave
the orders, and she paid me my wages.' There was much
laughter around the house. Maxine had discovered that he
liked to make up his face and put on funny noses and daub
himself with strange marks, so she offered to take him to New
York and teach him to be an actor, but his mother would not
hear of it. He saw their departure with regret.

The visit was not altogether a success. Maxine's old friend,
Jenny Willey, now Mrs. Bird, eagerly prepared to visit her,
but found herself sternly forbidden by her husband to asso-
ciate with a woman of the stage whose life could hardly be
moral. It was a sorrow to Jenny, who never questioned her
husband's authority but told her daughter Madeline that such
slights made her fully understand any lack of love for Rockland
that Maxine Elliott showed.

It had hurt Maxine. On Main Street she happened to run
into Ed Gould, then a rising member of the bar, who hurried
to greet her and expressed his admiration of her looks and the
elegant good taste of her costume. In his letter to the *Courier*
in 1933 he recalled that she became suddenly melancholy and
said, 'Thanks so much, "Happy Jack"—you evidently believe
in planting a rose where a thorn might grow, and do not hold
back from your friends the good things you could tell them
until after their death. Don't let some of life's experiences,
however bitter, change this disposition. . . .'

*

Jessie Dermot of Rockland, Maine, seemed to me a person I could at last recognize sufficiently for her to step out from behind the image of Auntie Dettie. In the exuberant school girl of the eighties was the beginning; in the large, ageing woman on the Riviera was the end. With these two aspects to guide me I felt that in my searches ahead, in New York to start with and wherever they would subsequently lead me, I would find the personality familiar, and in time the triumphant beauty, Maxine Elliott herself, would appear.

3

MRS. GEORGE MACDERMOTT

JESSIE DESCRIBED her life at Notre-Dame Academy in Roxbury as 'very quiet'. It was an interim period that left little impression; in later years the names and faces of schoolfellows were so dim that she could not remember them when ladies from Boston called on her, claiming her as classmate. Jessie, a travelled woman of fifteen who had sailed to South America and Spain, considered schoolgirl passions and interests now of little account. She went through her work in a dream and awaited freedom.

A fresh interest, friendship with a New York girl, aroused her enthusiasm. Mary Kiernan's tales of New York life filled her with longing; when she was invited to spend a vacation in New York City with Mary she jumped at the opportunity. Mary's mother was a MacDermott, and the coincidence helped draw the two girls together in an amused pretence of cousinship. These MacDermotts had an advantage over Captain Tom Dermot by having arrived in New York in a later immigration, when the Irish population of the city had become an accepted fact; thus there was no need to drop off the 'Mac', but Jessie noted with pride that they had a double T, whereas her own name ended with only one—a sign, according to her father, that she belonged to the gentry of the clan.

Jessie had seen New York several times. She had stopped there with her father on the way to South America and on shorter coastal trips when his last port of call before returning home was New York. She had been there chaperoned by the aunt of Addie May and Lizzie Crocker on an excursion that caused Mrs. Crocker profound embarrassment because Jessie attracted so much male attention in the streets. Jessie had loved it, but on each visit she was an outsider looking wistfully in, accompanied by family or friends who were not part of the city's life. A visit to the Kiernans meant that she would be included in a New York household of people who were not country cousins gawking at the sights.

The Kiernan residence was at 236 East 36th Street; the occupants were Laurence and Eliza Kiernan, the parents, wonderfully and surprisingly young; their three children, Edwin, Mary, and Paul (aged seventeen, fourteen, and ten respectively); and Mrs. Kiernan's brother George Mac-Dermott, a bachelor thirty years old. Besides the family there were seven gentlemen boarders who brought a tidy addition to the weekly budget, professional men who were out all day and had little association with the family except for a communal meal offered by Mrs. Kiernan at Sunday midday. Two young Irish maids, who lived at the very top of the house, struggled to keep it clean—a losing battle with two elevated railways which enclosed the city block, showering gritty soot over sills and onto Mrs. Kiernan's white lace curtains. The maids struggled up and down the steep house with shaving water for the gentlemen, and sometimes a little pleased yelp was heard if they happened to pass George MacDermott on the stairs.

The district was crowded and noisy, but to Jessie it possessed the magic of a great city full of raucous, vivid life. Families of tradesmen and office workers, predominantly Irish and German, crowded this East Side section, which in the 1880s was considered far uptown. It had been nearly forty years since the mass immigrations of destitute Irish and slightly better off Germans had flooded the downtown and West Side dock areas of New York, but another generation had been born, and those who prospered moved uptown and eastward. Quarters were still crowded, but respectability had come. If you walked west from the Kiernan house toward Fifth Avenue, you were soon among the houses of the rich. At 36th Street and Madison Avenue was the great mansion of J. Pierpont Morgan himself; only a few blocks farther was the reservoir (the present site of the Public Library), past which equipages of the well-to-do bowled up and down. A short stroll home again in the easterly direction soon brought you back under the clanging elevated railroad on Third Avenue, with restaurants, boarding houses, small shops, blacksmiths, stables, and carriage houses that leaped into crowded existence at the point where the private mansions and gardens ceased; but the life of privilege was close enough at hand to make the dwellers in the east thirties feel that in some measure they had begun to arrive.

Even if the Kiernan family, jolly, noisy, and untidy, had felt misgivings when Mary proposed bringing a New Englander to stay, they learned immediately that Jessie Dermot was delighted with everything. She stepped happily off the train at Grand Central Depot, and never flinched, as many a provincial girl did, at the onslaught of yelling cabbies who fought for fares, pulling the arms of bewildered travellers, or cracking their whips to assert availability. She was eager for everything, full of laughter, released to chatter about the house instead of living constantly on tiptoe for fear of her mother's headaches. She wanted to go and stare in B. Altman's store window; she wanted to watch the celebrities come and go at the Hoffman House; she drank in the details of city life and set the family in a roar with her comments. Mrs. Kiernan refused to believe Jessie was only fifteen. 'I'll send back home for my birth certificate to prove it,' said Jessie, and she did.

A girl who wished to get married would be expected to produce her documents. Jessie's request for her birth certificate may have been already the result of the meeting of eyes, the touching of hands, the stolen escapes from the rest of the household by Jessie and her friend's Uncle George. If seventeen-year-old Edwin had believed that he had the right to expect to escort his sister's lovely friend, he was passed over unnoticed in favour of Uncle George, a man the family proudly described as a real bachelor, not the marrying kind, always with a new and gorgeous stage actress upon his arm, a frequenter of the vaudeville, the race track, the men's clubs. He was precisely the sort of man who dazzled Jessie, making the high jinks of Art Hall fade into boyish pranks beside his worldly knowledge. She made it her business to be sophisticated in his presence, determined that she would never show herself as too young. He, too, in his turn was dazzled. Here was a glorious girl who would never be a drag with his friends, but was young enough to be his entirely, moulded to his ways.

Immediately he found delight in taking the young beauty to parade before cronies and put despair into the hearts of his ageing mistresses.

George MacDermott was a practising lawyer who had done a brief apprenticeship in the office of the mayor's city marshal in 1880—so brief, in fact, that it could have been only for the purpose of learning his way around before becoming first marshal himself within a few months. It was an appointive office, received from a new mayor just taking office, William R. Grace, who won the election of November 1881 on a Democratic Reform ticket. Among the predominantly Irish names at City Hall George MacDermott had friends, and these friends had helped elect the mayor, so George was one of the political debts Mayor Grace found himself obliged to pay in his struggle to win the nomination over a Tammany candidate. During the course of Mayor Grace's first term of office (for one year only), he delivered some shocks to those who had expected to treat him as a cipher, by bringing order into the city finances and reforms to the police and street-cleaning departments. George MacDermott, whose appointment as first marshal ran for a six-year term, settled comfortably in under the Tammany successor, Franklin Edsel, who ousted Grace in the election of 1882. When Jessie met him he had been established in Room Number One on the ground floor in City Hall for two years.

He was the most glamorous man Jessie had ever met. Her head was still full of romances; her experience had been small; her sophistication was only on the surface, and she was an easy victim. She fell deeply in love. George had the assurance of a man fifteen years older than herself; he talked of the theatre, of politics, of society, his conversation peppered with the names of the rich and powerful, all his dear, good friends. He claimed that a great political career lay ahead for him, with the patronage of ex-mayor Grace, still a business power in the city, and all he needed to realize his ambitions was a beautiful wife. Besides possessing worldly glitter, he was also tall and florid, with straight Irish features and red-gold hair; he decked his commanding looks in the latest styles, with fancy waistcoats, four-in-hand ties held by a jewel; he swung a smart cane as he walked, his grey bowler tipped boldly over one eyebrow. He was a lavish spender; he would adorn Jessie so that she would be the most admired woman of the city.

The office of first marshal in the eighties held considerable power and brought a salary of $2500 (equivalent today to about £3,700). Under him served a second marshal, three permanent clerks, and an army of hired men to be sent as bailiffs to carry out the marshal's orders. Today there are over eighty marshals in New York City to serve the courts, but then the marshal held the position equivalent to a Western sheriff and was himself arbiter and judge. George Mac-Dermott was never required to soil his hands by removing furniture for nonpayment; his roughnecks did this for him, often with extreme brutality. The bulk of his work consisted of checking licences and collecting fees and renewals—ten dollars a year for boarding houses, express wagons, vendors, vendors' pushcarts, coach drivers, porters, charcoal burners, kindling-wood salesmen, steamboat runners—with the revenue going to the city treasury, and ten dollars or sometimes five dollars a year for pawnbrokers, junk boats, junk carts, second-hand dealers, coaches, and cabs, to benefit the city's sinking fund. Informers slipped easily into the west door of City Hall, finding Room Number One immediately on their right, to tell of neighbours operating without licence (so that the city could swell its funds by imposition of fines), and the door was equally accessible to those who wanted, for a cash consideration, to avoid trouble with the marshal's office. George MacDermott found these deals profitable and the door convenient, often using it himself to disappear to the Brunswick Bar to pick up racing tips from the boys. If the tips were promising, visitors waited on the benches outside his office while he spent the afternoon at Belmont track.

Jessie knew nothing of his work, but saw him only as a man of substance, a respected, powerful city official. The great flag that stood in the corner of his office gave him dignity, impressive to a girl on a tour whose conductor was the chief official himself, causing clerks to rise at his entry, hats to be tipped in the passageways. She was impressed, too, by his private law office at 29 Broadway (the present site of the Woolworth Building) in the shadow of the monstrous Post Office that stood in City Hall Park and dwarfed the eighteenth-century elegance of the Hall itself. She was dazzled by the electric lights on Nassau and Pearl Streets—the first in the city—and the brand-new Brooklyn Bridge. George Mac-Dermott was cloaked in the glamour of a growing city, treating its vigour as his own particular plaything. When Jessie told her parents she had fallen in love and wanted to marry George MacDermott they had no reason to suppose it was not an ideal match. This was a man who could support Jessie handsomely, a professional man of good Irish background, patronized by men of position.

The exact date of the marriage cannot be traced, but it was probably during 1884, when Jessie was sixteen. The Rockland relatives, even if they retained some doubts, did Jessie proud by a whirlwind sewing bee which gave her forty dresses for her trousseau. They were not all in the precise taste that a Rockland woman would have chosen, but Jessie's pleas for strong, flamboyant colours in the latest styles of *Godey's Lady's Book* were faithfully fulfilled. She had not yet learned that her vivid looks bloomed more in restrained colours, but revelled now in teen-age delight at being a married woman who could wear what she pleased—brilliant reds, blues, emerald greens, tartans galore, with a plentiful spattering of bows, ruchings, inlets on skirts and sleeves, with hats that were bowers of fruit, flowers, and birds.

The George MacDermotts did not have their own house until June 1885, but when it was an accomplished fact it was proudly entered in the city's records under the name of Jessie C. MacDermott, at 155 East 46th Street. Almost simultaneously George acquired a new private office at 5 Beekman Street. Jenny Willey from Rockland visited them and reported that George was a charming, handsome man and Jessie terribly in love. There was a trip to Rockland, too, when the newly wed couple called upon the family—a flying visit because of George's work, a mere day spent between the overnight boat from New York to Rockland and the return boat the following evening. In the excitement of many cousins flowing to 12 State Street to inspect Jessie's husband the couple managed to miss the five-thirty p.m. sailing of the steamship *Katahdin* and were obliged to stay overnight. The household was unprepared for them, and Jessie went hurrying round to a neighbour, Mrs. Berry, to ask if she could provide a meal for her husband. Already she may have learned that George had a quick temper when inconvenienced. The MacDermotts did not visit Rockland together again.

With George's change of office he also discarded his city work, declaring that it was hampering his private practice, making him waste time sitting round for hours for a mere $2500 a year when he could make far more on cases sent his way by a wide acquaintanceship. Jessie, a wife of the eighties who expected to know nothing of a husband's work, accepted his judgment, and indeed was delighted to find George more available for long, cheerful lunches and mid-week excursions to the country. George left City Hall in the third year of his six-year term—of his own choice, according to his report, but in the records there is a sudden hiatus at this moment, followed by a painstaking, handwritten report of his successor, Thomas Byrnes, to account for expenditures in the first marshal's office. Total lack of documents at the time of George's departure suggests that he had either grown too careless to keep records or had removed them. Friends he still must have had at City Hall, because whatever happened led to no open scandal.

A year later George had become less available for long, gay lunches or little trips, but he could not be found at his office either. Sometimes he disappeared in the evening while Jessie waited supper for him and finally went to her bed alone, to hear him stumble on the stairs in the small hours of the morning. He began to lie late in bed, skipping his office altogether, and to emerge at the time when the men would be gathering at the Brunswick Bar. He became unwelcome at the Brunswick because he had borrowed money and failed to pay it back. Jessie became more and more worried as his ways changed, his temper shortened, and he became steadily more unreliable. She was alone much of the time, wondering where he was, daily more sure that wherever it was he was drinking. She faced him with it, and their first terrifying, violent fight crashed into the open. It was followed by other fights; verbal abuse gave place to physical violence. Jessie was horrified to find herself felled to the floor by blows. No amount of quarter-deck roaring from her father had prepared her for the experience that love could turn to bitter, brutal hate and that men and women who thought themselves civilized could hit and scratch and kick. It was impossible that it was happening. She tried to hide it from friends, but one of them, an actress named Ysobel Haskins, heard George's abuse and saw great welts rising upon Jessie's neck and arms.

All George's fine boasts of a good private practice remained unfulfilled because he had not power to apply himself to work and believed that talk would always get him through. When his weaknesses were revealed and clients were disappointed he covered up loss of face and anxiety over money by more talk, more and more drink, more and more trust in a horse that would come in, a man who would give a loan, a deal that would pay off. He grabbed at the easy, spurious ways of making money. Some unworthy deal became known to Jessie, still more intolerable than physical pain or betrayed trust. She barred her bedroom door and George sank into brooding suspicion or raging accusations. He began to taunt her with finding her pleasure elsewhere. He had her followed by rough-necks who had been in his pay as marshal, and Jessie knew there were characters lurking at the street corner who fell in behind her whenever she left the house. Furious and defiant, refusing to be cowed, she found a man who admired her, a figure of renown, and fiercely asserted her right as a woman to receive admiration from others if her husband denied it to her. John Montgomery Ward, star of the New York Highlanders baseball team (his batting average for 1887 was .371), became her escort whenever she could escape the eye of George and his spies. One day she went shopping for a hat with John—George's promised finery came no more—and an informer reported where she was, so at the shop door on Fifth Avenue, as she emerged with her arm on John's and a hat box looped to her wrist, the enraged husband awaited her. With flailing fists George sprang at John Ward, but his bloated force was no match for an athlete in perfect condition. Jessie's horror of failure and loss of dignity made her recoil from the man who slumped ignominiously on the pavement among the titters of passers-by, and she swept away with the victor.

Briefly she may have contemplated flight with John Ward,

but she had loved George and the hurt was deep. All that a new man could give her was temporary comfort and the assurance that she was still beautiful and lovable; she herself could not give love again so soon. She let John Ward accompany her to Rockland, so angered and injured that she was careless of her reputation, and stayed briefly at Stryker's boarding house. His presence caused comment that still echoed sixty years later but was disregarded by Jessie. She had come home bearing her own hurt, with a man who made her feel at ease, a gentle, friendly man who would not be overbearing with her mother and whose sporting prowess would delight her father—only to find that a hurt of a profounder, more solemn kind awaited her. Her mother had been found wandering in the streets of Rockland unable to tell where she lived or who she was. The decision had to be taken at last to send her away from home where her mental state could only do irreparable harm to the young children. She was taken to the State Asylum in Augusta and died there shortly afterward in April 1888 at the age of forty-five.

As Jessie fought through the last months of her marriage to George MacDermott, Captain Tom put his furniture up for auction, made over his house to his sister-in-law Clara Perry, sold his interest in the jewellery store back to his cousin-in-law, Thomas Hix, persuaded the owners of the *Will H. Case* to sell her to a San Francisco company, and sailed away round the Horn, giving assurances to Clara Perry that he would send for the younger children the moment he had a new home. In California he found his childhood sweetheart, Isabelle Paine ('Uncle' Paine's daughter), now a widow of forty-two, teaching at a school in Stockton, still holding a place in her heart for Tom. They married within the year and bought a house across San Francisco Bay in Oakland. When Jessie fled from George MacDermott's bed and board she was able to put a continent between herself and her misery and go to the arms of a childless woman who at last had won the man she loved from girlhood and who longed to mother his children.

Jenny Willey from Rockland, Ysobel Haskins the actress, and Jessie's sister Gertrude all said Jessie had been deeply in love. 'She adored him and he hurt her horribly,' my mother told me many years later. Undoubtedly Jessie's rapid growth into apparent maturity had caused her to love an illusion of a man. Full of romantic, high-sounding imaginings of a great life, she had mistaken George's vulgarity for gallantry. It was bitter to have been so tragically wrong. The defensive pride which she had developed under the burden of her mother's illness, her father's financial losses, her own humiliating mistakes in Rockland, had received yet another smashing blow. All the advantages of being beautiful seemed to be swept into the rubbish heap; the noble, romantic men of fiction did not seem to exist at all in the real world. She had been taught to distrust the emotions by quick and cruel strokes, but she came to Oakland with her head high.

The cosy, small-town domesticity of Mrs. Belle Dermot enfolded her. For a little while Jessie could give in to it—even to the gruff, bewildered sympathy of her father and his large vows to beat George MacDermott unconscious—but she had come back where she had started, back to the kitchen and the neighbourly gossip, the pie-making, the gardening, the busy, unpretentious home shining with soap and polish, designed to welcome the sailor-man home from his voyages. Even in pain she had smelled the life of big cities, the brush of worldly success, and a freedom of action that came with urban living. She was determined to recover and go on alone, pushing marriage behind her as an ugly deception, raging when 'little mother' assured her that a fine, decent man would come along in no time. As she recovered she knew she must shake off dependence on her father; he also was a man, part of this race that demanded subservience and might turn and rend you. She would make her own way in the world, wary now of the siren song of romance. She was not yet twenty-one.

4

'MAXINE ELLIOTT'

NO ONE in the Dermot family wanted Jessie to leave Oakland. Captain Tom urged her to savour the quiet life and keep her stepmother company while he made his long trips up to Puget Sound and Alaska as master of the *Portland*. Belle Dermot begged Jessie to have patience and wait for happiness. The girl laughed bitterly at the idea: she wanted independence, and she wanted glamour still, but the right kind, not the spurious version George MacDermott had to offer. May Gertrude, now a schoolgirl in Oakland taking singing lessons, felt despair that her wonderful older sister, so recently reclaimed, would disappear again. Although the brothers had nothing to do with the question, they believed, if they thought about it at all, that their sister ought to stay at home as other sisters did. Jessie was bound for New York and no one could argue her out of it.

During her life with George she had met theatrical people. Ysobel Haskins had become an intimate friend and there were undoubtedly others. On all sides she must have heard the words, 'You ought to go on the stage,' because of her beauty. She was well aware that self-consciousness had stood in her way at school when there were dramatic presentations; she loathed recitations, except when she was allowed spontaneously to give wicked imitations of ballads such as those that peppered the entertainment of the Grand Army gathering in Rockland. With hand on heart and rolling eyes she could reduce the Dermots to helpless laughter giving a spoof of 'Lasca the Cowboy' or 'The Empty Sleeve'. But the thought of actual professional acting terrified her. It was the one road to freedom, however. The alternatives were dismal; she could take in sewing, work as a governess; if she finished high-school work she might teach; she could learn to use a typewriter and work in an office. Whatever she did, the pay for women was infinitesimal. She had no desire to join the droves of humble and distressed ladies who educated the children of those more wealthy, or battle in the business world, where women were accepted on sufferance and only at the bottom of the ladder. She had much bigger visions of herself, and where could they be better realized than in the theatre? She had the asset of beauty, which had failed her in love; it must be food for something.

The thought of a woman of the Hall family going on the stage was appalling. She knew that some aunt was bound to say, 'Thank God your dear mother never lived to see the day.' Belle Dermot was filled with worry; Captain Tom suggested that damnation might be not far off, but he did not mean it in the way the Halls and Hahns would have. It was not her eternal soul that was worrying him but her splendid, inviting body, and he believed her to be quite 'a damn fool'. He feared she would land herself in some stupid scrape and have to be hauled out. Jessie flared at the suggestion. Inside her, however, the early religious training of her mother, grandmother, and all members of the staunchly Methodist family made her feel that perhaps this was a step of desperation. The sense of sin was powerful. When she left for New York to seek work in the theatre she had finished her argument with God. He had failed to preserve her mother's spirit in tranquillity. He had never seemed very helpful in her own decisions so far. If He was going to damn her now, she was ready to take the consequences. Jessie gave up going to church, except on the occasional visit to Rockland when it pleased Aunt Clara; then she marched up the aisle, her best feathers nodding, defying the congregation to criticize, enjoying the turning heads of the men. 'Put yourself into God's hands, my child,' she had been told so often. It had never seemed to work. The only hands she trusted from now on were her own.

If Jessie was as careful of her reputation and her money then as she was in later years, she must have found another woman to share her lodgings when she first came to New York alone. New York was honeycombed with lodging houses in that period, so the mission to be accomplished was to choose one among them that was respectable. Some offered meals at a communal table; some allowed cooking in the room. An overworked maid brought bowls and heavy pitchers of water for each lodger's washing requirements, and made the beds and cleaned the rooms. In the hopes that she might meet people helpful to her career, Jessie probably chose one of the lodging houses that catered chiefly to actresses, where theatrical landladies did not object to much washing and pressing of clothes, and were lenient on late hours. She tacked the C on the end of Jessie to make the more romantic name Jessica, and threw away George's 'Mac'. She presented herself at the Madison Square Theatre as a prospective student in Mr. Dion Boucicault's drama classes. She had the fee, and she was beautiful. She found no difficulty in being accepted and enrolled.

In 1890 Dion Boucicault was sixty-eight and had behind him a career of fifty years as playwright, actor, and director. He had started in London, a poor boy from Dublin determined to make his way in the theatre. He was almost starved into an ignominious return home, but finally managed to slip past the vigilant stage doorkeeper at the Covent Garden Theatre and present the manuscript of his first play to the great comedian Charles James Mathews and his wife, Madame Vestris. At eighteen, in 1841, Boucicault was the author of *London Assurance*, which Mathews produced; fifty years later it was included in every stock company repertory. One hundred and forty more plays followed, some original, some adaptations. They were melodramas filled with floods, fires, noble heroes, black villains, battles, rescues, mistaken identity, long-lost children, and heroines pure as snow. Boucicault's greatest successes included the Irish plays he performed himself—*The Colleen Bawn*, *Arrah-na-Pogue*, *The Shaughraun*. In 1890 theatre fashion had abandoned him, turning toward the smart drawing-room comedy of Arthur Wing Pinero, while the *avant-garde* discovered Ibsen. Boucicault was cynical about public and critics, and financially harassed by much litigation; he found the offer from A. M. Palmer to direct a drama school a convenience he could accept. He had made many enemies in his life, but Palmer remained on good terms, often asking him to direct plays in his string of theatres.

Mr. Boucicault was a cocky little man with a large, domed head carrying a frill of luxuriant fluff around its edges. He considered himself a judge of beautiful women, and probably expected to be irresistible still. He examined the splendid newcomer to the school, Jessica Dermot, pleased with a speech nearer his own original Dublin English than was usual. He assured her he could teach her much. Stagecraft he knew backward. Perhaps a greater gift he had to offer was an attitude of mind expressed without much friendliness by the critic William Winter in the words, 'He assumed greatness.' This could be useful in making others believe you. He was not always tactful, however, sometimes too broadly a courtier of the important, mistakenly ignoring those who might become great. His way had been to flatter the public while at the same time he despised it.

To become the favourite pupil of his was a matter of luck; it would be caprice if he happened to like a young student or was capable of continuing to like her. Jessica Dermot was singularly well equipped to remain on his right side, because she had no desire for close relationship with him and could titivate his vanity by using the worldly wisdom she gained. She could defer to his opinions, or make the caustic comment which appealed to his wit. It pleased him also to be seen in a restaurant accompanied by a beautiful young woman. He gave Jessica much information about how to get on, whom to know, and whom not to know.

The theatre which housed the drama school was the Madison Square, created in Steele Mackaye's great dream of making a cultural centre. Mackaye, playwright and inventor (father of the playwright Percy Mackaye), had made it beautiful in white and gold, filled it with his own inventions (an elevator stage, a cooling system, seats that folded back) and nearly bankrupted the owners, the Mallory brothers. They were a curious parsonical pair engaged in theatre management—one the editor of the *Churchman* and the other a retired pastor of the Madison Avenue Episcopal Church. The Mallorys decided their theatre property must be put back on a paying basis, so Steele Mackaye took his idealistic enterprises elsewhere and A. M. Palmer came to bring solvency and add the Madison Square Theatre to his numerous others. The idea of the school remained, designed to provide supers and bit players for productions as well as instruction to beginners, and Dion Boucicault was made its director.

The students climbed to an upstairs rehearsal room near Mr. Boucicault's own office for their voice and movement exercises. (Often Mr. Boucicault retired to the couch in his office to listen more comfortably.) Sometimes they watched him rehearse a production in another of Mr. Palmer's theatres —the Union Square. Their small theatre world of study and talk and hopeful association with professionals was bordered by 14th Street on the south and 30th Street on the north. Perhaps Jessica Dermot learned a little to project her voice and move with some assurance. She did not discard self-consciousness, however, under Dion Boucicault's tuition, and it may not have seemed necessary because soon, he assured her, he would see she found confidence on a real stage. 'Learn by doing it; it's the only way,' he said.

There was no time, however, for his plans to work for her. The New York *Herald* of September 18, 1890, described Mr. Boucicault as feeling unwell. A group of his students, the newspaper reported, anxiously called upon him, and 'He went with one of them, in whom he took a special interest, to the stage on the floor below and there conducted a rehearsal'. This was the last time Jessica Dermot saw her first mentor. Boucicault complained of the depressing rainy weather, shut himself in his office for a while, and then huddled home in a cab. Mr. Palmer, knowing that he had already had several small heart attacks, hurried in anxiety to call on him, but was turned away. Boucicault died two days later.

At the time, his death probably seemed an irreparable blow to Jessica Dermot. She was surely one of the congregation at the Little Church-around-the-Corner at 29th Street and Fifth Avenue, and surely wept when the choir sang 'Lead, Kindly Light' and 'Abide With Me'. Pallbearers included Mr. Palmer, T. Henry French, Daniel Frohman, and Henry E. Abbey. The 'Profession' was represented by W. H. Crane, Sol Smith Russell, and Henry Miller, and the family came in the person of his daughter Nina Boucicault (in later years the first Peter Pan), leaning upon the arm of Edward H. Sothern. Jessica may have remembered Mr. Boucicault's voice telling her that this was an important occasion for a young hopeful in the theatre to attend because it never did any harm to be observed among the leaders of the theatre world. Every pall-bearer was a manager.

Bleakness and uncertainty descended. There would be no class tomorrow. She sought out fellow students, and one of them, Robert Hilliard, who was further advanced in a career, helped her pore over newspaper announcements of autumn productions. The time of year was good; now all the established companies were casting. Obviously the first management to try was Palmer's; his theatres were numerous, he might possibly have noticed her trailing in Mr. Boucicault's wake, but above all Robert Hilliard knew him and gave her a letter. 'You've always got to know someone,' Mr. Boucicault had told her.

All his advice amounted to nothing beside one precious legacy. Boucicault had helped invent the name she would present to Mr. Palmer when she requested an appointment. He had told her to study her assets—statuesque beauty, lady-like speech, dignity, and grace. A name of importance must be found, nothing as comfortable as Jessie or Jessica Dermot. Starting with the first name, he had asked for the grandest name she knew. They laughed at the romantic Rockland names commemorating seaports, such as Odessa, and the Puritan ones—Charity, Prudence, Experience. 'The grandest name I know,' said Jessie despairingly, 'is a man's name, so it won't do.' It was Maximilius, the name of a school friend's father. Mr. Boucicault felt it had the right ring, but Maximilia upon a marquee or a programme was too long. After passing through Maxime they invented Maxine, and Mr. Boucicault pounced upon it. So they went to work on the last name. Jessie recited all her Rockland ancestors: Halls, Perrys, Youngs, Tolmans, Hahns, Hixes—all too plain or abrupt to couple with Maxine. Finally a more harmonious name came to her memory; it was Elliott, borne by two remote Tolman ancestors as a first name, in memory of the maiden name of a grandmother. It too attracted Mr. Boucicault's experienced eye and ear; he well knew the power of the Irish-French mixture of his own. In final pleased surprise he pointed out that the name Maxine had now an added significance; Elliott was an old family name from her New England past, and if you eliminated the middle *x* in Maxine it spelled Maine, her home state. 'That,' he said, 'is excellent theatre'.

Miss Maxine Elliott requested an interview with Mr. Palmer and was told to appear at his executive offices on 30th Street. He was the most powerful man she had met, a man who has bestowed favours on her master. She dressed with meticulous care, but not too flamboyantly, for this gentleman of distinction. Mr. Palmer in 1890 was at the height of his power in management, beloved for his support of native talent, which he encouraged as enthusiastically as he beckoned to the great names of England, France, Germany, and Italy. He had helped American playwrights gain self-respect; plays by Bronson Howard, William Gillette, Bartley Campbell, and Augustus Thomas had been given productions by Palmer when other managements stuck slavishly to the writers first tried and acclaimed in London. He had fought for a fair copyright law to protect their works from piracy. He had the reputation of greater conservatism than his rival, Augustin Daly; he was fair, courteous, deeply devoted to the theatre, but determined that it should pay its way. He was prosperous and social, friend of the great everywhere, to whom he offered distinguished entertainment either in his mansion on Madison Avenue or in his house at Stonington, Connecticut, and each summer he and Mrs. Palmer took the trip to Europe. He was splendid in high-winged collar, frock coat, and flowing side whiskers as he graciously bade her be seated before his desk. The face of General Sherman gazed at her from a silver frame.

Now she would learn whether her beauty could serve her. She could not hope to be offered employment on the basis of acting experience; her only credits were the class work she had done with Mr. Boucicault and one appearance in an amateur group, run by Mr. Warde-Bingley, which boasted the grandiose name of American Théâtre Libre and had presented a play, *Aftermath*, on September 13, just before Mr. Boucicault died. She had, however, the luck to appear at the right moment. Palmer was casting for the English company of Edward S. Willard and would need several small-part players with accents that would not clash too glaringly. He could see this young woman in a series of roles in the Willard repertory;

she had an air of distinction and wore her clothes well—an ability more important than acting experience, which she lacked. Maxine left her first job-seeking interview with precisely what she had come for. She would get twenty-five a week (worth about five times the present value) but must provide her clothes: if her work was satisfactory she would be assured of employment for many months, because a tour would follow the New York opening.

E. S. Willard had recently achieved huge success in London with the play by Henry Arthur Jones, *The Middleman*, which was to open his New York season. It had come as a surprise that he could play a gentle, idealistic maker of fine pottery, because London audiences had known him long as portrayer of snarling villains (such as the original Spider in *The Silver King*) in the company of Wilson Barrett. There was nothing villainous in his looks, to be sure; the company who assembled to bid him a respectful good morning at the first rehearsal saw a man who resembled a popular preacher, with sad, deep-set eyes and hair that formed a halo effect of grey-brown.

He came accompanied by several dependable English character actors needed for a play on a political theme—the clash between labour and capital. Mr. Palmer provided the young leading lady to play his daughter, a regular of his repertory company, Marie Burroughs. Numerous second women, second girls, second old men, and second young men waited to be told their English star's requirements, among them Maxine Elliott.

Maxine's association with Mr. Willard was confined to an occasional bow. Outside the theatre, lionized by hostesses and housed in an elegant hotel suite which he furnished with rare first editions, he lived a life untouchable for her. Her friends must be sought among the girls she dressed with, who gave her tips on make-up. She was terrified of her inexperience and thoroughly surprised that everyone was twice as friendly when they found out this was her first job. She would step out onto a public stage as Felicia Umfraville, a young lady of breeding but no fortune. On November 10, 1890, the opening night was upon her: the overture music was playing, the hum of an assembling audience could be heard through the curtain. Maxine was sure she was going to be sick, faint, or die. She did none of these, and delivered the most awkward first line without stumbling: 'What a charming collection of people a political candidate gathers round him in the course of his career, Mr. Chandler.'

By the final curtain the nervous company knew they had a success. Mr. Willard's 'strong scene' brought down the house, and he had become a new favourite on Broadway. The play was skilful and serious by the standards of the day, though impossible today in its triteness of situation and unreal dialogue. Very few of the lines were delivered by Maxine, who sat one whole act in her dressing room while Felicia Umfraville faded from the plot, but a few of the critics noticed her. They remarked that she was beautiful.

Mr. Willard had a repertory to present, so after *The Middleman* came *John Needham's Double* by Joseph Hatton (it had a tiny part, Virginia Fleetwood, an American heiress, for Maxine). There were some evenings and matinees of one-act plays—more small parts for Maxine. The Willard company closed in New York on April 11, 1891, then played three weeks in Chicago and one in Boston. The whole season ended in May, but with good news; most of them, including Maxine, were re-engaged by Mr. Palmer to tour with Mr. Willard for eight months from next September through the following spring.

It was a beginning. She had collected no reviews that said anything about her acting. She earned a small salary, into which her own clothes costs bit heavily. She was learning the tricks, however—how to get a costume to look rich for the least money, where to eat cheaply. She had learned how to stretch and squeeze and pinch her salary so that she had saved enough to let her go back to Oakland for the summer, where she lived rent-free, making new costumes all the time. Gertrude goggled to hear all her tales of life in a theatrical company, and, though Maxine told her that it was a weary grind, to Gertrude it sounded magical, a world she longed to join.

Maxine rejoined the Willard company at the Chestnut Street Opera House in Philadelphia in September 1891. The two weeks were followed by a week in Baltimore, a week in Washington, a week in Pittsburgh, a return engagement in Chicago of a month at Hooley's Theatre, then on to St. Louis,

Cincinnati, Peoria, Davenport, Des Moines, Omaha, Kansas City. By a joyful coincidence, the company opened an engagement in San Francisco on December 14, May Gertrude's sixteenth birthday, and stayed there for Christmas, so she could celebrate it in the bosom of the family. The tour continued to Los Angeles, then had two more weeks in San Francisco, two nights in Oakland—right down the street from the Dermot home at the McDonough Theatre—then Salt Lake City, Denver, Kansas City again, St. Joseph, Jacksonville, Peoria and Chicago again, Milwaukee, Grand Rapids, Toledo, Detroit, and back again through Cincinnati, Pittsburgh, Philadelphia, Washington, two weeks in Brooklyn just across the river from home base, and a final seven-week engagement at the Tremont Theatre in Boston. By June 4, 1892, Maxine would have been happy never to see another train; but ahead of her lay another nine and a half months of touring with Mr. Willard. She had graduated to the part of Sophie Jopp, the villainess in *Judah*, also by Henry Arthur Jones, and there was one other play added to the repertory, J. M. Barrie's *The Professor's Love Story*, in which she appeared. Otherwise it was three solid years of dreary Umfraville and equally tedious Fleetwood.

These enormous tours were comparatively comfortable for the star: he had his special private coach in which he and Mrs. Willard could have their books, their dogs, and almost a settled home life. The company travelled by special coach also, but not separated from one another. They broke up into the card-playing group, the pairs of lovers, the girls who trimmed hats, knitted, and gossiped to pass the time, the men who disappeared in clumps to drink, sharing hip flasks in the corridors when the train was passing through a dry state. Maxine learned all the tricks to preserve her clothing from too much wear and tear. She kept in her bag the list of boarding-houses in each city, where she knew that the first thing to check was a decent looking-glass and an iron and ironing board. Once the room was selected, the shirtwaists were pulled out, to be pressed immediately, the handkerchiefs were washed and stuck on the looking-glass to dry, and the gloves were hung in a limp row on a towel laid over a convenient chair back. Skirts had to be hung, and their creases could be

more rapidly removed over a steaming bath. The landlady's
food was sampled, and Maxine and other members of the
company who shared the same lodgings would nod and say,
'Just like Mrs. Thingummy's in Cincinnati,' or 'Not so good
as Mrs. What's-it's in Saint Joe'.

There was inevitably a good deal of companionability in
this community life, which depended so completely on itself.
If there was any member of the company who was her special
friend, male or female, the name has not survived. Members
of the company were invited out, but could never become
quite a part of the cities visited. Mr. and Mrs. Willard, of
course, were entertained by the dignitaries of each town, and
the lesser members, if female, could find admiring gentlemen
at the stage door offering to give them supper. Sometimes
there were relatives or old friends in a city, but the good-byes
came fast, and the touring actors moved on, envying the
solidity of the homes they had visited, and being envied by
the stay-at-homes for what looked on the outside like a
glamorous life.

It was in fact an intolerable grind. Maxine stuck with the
Willard company for three years, because it gave her security,
and she had not made sufficient impact upon the managers of
New York to be offered anything else. In September 1893
Maxine joined the management of T. Henry French in a
drama called *The Prodigal Daughter*. The play had opened at
the American Theatre on May 22, and Maxine was a replacement for Charlotte Tittel in the part of Violet Woodmere.
The American Theatre (it has long since disappeared) was a
new mighty building at Eighth Avenue and 42nd Street. Its
capacity was twenty-one hundred, including seating in boxes
and standing room. It was lit entirely by electricity, and on its
roof there was a separate cabaret and restaurant. Everything
was done on a large scale by Mr. French, who had already
run the Grand Opera House and the Garden Theatre at a
profit.

When Maxine found herself established in New York at
the American Theatre she wrote to her sister that she could
come to live with her. Now that May Gertrude had been
graduated from high school in Oakland, she wanted more
advanced singing study, and a chance to be nearer New

York City, where the seat of a real career seemed to be. To calm the Captain and Belle, who were horrified at the thought of little May's being exposed to city life and Maxine's theatrical friends, Maxine stressed May's right to higher education, suggesting that she work for a degree at Hunter College while she also studied her singing. It was with extreme reluctance that the Dermots let her go. They placed her on the train for the transcontinental journey with a thousand admonitions and all but a label round her neck. When the train drew in to Grand Central Station she jumped out eagerly, searching the crowds for a sight of her sister. She saw her, a tall, majestic woman in a splendid hat that sported feathers, flowers, and fruit. May rushed to greet her.

'Heavens, what have you got on?' said 'little Dettie'. With horror she looked over May's boater, middy blouse, and serge skirt, whose girlish length exposed her ankle in button boots. May was, in fact, eighteen years old, but she could have passed for fourteen. As quick as lightning, Maxine shot her to a cab, and drew down the side blinds for fear anyone should see her. 'You don't think anybody is going to take you seriously as a singer looking like that, do you?' she said.

May Gertrude felt no resentment at this authoritarian treatment. She was willing to believe that everything her sister did was right; at the boarding house she submitted with surprised little cries as Maxine temporarily pinned her into one of her own dresses, pushing and poking angrily at her when she found insufficient bosom and hips to fill the dress. Maxine whisked May's hair out of its back hair ribbon and piled it with a fashionable puffing of the front hair over the forehead, and on top of all she set one of her own elegant cartwheels, which May was sure would not stand the impact of even the slightest breeze. Some of Maxine's friends fetched them out to dine in a restaurant, where May nervously watched which forks, knives, or spoons her sister used.

May Gertrude started work at Hunter College, and a singing teacher was found. Maxine moved them both into lodgings farther uptown in the sixties, so that May could easily walk to school. They had two rooms on the ground floor of a brownstone house, with meals provided by the landlady. Maxine went nightly to the theatre, and often stayed out for late supper. May was too young to be included in her social life, and much too shy to want it; besides, the separation of existence between an ex-married woman and a young girl was far more rigid then than it is today. The conversation of her elders would immediately have changed if May had been of the party. She was not permitted evening dates of her own, unless in the company of an older woman, and the suggestion that she might go out with a boy of her own age would have been rejected out of hand. It was also supposed that a girl still studying had to keep the hours of a child, for fear that she might overstrain her strength. Thus May's evenings in New York, although she felt herself blissfully lucky to be living with her big sister, were totally lonely and filled with fears. She was supposedly in the charge of the landlady, and no one could have entered the front door without this lady's knowledge, yet May sat long hours till Maxine returned, jumping at every sound, unsure if she was more afraid of a living human being who might break in or a shadowy one out of her own imagination.

Some of this fear was unwittingly created by Maxine herself. May was constantly anxious to say and do the right thing, to look just the way Dettie wished to see her. She wanted to reach this magical being, who was often subject to the blackest moods of depression, which May saw, but of which the social world knew nothing. Very small setbacks could send Maxine into moods that produced tears, and remarks that could be strangely cruel, although she was probably unaware of their effect. She worried about her career, finances, engagements, clothes; she often exploded over trivialities with a force that was out of all proportion and could be terrifying—the landlady had not changed the towels, or Maxine had been unable to match material for a blouse. Frequently she could whip little May into a frenzy of anxiety and confusion, so that to May also the reason for worry became magnified, and she did not see that it was Maxine's over-tension and not the thing itself which was the cause. Without husband, children, or anyone but herself and her small sister on which to expend her emotion, Maxine could often produce the effect of a tornado, all directed on a missing button.

An incident in the street one day added to May's anxieties.

Walking along Lexington Avenue on her way to class on 68th Street, May ran head-on into George MacDermott. He grabbed her by both shoulders and thrust his red, perspiring face into hers. 'Where is she? Tell me, where is she? Where is she living?' May pulled herself free and ran and ran, then collapsed into class. Her classmates remember her as always quiet and gentle, and at this time, too, she probably showed no signs of what she had been through. 'Little Dettie' must be protected at all costs. The grown-up world was indeed a terrifying place, and men were horrible.

Another day she took her school friend, Lulu, home for tea. Lulu remembers the elegantly dressed woman who came in after the two girls had been together for a few minutes. She got the impression of a mother or an aunt, rather than of a sister. She also felt her presence unwanted, and saw that the chatter about doings on the campus was tedious to the older woman. Lulu went home quite soon. Maxine was never able to enjoy the callowness of young people. It was as if some part of her emotional development stopped at the moment of her rapid burst into maturity at twelve, when an object aged merely ten or eight was infinitely below her dignity. She seemed immensely 'grown-up', but perhaps she was still trying too hard to make sure that she had indeed been graduated into the adult world.

*

The American Theatre had a stage seventy-five feet wide and fifty-five feet deep. The show whose cast Maxine now joined was *The Prodigal Daughter*, a spectacular production piece rather than a play, with a speaking cast of twenty-five and an army of supers, while the 'stars' of the company took up most space of all, because they were ten racehorses and a pack of hounds. The high point of the evening was the final stretch of the Grand National, presented on a revolving stage, the audience supposedly in the grandstand, and nightly the leading actor (a man), battled for supremacy over the last jump with the racehorse Roquefort (once the Duke of Hamilton's, winner at Aintree in 1885). All other horses wore the correct colours of real owners, and it was the delight of the knowledgeable in the audience to show they knew which was

Leopold Rothschild's, Lord Randolph Churchill's, or the Duke of Beaufort's.

When she got to the theatre at night Maxine frequently had to give precedence to the ten horses in their blankets and blinkers, which had been led unhappily through New York traffic by their grooms from the stables. Boys stood posted in the backstage corridors with brooms and shovels to tidy up after any indiscreet show of nerves. The hounds sometimes vied with the overture music in a community howl if something disturbed their nervous equilibrium. One actress who had frequently to be admonished by the kennel men was Maxine, because she always brought titbits to her favourite colleagues, the dog actors.

The play attracted a noisy kind of playgoer, tempted to place private bets and yell encouragement from the orchestra stalls. This enthusiasm was startlingly different from the decorum of Mr. Palmer and Mr. Willard. 'Stage-door Johnnies' were far more troublesome, and inclined to mistake the actresses in *The Prodigal Daughter* for the cabaret artistes from the roof garden. Lady members of the cast made their exit from the stage door in groups.

Maxine was in *The Prodigal Daughter* for two months. At the final matinee of December 16 she reported as ill, and Anna Erroll Boyd replaced her. Her affliction was evidently not grave, because she opened the following week, December 23, in the next production at the American, *The Voyage of Suzette*. It was another spectacular presentation, with an Oriental setting. Maxine wore twisted golden snakes as bangles, Turkish slippers, and a piece of floating gauze which passed for a yashmak. For the Christmas season a pantomime was included, complete with Clown, Pantaloon, Harlequin, and Columbine. Some distinguished actors took part in this hodgepodge—Nelson Wheatcroft, Harry Davenport, Vincent Sternroyd, William Simpson, and Sadie Martinot, as well as Fannie Ward in a small girl's part. But *The Voyage of Suzette* was a ghastly failure and closed in less than a month; then came *Sister Mary*, which collapsed after only two weeks. In this play two people appeared who did not vanish from Maxine Elliott's life as so many temporary associations during the run of a play were inclined to do. One of these was Elsie de

CAPTAIN THOMAS
DERMOTT

MAXINE'S PARENTS

ADELAIDE HALL
DERMOTT

MAXINE AGED 14

GERTRUDE AGED 12

Wolfe, who was still visiting her (as Lady Mendl) the year of Maxine's death, and the other was T. Daniel Frawley, who played an important part at one of the decisive moments of Maxine's future career.

The engagement with the American Theatre was finished. It had given Maxine far greater publicity than she ever had with Willard. It also brought with it a rumour that persisted but which cannot be proved. It was said that the handsome Richard Harding Davis, first of the foreign correspondents, kept a little apartment opposite the American Theatre, as 'a hideaway where he could meet Maxine Elliott'. Dickie Davis was twenty-nine at the time, just becoming a man whose work and personality were observed; he had made a stir with articles in the *Sun* and was doing special pieces for *Harper's* (including the report of an American cricket eleven, which he accompanied to England). He was handsome—firm-jawed, straight-nosed; Dickie Davis and Maxine Elliott together, if they ever were together, must have looked like models for a drawing by Charles Dana Gibson.

An offer of work followed at once—encouraging indeed, if fresh jobs would flow one after the other to assure her a rising career. Rose Coghlan, a veteran dramatic actress, needed a second leading woman for her repertory company, and sent for her. Maxine was advised to play down her self-confidence when presenting herself for an interview with Miss Coghlan, a strong, temperamental woman. The interview progressed satisfactorily; Miss Coghlan's manner could be breezy and affable. She decided she liked Maxine—the dark girl would be a foil for her own red-gold hair—and told her that she would do. The tour would start on September 1 at Saratoga Springs, New York.

Maxine's face fell. She had thought the engagement was for New York. She had decided never to take a touring job now that Gertrude had joined her in the city. How could she go out on tour and leave the child alone?

'I don't think it's possible, Miss Coghlan. I don't think I can leave the city. I have a little sister I am responsible for.'

'I can't have children in my company. I have enough trouble with my daughter and my pug dog.'

'My sister isn't a child. She wants to be a singer.'

6

'I need an *ingénue*. Can she act? Is she pretty?'

The scramble to rig May Gertrude out suitably was appalling, and Maxine swept her to the American Theatre more dead than alive. Miss Coghlan had her read a few lines; her brother Charles, who joined the interview, declared her utterly charming, and there and then created the phrase that haunted Gertrude Elliott for many years—'She's the carbon copy of her sister.'

Gertrude had learned from her singing teacher that she did not have an operatic voice. It was true, high, and pure but she could never hope to develop it, said her teacher, into a volume that would be anything more than a voice for ballads, for the drawing room. It was no wrench, therefore, to leave singing teacher and college in one enormous, breathless step and join Rose Coghlan's company at the side of her big sister. In fact, it was the realization of a dream at last.

After opening in Saratoga Springs, the Coghlan company would tour New York and other Eastern states and come into New York City for a month at Christmas. Maxine worked furiously on her clothes and Gertrude's. She also delivered long lectures about the rakish atmosphere of Saratoga, dominated by Diamond Jim Brady and Lillian Russell, and warned that if ever Gertrude should find herself alone in her lodgings when Maxine was out she must keep her door locked and open it to no one.

Oscar Wilde's *A Woman of No Importance* was the first production of the season, and in it Gertrude, briefly billed as Gertrude Elesmere to avoid family conflict, made her first appearance on the stage on September 1, 1894. Maxine was in an agony of nerves for both of them. Playing Mrs. Allonby, she was constantly on the watch to see how Gertrude, as Lady Stutfield, was making out. Suddenly there was one of those stage silences which the actors find interminable and the audience frequently fails to notice. Someone had dried up. Maxine glared at Gertrude, and Gertrude threw Maxine her own lines. The jubilation in the company that little Gertrude had sailed through her own part so triumphantly, and prompted her sister besides, was enormous, and filled Gertrude with such delighted confidence that the following night, as the well-trained maid in *Diplomacy*, she removed the slippers of Dora, played by Maxine, tripped out with them, and forgot ever to bring them back. Maxine had to finish the act in her stocking feet.

The tour was brief and awful. Miss Coghlan had already worked her way through every major city in the United States over and over again, and was now scraping the barrel of every small town that boasted an auditorium. In New York State alone they played in twelve cities, one-night stands, travelling by day and acting at night, or packing up after the performance and struggling on to trains that delivered the milk in the dawn hours. Miss Coghlan was moody and tired after a career of some forty years. It was advisable not to cross her.

Maxine in particular seemed to irritate Miss Coghlan. Perhaps ambitions of becoming a lead herself made her less the pleasant, respectful girl who had joined the company, so touchingly bringing her little sister. The family situation of the sisters amused Miss Coghlan at first, but Maxine, by her over-protectiveness, could also have turned it to a nuisance. As they neared the final days on tour Maxine was determined to look for other work when she reached New York. Gertrude passionately agreed with her. A small beaming *ingénue*, she got on without trouble with the star herself, but loyalty made her fiercely declare, 'She's got a voice like a corn crake.'

In New York City Rose Coghlan was going to present a new play, *To Nemesis*. How hard it was for a girl in Maxine's position, on the way up, to figure out whether the new play might do more good to her career than a break from the Coghlan company. There was little time to seek work, with nightly performances of *To Nemesis* at the Star Theatre and rehearsals all day. All was not well with the script. Rehearsals were stormy, with Rose Coghlan and the authoress often in hot conflict over a line. In the dark theatre the little Coghlan girl whined and Pujoss the pug yapped. Maxine felt she had had enough. Wasn't it better to throw up the job and put both herself and Gertrude out of work? Gertrude listened nightly to Maxine's debates with herself, sometimes offering advice but ready to do whatever Maxine decided.

To Nemesis opened and reviews were poor. It was an irritable Christmas season in the Star Theatre. 'If only we could join a management that's really distinguished,' said Maxine, young enough to cast aside the long career of Rose Coghlan as finished. And the answer came, the best, the one so good that it had not been even dreamed. A polite gentleman came with a note for Miss Elliott from Mr. Augustin Daly saying he wished to see her at once with a proposal to make.

'Daly's!' The sisters shouted the name at each other in rapture.

5

DALY'S

THE COMPANY of Augustin Daly offered the prestige that Maxine's career had lacked. You became a lady or a gentleman of the Daly company, not just a working player. You had stature in your profession and outside it too, even among the narrow social world of New York, which still considered actors beyond the pale. Every critic saw you; every person of distinction visiting the city felt it a duty to attend a performance at Daly's. Once you were marked as someone who had been with the Daly company, future work was assured.

Mr. Daly heartily agreed with this opinion. He offered an engagement as if conferring an honour. He was bitterly shocked if actors left his company—and, it had to be whispered, actors did leave Daly's. Maxine knew she would receive a much smaller salary than either the American Theatre or Rose Coghlan had given her. It was equally well known that a successful Daly player when he left the Guv'nor had raised his own value so that he could demand ten times the amount. There was no need to stay forever, and now every sacrifice was worth making for a step that could lead anywhere. It changed her from a publicized 'stage beauty' treated without seriousness to a member of the upper crust of theatre hierarchy. A sacrifice beyond money would have to be Gertrude; Mr. Daly would not employ members of the same family. But Gertrude, now firmly billed as Gertrude Elliott, had also been noticed in her brief appearances with Rose Coghlan and landed work all on her own in the company of Marie Wainwright. The sun had risen on the Elliott girls.

The theatre Maxine now joined was the last of several empires and several careers for Daly. He had been a New

York drama critic at twenty-two before the Civil War, took
on five more newspapers, and wrote or adapted plays in his
spare time. But he had thrown aside everything in his New
York life when he saw Adah Isaacs Menken (who thrilled
audiences as Mazeppa, strapped to the back of a horse), and
began to take care of her bookings throughout the nation.
He had his first theatre in 1869 on 24th Street near Broadway;
suddenly New York was shocked and entranced by plays that
mentioned forbidden subjects and a series of actresses who
dared to play divorces and fallen women with passion and
realism. Among his creations were Clara Morris, Agnes Ethel,
Kate Claxton, and Fanny Davenport, who adored him and
raged at him for poor salaries and sudden demotions from
stardom if he thought them growing too big. 'I put them all
in a line,' he said, 'and then I watch, and if one head begins
to bob up above the others, I give it a crack and send it down
again.' They left him, heartbroken, to become great stars. His
theatre burned, he took another, and by 1877 the first Daly
empire fell.

He went to examine the London theatre and within two
years gave New York a new formula—lavish musicals like
those that George Edwardes presented in London, varied by
dramas (usually adapted by Daly from the German or French)
and tremendous Shakespearian productions. He had turned
the old Wood's Museum at 30th and Broadway into Daly's
and assembled 'the big four', pillars of Daly's palace, three of
them till death—Ada Rehan, aged nineteen, an astonishing
new personality of ardour and earthiness; John Drew, the
perfect worldly hero; Mrs. Gilbert and James Lewis, the
character woman and character man. The battling of John
Drew and Ada Rehan as Petruchio and Katherine made
history (Miss Rehan knocked Mr. Drew senseless one
night). A Daly first night had an air of breathless excitement
as the public waited to see what their darlings would do
next.

Thirteen years ended this era. The change came from only
one person, John Drew, finally fed up with a salary he felt
insulting and bonuses handed him like Christmas presents.
He left for the star billing and fortune offered by Charles
Frohman at the Empire. Other lesser actors fought Daly's

paternalism and autocratic rule with less success. George
Clarke declared, after returning to Daly management for the
third time, 'I could not keep away. I was able to make a
great deal more elsewhere, but I never found elsewhere the
artistic atmosphere, the home of art, that remains unchanged
here as always.' Mrs. Gilbert and James Lewis stayed, and
the adored Ada Rehan stayed, and through her a new Daly
era began. Ada Rehan finally forced out of him star status
and a star's salary. She was the only one who ever succeeded
and was not herself pushed out. Now a company was run for
the precious personality of Mr. Daly's creation, his joy and
Galatea, for whom he selected his plays, but whom he treated
with the same autocratic hand as always. People whispered
about Mr. Daly and Miss Rehan, but no one was sure. She
was an enslaved star, as obedient as the rest of the Daly
players. She had become his theatre, an embodiment of a
single-minded passion for his ideas of management. She
seemed his woman, too, but there was a Mrs. Daly who
travelled with him in perfect harmony, and they shared the
tragic memory of two sons lost in a diphtheria epidemic. The
family threesome of the Dalys and Ada Rehan fascinated the
public and perhaps Ada Rehan herself. Daly had succeeded in
fascinating and confusing all his famale stars in turn. He
protected Ada Rehan personally like a tiger, never allowing
her to be seen in public. In this he probably had little difficulty,
because outside her own art she was a shy woman with no
interest in social life, happy to live as a recluse in her non-
working hours.

One day a small child, Mercedes de Acosta, attracted Mr.
Daly's attention in church. He made an attempt to adopt her
and learned to his chagrin that she was the child of an extremely wealthy family (her sister was Mrs. Leiter, famous for
her elgance), but from then on gained permission to take her
out to tea or for drives in Central Park. Madame de Acosta
smiled on these visits with amused indulgence until Mercedes
let drop that 'the lady' was there. 'The lady' was identified as
Ada Rehan, and so the visits were forbidden. Society believed
that this was an illicit affair and acted accordingly. Maxine's
engagement with the Daly company was during the Ada
Rehan ascendancy, but except for the addition of a permanent

star nothing had changed in Mr. Daly's way of running a
theatre.

A newcomer joining a management of such powerful identity could do so only with trepidation. Many stories were told
around 'the profession' about the Guv'nor; he was said to
pass members of his company inside the theatre without even
a good morning, but to see across a restaurant, or receive
reports from his spies, if the same members had failed to
behave in public according to the strictures of the Daly management. A woman could find herself reprimanded for having
worn too low a *décolletage*, a man admonished for failing to
wear gloves in the street. It was told that there was no such
thing as rest in the Daly management; whatever you were
playing at night, inexorably you were commanded to appear
for rehearsal at ten-thirty every morning. It was said that
Augustin Daly never missed a performance; no relaxation on
stage could be risked even if his own box happened to be
empty, because in the back of the orchestra seats or far up in
the gallery, somewhere always flitting silently about his house
he was listening, marking in his memory any slackening of
pace, any rebellious attempt of an actor to insert some inter-
pretation of his own which Mr. Daly had forbidden in rehearsal. The notice board bristled with orders: 'Be distinct; be
earnest; do not trifle.' He pinned up written lectures (after
ferociously delivering verbal ones) on the unpardonable crimes
of inaudibility, whispering, giggling, hurrying, dragging, and
bad timing which allowed a laugh to slip or a line to get lost
in the audience's laughter. 'The spirit that can permit such
a condition of affairs,' he wrote, 'is unworthy of my company.
Out of it grows grumblings and mutiny—a spirit natural to
the rabble and not to the ladies and gentlemen who are treated
with such extreme consideration with which I treat my
company.'

Maxine was invited to join the company in mid-season
after New Year of 1895. Her dark beauty was hand-picked
for several plans he had: a fantasy with a young Oriental
heroine, lovely Silvia in *Two Gentlemen of Verona*, 'proud
Helena' in *A Midsummer Night's Dream*. Her debut was
challenging; she had the title role in *The Heart of Ruby*, the
Japanese fantasy that had attracted Daly by its opportunity

for dazzling sets. Justin Huntley McCarthy had translated it from the French of Judith Gautier into gaudy declamations. Maxine appeared as Heart of Ruby, undoubtedly wronged and tragic, her eyes rimmed in slanting black, her own hair piled high with combs. Cherry blossoms and little peaked bridges were hazards of the set, and it was essential not to spoil Mr. Daly's precious lighting effects by casting a shadow across the smoking peak of Fujiyama on the backdrop.

Amid the brilliant first-night audience sat the Japanese consul, Mr. Hashigucki, accompanied by the Japanese minister to Great Britain, Mr. H. E. Kato, who happened to be visiting New York, and they diplomatically declared themselves enchanted. 'The scenery reminded us of our sweet home. During the whole evening, we were transported to Japan.'

Maxine had reason to be relieved on two counts. She had feared resentment from Ada Rehan, whose part was nothing more than a chorus to open and close the play. Miss Rehan proved the most comfortable of colleagues, to be feared only for the contagion of her wicked humour, and in *The Heart of Ruby* it was easy to be overcome by giggles. The second fear —whether she could get through the part at all without falling down or bumping into someone else—also proved groundless. But, though her part was the leading one, Maxine felt no regret when *The Heart of Ruby* closed at the end of the week, all the effort and expenditure having totally failed to interest the public.

Following the characteristic Daly formula, after *The Heart of Ruby*, Maxine was immediately demoted to a small part in *The Orient Express*. It was not an unhappy time, however, because the great comedian Henry E. Dixey had been called in for a special engagement in the second play, and his irreverent manners relaxed some of the Daly solemnity. She began to know her way around and breathe more easily. In such a company as Daly's, where actors and actresses had been associated for years, it was natural for newcomers to draw together. Maxine found an immediate friend in Frank Worthing, an Englishman playing young leading parts, a newcomer since John Drew's defection. He was dark, with enormous deep-set eyes, a romantic-looking man who reminded Maxine

of all her brothers. The other personalities of the company
sorted themselves out. Mrs. Gilbert was always kind, a self-
elected mother hen to all the girls. Maxine learned not to take
personally the silences and abruptness of James Lewis, who
lived within his own shell, never meaning to be rude, merely
unnoticing. Even the appearance of Mr. Daly's conical hat and
drooping moustache ceased to be terrifying, because on most
of his bugbears Maxine would never give offence. She was an
indefatigable worker, always in time, always ready to try,
always ready to go over and over a scene while other members
of the company openly showed impatience. With Ada Rehan
there were no terrors at all. You met the precious, protected,
nurtured star upon the staircase, and there was nothing in her
to suggest the frail flower about whom the public was informed
from Mr. Daly's press office. Shy in public, she was friendly
with the cast, enjoyed jokes, and assumed no leading-lady
airs. Finally, there was the pleasant friendship with Frank
Worthing, growing in flirtatiousness, which made daily life—
and it lasted from morning rehearsal through to the final
curtain at eleven-thirty—thoroughly entertaining.

Maxine at last faced her first attempt at Shakespeare, and to
prove herself now was all important. Too often had she heard
it asked whether, though she was beautiful and possibly even
competent as an actress in the melodramas and drawing-room
comedies, she could play Shakespeare and speak verse. Her
recitations at home for Captain Dermot told her that she
could, but she dreaded the first rehearsal, when she would be
asked to blend her speech with the curious, rippling, breathless
verse speaking of Ada Rehan and the classical training of the
English members of the company.

On February 25, 1895, Daly gave a production of *Two
Gentlemen of Verona*. It was, of course, a production beautiful
to behold. High on a balcony stood Maxine in a square-cut
blue velvet dress, a little jewelled cap upon her head, and
beneath her a voice sang, 'Who is Silvia, what is she, That all
our swains commend her?' Ada Rehan, always most pleasing
to her admirers in the parts of Shakespeare's girls who assume
boys' clothing, thrilled the audience as she mourned Sir
Proteus's attentions to the fair Lady Silvia. But it came as a
surprise to New York critics and audiences that Miss Maxine

Elliott's voice came out low and lovely, the measure of the verse perfectly kept.

> *'Return, return, and make thy love amends.*
> *For me,—by this pale queen of night I swear,*
> *I am so far from granting thy request,*
> *That I despise thee for thy wrongful suit;*
> *And by and by intend to chide myself*
> *Even for this time I spend in talking to thee.'*

'Good Heavens! The beauty can play Shakespeare too!' Overnight had come another rapid change in her status as an actress.

Some minor plays continued the Daly season, then a revival of an earlier production of *A Midsummer Night's Dream* had a week's run. Ada Rehan as Helena and Maxine as Hermia tore each other's hair and scratched at each other's eyes, and everyone was delighted. Once more it was noted that Miss Elliott could play Shakespeare. The season closed on April 20, and the company went off immediately on a six-week tour. It was the usual grind, all too familiar now to Maxine, but she was walking on clouds. Mr. Daly had announced to his company—always the last to be informed of the Daly company movements—that he was taking them for a short engagement in London in July.

*

Maxine's trip to London with the Daly company was, she told the British press, her second visit to England. Before, she could have come only on a modest budget, perhaps as the schoolgirl on the *Will H. Case*. Now, as a member of Daly's company, she was not just peeking in on English life, but was an accepted member of a group already popular in England. She may have had an instinctive liking for the country from the start—the people did not rush her, she liked their good manners and their quiet voices—but she could have had at first that tantalizing experience of the foreigner who feels that all English life is behind closed doors, gaieties happening but unavailable unless someone is there to open those doors. She was in London now in the summer of 1895, in full season, with the sun shining benignly, carriages crowding Hyde Park, welcomed as an old friend because she was part of the

Daly group who had come back. Nothing is more reassuring
to the English than to have friends return; Mr. Daly had his
own theatre in London, and was thus identified with English
commercial life; Miss Rehan, with her cottage in Surrey, was
a householder who could ignore transient hotels. The Daly
company had come to England three times since 1884, causing
a sensation as the first all-American Shakespeare company to
play at Stratford-on-Avon. Within this setting a new and
beautiful face was also delightedly received.

London proceeded to go mad over Maxine. Here for the
first time she was not one of a crowd of beautiful girls fighting
for attention on Broadway, pushing to get her pictures in the
papers, trying to be in the right place at the right time where
someone might be who could further her career. London
sought her out. The smart magazines sent their interviewers
and photographers to beg appointments; the press was full of
her, hostesses fought for her. For the first time, her inner
belief in herself as a queen was being realized.

Suddenly life was no effort. She told *The Illustrated Sporting
and Dramatic*, 'I think England is the best place in the world.
All you want is leisure and money. You take everything so
leisurely here. Even your elevators catch the national characteristic. In America, one goes up like a rocket, and the
difference in that respect represents the difference in our
respective modes of life.'

For the English, Maxine had everything—beauty, manners,
a sense of fun. They adored her foreignness, her free-swinging, healthy, Juno-like quality that enabled them to say, 'Yes,
yes, that's exactly how an American girl ought to be.' And in
the matter of the important national difference which causes
so many insults to fly in both directions—the quality of the
speaking voice—she had just the amount of lilt and emphasis
to make her sound American, and none of the nasality which
the English claim makes American speech strident. When
they raved over her 'accentless' speech, it was Captain Dermot's fierce Irish antagonism to the Yankee twang that she
had to thank, and did so, charmingly and modestly. 'All my
family have the same pronunciation,' she said.

It took all Maxine's tact and good manners to keep relations
with the rest of the Daly company unmarred. In particular,

Miss Rehan was suffering a fierce attack upon her by Mr. George Bernard Shaw. His attack was directed more fully upon Daly as the destroyer of Ada Rehan's talent; his columns in the *Saturday Review* advised her to run for it, to get out, to come alive again before it was too late, or, he said, delivering the worst insult he could think of, she would become as stylized and meaningless as the barnstorming ham, Barry Sullivan. Even the worshipful Max Beerbohm was not so enslaved as before. The gentlemen of the press were rude enough even to remark on the thickening of her waistline. The productions were none too kindly treated either. The dancing, singing, and incidental music of *Two Gentlemen of Verona* made one critic describe it as an operetta. The use of heavy gauzes and twilight lighting for *A Midsummer Night's Dream* was described as affected, and Mr. Shaw merely said it was vaudeville. Among these insults, Maxine was picking up nothing but compliments—'A Silvia of finely contrasted beauty and temperament by Miss Maxine Elliott'; as Hermia, 'rare beauty and attractiveness in Miss Maxine Elliott'; 'Miss Maxine Elliott, who is remarkably handsome, was graceful, courteous, and unaffected as Silvia'; 'Miss Maxine Elliott is a handsome Hermia, playing the part with care and good judgement.' During the season, Miss Ada Rehan's face did not appear once upon the covers of the glossy magazines; Maxine's appeared three times. She might have been made to suffer, but the Daly management was different. Mr. Daly had always enjoyed putting mettle into one of his actresses through the success of another, and in Miss Rehan, Maxine had the luck to encounter a woman of generous soul. Daly and Rehan, licking their wounds, both kindly assured Maxine that her personal success did the company good as a whole.

All sorts of delightful things happened outside the theatre. Maxine went boating, on what she called 'up river'. One assumes this was a day when she took the train to Taplow, joined the scramble for a hackney carriage, and sped to Skindles at Maidenhead to be wafted away in a punt, trailing a languorous hand, while a young man in gleaming whites and tilted boater propelled her through the peaceful waters of the Thames. Ascot Week was on during the first days of the Daly engagement. Could she have squeezed a few hours there amid the picture hats and blowing frills and skirts, with an occasional glimpse of a horse?

There was fascinating political discussion, too, so seldom part of American conversation in the 1890s. Here in England it was colourful, rather like a wrangle in one big family of title. She learned that everybody of every class in London was in a state of wild excitement the night before the Daly season opened, and it was because 'the Government had fallen'. The very words had beauty. The defeated Prime Minister was the Earl of Rosebery, aristocrat of aristocrats, and yet, in the fascinating mystery of English politics, the leader of the Liberal Party—one of England's greatest landowners leading the party that was the enemy of the landowning class. Before she went to the theatre on opening night, she heard the words, 'The Queen has sent for Lord Salisbury.' The Marquis of Salisbury was leader of the Unionist Party (Conservative), bitterly opposed to the Earl of Rosebery. For the moment, it made no sense at all, but it sounded splendid. Salisbury, a great dreamy man with untidy suits and an enormous beard, would take the train to Windsor Castle and assure Her Majesty that he would try to form a government. Rosebery was fastidiously sorting his papers at No. 10 Downing Street before closing the door and driving off with deep relief to put high office behind him. He would settle himself in one of his six properties, where he would sit beneath a Rembrandt amidst rare editions. They were all dream people, living in a fairy-tale world, inaccessible, and yet . . . London already showed that it might hold a miracle of living in which worlds met worlds and nothing was impossible. She even met people who knew Lord Rosebery and Lord Salisbury personally and were also enchanted to talk to a young American actress. The houses of the Liberal Earl—Mentmore, the Durdans, Dalmeny, Rosebery, Barnbougle, and 38 Berkeley Square—were already a little closer than Mrs. Cornelius Vanderbilt's house on Fifth Avenue.

Whenever Maxine was away from actual work in the theatre, she asked questions and she listened. The ability to do so was one of her greatest gifts, providing her with information and allowing others to feel they were brilliant conversationalists. Everyone in England seemed ready to talk politics; the stage hands in the theatre were as full of opinions as the partners she was given at after-theatre supper parties. It still seemed to her that it would have been simpler if all the lords were on one side and all the non-lords on another, but apparently it didn't work that way. As the general election fever began to mount, she was enchanted with the terms in which it was presented.

'If the noble lord will do me the honour to search back into his own memory . . .'

Thus a member of the House of Lords called another member a liar. Who can tell now who were Maxine's friends at this time and if she cared whether Liberals or Unionists came to power? It was somewhat like the temporary excitement about who is going to win the Ascot Gold Cup when you don't happen to have money on a horse. It was picturesque and above all intimate; the battling aristocratic leaders of the country seemed to be the property of every citizen. The movements of the Royal Family were discussed as if they were relatives. The London season was in full swing, and it seemed almost possible to peep into every ballroom and examine every dress. And yet she was not inside those doors, and she longed to be with all her heart.

Her colleagues in the theatre who were English-born (Mrs. Gilbert, Frank Worthing) were eager to point out to her another startling difference between English and American life which vitally affected their own profession. In the Birthday Honours of June 1895, Her Majesty Queen Victoria had delighted to honour a member of the theatrical profession by giving a knighthood to Henry Irving. By this step, and in the person of Irving, actors and actresses were lifted from their centuries-old position on the edges of society into total acceptance. Many members of the profession had been received in the social drawing rooms for years, but this knighthood gave the final touch of respectability.

A great gathering had been called on July 19 at Sir Henry's own theatre, the Lyceum, to enable his professional brothers and sisters to do him honour and to give him their thanks. The leading members of Daly's company were of course included at the theatre, which bulged from gallery to stalls with all the leaders of the profession who did not happen to be away on tour or in bed with a cold. Everywhere Maxine turned amid the gold and plush of the old auditorium, there were faces she knew or who were identified for her by Frank Worthing. She could bow on what seemed equal terms to her old boss, Mr. Willard. There was the lovely, eager, golden head of Ellen Terry. Frank Worthing greeted his own old boss, Charles Wyndham. She peered across the aisle at the strange new personality everyone spoke of, Max Beerbohm's half-brother, Beerbohm Tree. On the stage itself Sir Henry, just returned the day before from Windsor Castle, where he had received the tap upon his shoulder of the royal sword, sat crouched within his coat collar, struggling to control his emotions. To Maxine's delighted eyes, the leader of the English stage looked to her exactly like the pictures she had seen of the Old Leader in politics, Mr. Gladstone. At his side rose the distinguished figure of the actor-manager Squire Bancroft, black ribbon floating from the spectacles through which he viewed his address. His duty for the afternoon was to present to Sir Henry a casket containing a scroll signed by four thousand fellow professionals to express their thanks for his gifts to them all. Arthur Wing Pinero, the playwright, had written the words.

Sir Henry rose to express his thanks.

'My brother and sister actors . . .' The theatre rang with cheers. When he was allowed to speak Maxine listened to the most distinctive voice on the English stage and observed the oddly awkward body and pale poetic face.

'This beautiful casket, and its most precious contents, will ever be a shrine of loving memories. . . .' Irving clasped the crystal-and-gold casket shaped like a small Parthenon. Maxine saw heads turning toward a handsome young man in the audience. It was Johnston Forbes-Robertson; he had been asked to design the casket—a happy choice combining his past beginnings as a painter with many fine performances as one of the younger classic actors to whom everyone was pointing as Irving's successor if the old man abdicated. She heard the whispers—'Beautiful, Forbie, beautiful.' The English were truly extraordinary, and she loved the way they did things. Their actors looked like statesmen, artists, or country gentle-

MAXINE IN *TWO GENTLEMEN OF VERONA*

NAT GOODWIN AS *DAVID GARRICK*

GROUP AT JACKWOOD

(*left to right*) Ysobel Haskins, Max Beerbohm, Nat Goodwin, Maxine, Clyde Fitch, Paul Arthur

men, and this moment of elevation of the whole profession called out in them both ritual and tearful affection.

Life seemed an anticlimax when the Daly company scrambled ashore in New York and went off on tour for six weeks. Maxine had come home so terribly English that she made her friends chuckle. She performed her third Shakespearian part when the company reopened in New York in November. Everyone was warmly complimentary about her Olivia in *Twelfth Night*.

A real chance seemed to be offered in a play which gave her and Frank Worthing the two leading parts. She was pleased that Mr. Daly had noted her success in London and would build her in the future. Her confidence was high. The play was a drama, adapted from the German by Sydney Rosenfeld, called *The Two Escutcheons*. The theme of the play was conflict between an ancient aristocratic house of Central Europe in the person of Frank Worthing as von Vinck, and an American meat-packing fortune represented by the widow Stevenson, played by Maxine. The two handsome young people were warmly received by the public.

Then the Daly axe fell. *The Two Escutcheons* was withdrawn after only three weeks, although a popular success, to give place for a new vehicle for Ada Rehan.

'There's no chance for a woman at Daly's,' raged Maxine.

Frank Worthing was equally angry. The part had been good, and he liked himself in it. The author, Sydney Rosenfeld, was also incensed, feeling his play had not been given a fair run. Maxine had reason to feel that she at last counted for something in the theatre. She had a folder of fine English reviews. She had been able to bring in the paying customers in a play carried only by herself and Worthing. She felt the need no longer to be always in the position of second fiddle to Ada Rehan. Maxine Elliott and Frank Worthing simultaneously submitted their resignations and left the Daly company on January 27, 1896.

A month later, Sydney Rosenfeld had raised the money and assembled a company to present a new production of *The Two Escutcheons* at the Garden Theatre. The supporting cast was in no way comparable to Daly's. The play did not go as well as had been hoped, but Rosenfeld, ever resourceful and

7

prolific, had a new play for Maxine Elliott and Frank Worthing to try out. But in spite of much better casting, which
included Henrietta Crosman, E. L. Davenport, and Maxine's
old friend Ysobel Haskins, *A House of Cards* lasted only two
weeks.

Another old friend was beckoning, however. T. Daniel
Frawley, a colleague from the engagement at the American
Theatre, now ran a repertory company in San Francisco and
asked both Maxine and Frank Worthing to join him, promising them a production of *The Two Escutcheons*. He was willing
to add another *ingénue* to his company, so joyfully Maxine
could once more annex her little sister Gertrude, who had
been unhappily cooling her heels in Oakland; her own engagement with Marie Wainwright had ceased during the summer
when Maxine was in England. For all the loving care of her
stepmother, Gertrude was miserable at the interruption to her
professional life, but obediently had gone home to await her
sister's return.

In June 1896 Maxine Elliott and Frank Worthing left for
the Coast. Naturally, the gossip of New York suggested that
they had an understanding which was more than professional.
Nevertheless, clever Maxine managed to have Ysobel Haskins
travel with her so she did not cross the country alone with a
man, and, of course, little sister Gertrude was eagerly await-
ing the arrival of the transcontinental train at the other end,
hungry for a sight of 'little Dettie' and hoping her clothes
would be approved.

The decision to leave Daly's and strike out for a position
of greater prominence and more money may have been preci-
pitated by that summer in London. Maxine had caught a
glimpse of the sort of life she wanted. 'Money and leisure,'
she had said. Taking the long view always, she knew that to
attain money and leisure meant very hard work ahead, but at
this point even unconsciously she may have received the incentive her life hitherto lacked. During the months at Daly's, she
tried hard to improve her art and, indeed, did. Possibly, if she
had stayed with Augustin Daly till the closing of his company
only two years later, she could have gained still further depths.
Inside, however, a voice was asking her if it was indeed total
excellence in the theatre and total dedication of her life to it

that she wanted with all her being. The call of a leisured sunny Sunday upon the Thames had gained the upper hand.

When she was asked why she had thrown over the distinguished Daly management to go to join lesser managements, she said the time had come to go for leading parts and big money. 'I don't want my brother actors to bury me.'

6

NAT C. GOODWIN

MAXINE had time to visit Captain Tom and the beloved 'little mother' before her season with Frawley's company began in June 1896. Once the season opened, the distance between Oakland and Frawley's Columbia Theatre would be too great for Maxine and Gertrude to think of staying with the Dermots. A trip on the ferry twice a day was impossible.

There was some further personal business to be attended to. At last Maxine had decided that she would end her marriage to George MacDermott by legal action. She could claim residence in the state of California, using its more palatable laws of cruelty and incompatibility instead of New York state's crude demand for proved adultery. She claimed that she had tried to reach George to ask for financial support or suggest a reconciliation, moves that she had made on advice from her lawyer, Peter F. Dunne, but without any desire ever to lay eyes on George again, and fortunately he had not answered. Gertrude agreed to testify to the validity of her California residence, and Ysobel Haskins was willing to tell of furious abuse she had heard and bruises she had seen. The plea was filed in May, and if George did nothing to fight it the chances were good that it would become final within six months. To assist George in accepting the situation, she claimed no alimony and let him know that she was so doing. George received notice of the suit and let it go by default; Mr. Dunne happily assured Maxine that he foresaw no further problems. It was merely a matter of waiting from May 20, when the suit had been filed, to the end of November, and she would be free. Whether or not Frank Worthing's devotion had anything to do with her decision cannot be guessed. Most people knew nothing about Maxine's marriage, and she had a masterly capacity for leaving unmentioned something she did not wish to discuss, so in all likelihood Frank believed her to be single. Maxine was sure that a divorce filed in the name of Jessie C. MacDermott would pass unnoticed. If marriage became a state that she could contemplate again with Frank or anyone, there would be time enough to reveal an event which by then would be neatly and legally folded up and put away in the past.

The season opened with *The Two Escutcheons*, which played two weeks. Maxine and Frank created a great stir in the Frawley company as the newcomers from New York and this was very much their play, but the whole cast was excellent. There were Mrs. F. M. Bates, an old California favourite, and her daughter Blanche Bates, already in a second season with Frawley, only twenty-three, a young woman of intense seriousness and emotional power; there was Madge Carr Cook (whose daughter gained fame in two spheres of activity, as Eleanor Robson, a fine actress and interpreter of Ibsen, and as Mrs. August Belmont, President of the Metropolitan Opera Guild); there were Maclyn Arbuckle, Tyrone Power—as handsome as the son who inherited his name—Harry Corson Clake, and George W. Leslie. Little Gertrude Elliott was there, too. The reviews gave Maxine some irritation because as usual her beauty was acclaimed but her emotional gifts were compared unfavourably to those of Blanche Bates. Tim Frawley, keeping the peace, assured her that Californians were intensely loyal to their own.

The New Yorkers felt themselves particularly lucky to be in California when they read newspaper stories of distress in the acting profession of Broadway. The country had not fully recovered from the financial panic of 1893, and money was tight. When the New York theatres closed down for the summer, allowing the stars a rest, the less established players found fewer opportunities for work in repertory companies, touring companies, or provincial theatres to tide them over, for many had been knocked out of existence. People who suffered serious losses when the banks were closing and capital was no longer available for industries and businesses were not going to hurry to spend their salvaged money on theatregoing. As the country started to recover, numerous theatres failed to do so, and there were fewer jobs for everyone. Solvent actors helped to raise funds to save some of their professional brothers from actual starvation. Maxine felt that anxiety about employment had disappeared since her engagement with Augustin Daly's company, but the cheap boarding houses were not so very long ago and not forgotten.

This feeling that a career was opening was something to be appreciated; offers were coming in, and a belief in her earning capacity and perhaps important money around the corner was to be enjoyed as the security of Frawley's summer engagement was being enjoyed, as comfortable rooms in the lavish Baldwin Hotel were too; but the theatrical profession was in a chaotic state, and nothing was to be taken for granted. No one knew yet how the lives of actors and actresses would be affected by the formation of the new group called the Syndicate. It seemed to be an agreement between theatre owners and booking agents, such as Charles Frohman, Klaw and Erlanger, and others, to standardize booking fees throughout the country. Now the struggling actor might be able to expect some guarantee against finding himself abandoned penniless on the road. Many of the important leading actors, however, were in full rebellion, furious that any businessman should think he could step in and dictate the fees that they had been in the habit of fixing to suit themselves. Maxine, in between the actor who barely made a living and the favourites who could command what they liked, could not yet clearly see what these developments would mean in her own professional life.

But for the moment, San Francisco in summertime was a delight. The changes of bill were not going to be too rigorous, and Maxine was looking forward to playing Lady Gay Spanker in *London Assurance*, the part that Rose Coghlan had acted when Maxine supported her. The weather was perfect, so the first Sunday after the opening Maxine, Gertrude, Frank, and some others of the company decided to indulge in the new and fashionable sport of bicycling. They were full of laughter, amusing themselves with all the new cycling terms that were entering the language—'bicycle face', an expression of acute anxiety; 'high wheel', an old-fashioned fuddy-duddy; 'cyclo donna', a lady bicyclist. It was observed by a local gossip writer that Frank Worthing obviously found Miss Elliott the cyclo donna of his choice.

*

The doings of the Frawley company rapidly became of secondary interest to the theatre-going public of San Francisco when Nat C. Goodwin and his company arrived in town. He was the most celebrated, beloved, and talked-about comedian of the day; every one was always waiting to see what Nat would do next, counting on a laugh, a touch of scandal, something unexpected either on or off stage delivered with Nat's peculiar touch. He was pausing on the West Coast for a short engagement before setting sail for Australia—droll indeed were Nat's groans at having to organize winter clothing in summer for his August arrival in Melbourne. In fact, he paid no attention to all the travel advice he got, feeling joyfully free with a divorce impending from his second wife and delightfully noble after abandoning his pursuit of a Kentucky heiress whose family disapproved of actors. He was looking for fun, and San Francisco was always fun for Nat. The Bohemian Club was ready to entertain him royally, and old friends were eager to assist him in his last lark on American soil. He was dubious about the Australian tour, darkly suggesting that he was embarking on a mission of great peril, and he was already bored with his leading lady, Blanche Walsh, who was far too serious and dedicated an actress to romp with Nat. George McClellan, his manager, just hoped that Nat would stay out of trouble for a little while.

Nat, his tall hat cocked at a rakish angle, his kid gloves gleaming, his long, tightly buttoned cutaway showing a waistline no longer quite as trim as it had been, sallied gaily forth from the Palace Hotel into the beloved streets of San Francisco, fortified with bourbon and branch water. It was his first day in town, with his play opening the next night, and he had promised his old friend Tim Frawley to come over to the Columbia Theatre later, so why couldn't the whole bunch of them go over there together? Yes, he had heard that Tim had got the beauty Maxine Elliott as his leading lady this season and he remembered from a casual meeting a few years ago that she was quite a looker, but a cold New England fish

—a piece of codfish, he'd heard—and she couldn't act for sour apples, but Tim was an old friend, and if he thought Nat's presence would help business he'd put in a free evening at the Columbia any time. But he was side-tracked—it was always easy to side-track Nat—and that evening he didn't get to the theatre. The tickets held for the Goodwin party remained un-claimed, an empty row of seats in the best part of the house only too noticeable to the company on stage. Maxine and Gertrude agreed with rather poor grace when Tim Frawley said that it was just Nat and he must be forgiven, and they must consent to come to a party he was giving for Nat at the old Bohemian Club within the next few weeks. Frank Worth-ing and Tyrone Power were invited to escort the sisters, although Frank was nervous, fearful that Nat's famous after-dinner stories might not be for their ears.

Nat Goodwin's next birthday would be his fortieth. It seemed as if he ought to be older, because ever since Maxine and Gertrude could remember anything about the theatre the name of Nat C. Goodwin, Jun.—or Nathaniel C., as he was beginning to be billed—had been as familiar to them as Joe Jefferson's. In Rockland he was hailed as a fellow New Eng-lander, Boston born, a nonsensical vaudeville performer who had toured the New England circuit (and the whole country) through the late seventies and all through the eighties, when the Dermot girls were children. He brought something special to creaky farces, first as supporting player then co-star to his enchanting wife Eliza Weathersby, a gorgeous blonde cockney girl who had come to America with Lydia Thompson's com-pany of British Blondes. Eliza, whose three sisters joined her as each grew old enough, and Nat had formed a team after their original meeting in E. E. Rice's production of *Evangeline*. The audience always felt that it knew Nat and the Weathersbys like dear friends. They floated in and out of character; Nat stopped to do an imitation, Eliza danced and sang, one moment intensely absorbed in wild, farcical business, the next coming to the footlights to chat about the horrors of public transport in the town they were playing or to carry on back-chat with the mayor. Everything they did was funny, every-thing seemed improvised, and above all everyone seemed to be having a good time; it was like a big, uproarious family party. Joyfully their admirers greeted the marriage of Nat and Eliza, the groom only twenty and the bride, who did not tell her age, nearly ten years his senior. Then the farces became a little more brushed-up, a little more written. The company put on *Cruets*, *Hobbies* (Nat borrowed a hundred dollars from the Mayor of Albany and gambled it into the sum of two thousand to buy the script), *Cinderella at School*, *The Member for Slocum*—slim, slapstick stuff illumined by the genius of Nat and the adorableness of Eliza.

The lark with Eliza Weathersby lasted ten years, but behind the public nonsense it was not always so rosy. Sometimes they made no money at all, and on Christmas Day once in Ogden, Utah, Nat and Eliza exchanged cuff buttons as gifts while snow drifted in through the cracked window of a tenth-rate hotel. Sometimes they were riding high, making money to pay off their debts, but Nat could gamble away all their profits in one night. Even when Nat won Eliza hated it, distrusting money made in this fashion. He got drunk and Eliza suffered as she nursed his hangovers, so Nat felt guilty and got drunk again. Then suddenly it was all over. At the age of thirty-nine Eliza underwent a major operation and died. Nat found that her love for him had been great enough to conceal some of their earnings without breaking into them even when they seemed to be down to their last dollar. She left it all to him— twelve thousand dollars—in her will.

Nat began to listen to the voices of his critics. He wanted to do better plays; he wanted to be a proper actor. He put on a real play, *A Gilded Fool*; he played David Garrick; he played a noble Western sheriff in *In Mizzoura*: everyone agreed that his Lucius O'Trigger, in an all-star revival of *The Rivals*, put him in the position of heir apparent to Joseph Jefferson in classic comic roles. During this period of emergence from vaudeville to high comedy he took another wife, this time a woman of the social world, Nella Pease Baker, who believed she could tame him entirely. They had a son, who died, and their brief marriage ended in bitterness. Through it all, Nat had managed to collect for himself the reputation of a man with whom no woman was safe. He was adored, he was followed everywhere by a delighted public and eager newsmen, ready to report each new Nat Goodwinism—a new woman, a new fortune lost, a new drunken episode, a new tomfoolery.

He was not the sort of man with whom the Elliott sisters would have anything in common, but Maxine's practicality told her that a party in his honour would call out many people of importance in San Francisco; Nat was the man of the hour and the indefinable 'everybody' was bound to be there.

Tim Frawley and the Bohemian Club did Nat more than proud. Banks of sweet peas filled the centre of the table with interwoven carnations and the wild flowers of California. There were toy balloons that hung from the ceiling, streamers sewn with American flags, a centrepiece in the form of a dainty bronze anchor lodged amid the flowers. The lighting was a soft pink glow from red shades set upon all the bulbs. California offered its flowers to Nat, the American flags proclaimed him the most American of exports, the anchor wished him a safe journey, and, as for the rosy light, perhaps it was intended to express the pink glow in which most of Nat's impetuous life was lived.

The guest of honour was hardly impressive. He was very short; his ginger hair was thinning; his eyes were pale and washed out. Delicate artist's hands of extraordinary whiteness gestured constantly; equally dainty and slim were his inimitable feet, which could do such special, speaking things upon a stage so that a tiny twist of a toe or sag of an ankle could express a whole life situation or the inner tumult of the character Nat was playing. He was the centre of the group; his friends hung on each word or gesture of his, and roared with laughter at everything he said. A long forefinger was hooked around his cigarette holder; a heavy signet ring hung on the last finger; diamonds flashed from the front of his shirt. For all his comicality he had an air of expensive, worldly elegance. Other men in the room had more physical charms than Nat, but it was hard to be aware of anyone else.

Tim Frawley introduced Nat to the party just arrived. Nat never missed any detail. He was immediately aware that the dress worn by Maxine Elliott was not the work of an expensive dressmaker. He knew at once that Frank Worthing was in love with her but that she was probably not in love with him. He knew that she was respectable and careful, for all her flamboyant looks, less easy to communicate with than

Blanche Bates, who was immediately familiar, a fellow player. Maxine seemed less approachable than the usual young actress on the make, or the usual young society woman seeking a temporary thrill of flirtation with an actor; she had none of the forthright camaraderie of his dear dead Eliza, none of the pretensions of that ghastly mistake, his second wife Nella. This was a New Englander like himself, and all the stories of her coldness, her resemblance to a codfish, were part of the nonsense forced upon the people who held in them the dignity of the New England states and were forever misunderstood by outsiders. She had none of the cloying sweetness of that damn woman from Kentucky with her Southern treacle. Nat's hopeless, bounding romanticism leaped off on its fateful way; this was the sort of girl he would like to take home to his mother. She was more beautiful than any woman he had ever seen.

In the hierarchy of San Francisco's artistic world and its distinguished visitors of the moment, Maxine's rank did not allow her to be Nat's dinner partner. Tim Frawley bade him offer his arm to Alice Rix, who was also beautiful, a brilliant newspaperwoman with more to say than Maxine Elliott. He might have concentrated his attentions upon Miss Rix for the remaining two days he had in San Francisco before he boarded the s.s. *Alameda* for Australia; but he had seen Maxine. He watched her take her place at table, between John Drew and Herbert Kelcey. There were twenty-two guests in all, and a remarkable preponderance of beauties among the eleven ladies, but Maxine outshone them all: 'How I chafed at the etiquette which prohibited my being at her side!' said Nat in his autobiography.

As he took his eyes off Maxine and turned to Miss Rix, noticing that Maxine had smiled most sweetly in her direction, Nat was reminded of something he had recently read on the train to the West Coast. At Denver his boredom with the long transcontinental journey had been lightened by a brilliantly caustic article he found in the Denver *Post* when it was brought on board the train; with artistic venom it had dismissed the performances of Maxine Elliott in the Frawley company as beneath contempt. Nat saw Miss Rix shoot a sharp look across the table in Maxine's direction, and an

equally sharp look shot back at Miss Rix; then there reap-
peared the same charming smile he had seen Maxine give
before—not placating, not frightened, merely casually gracious
—and he saw her turn to listen to John Drew, apparently
entirely at ease. Respect for Maxine was now added to his
admiration; she was the injured party and also the working
actress who needed the public approbation of newspaper
writers. She was not going to show hurt, or even behave as if
Miss Rix were a dangerous power; she was playing this scene
as a cheerful woman enjoying a delightful party. 'Clever
Maxine,' he said, 'tactful even in her respectable poverty!'

Nat says Maxine sat 'stately, majestic, Juno-like . . . totally
unconscious of the appetites she was destroying, absorbing
the delicate little compliments paid her by that prince of
good fellows, John Drew.' Undoubtedly Maxine was perfectly
aware that she had made a telling impression on Nat Goodwin, which made Alice Rix's presence in the seat of honour a
little more tolerable. Undoubtedly too Nat was wrong in
thinking that delicate compliments were passing between her
and John Drew; she already knew Mr. Drew quite well, and
he was probably applauding her decision to leave Augustin
Daly, as he himself had, to be turned into a 'star' on a high
salary by Charles Frohman, but also assuring her of his
respect and gratitude to Daly. Nat saw how the red hues from
the lamps made a sort of aureole above her black hair and
brought the depth of her eyes and the illumination of her skin
into startling contrast.

The party was long and late. Soon the individual conversa-
tions were broken up. Nat was begged to tell this story, tell
that story; he obliged, and the waiters who whisked the succession of dishes on and off the table and kept the decanters
of wine circulating were as helplessly convulsed as the guests.
Jimmie Swinnerton, the cartoonist, presented a drawing of a
kangaroo, wallaby in pouch, greeting Nat. It was passed
around the table, and everyone signed it; fat tears of gratitude
and good fellowship rolled down Nat's cheeks. At the shank
of the evening, the twenty-four-year-old drama critic of the
San Francisco *Call*, Ashton Stevens, produced his banjo and
played some old favourites, and even some classical music.
'This came at the tail end of the evening and much to my

sorrow,' writes Nat, 'the party broke up then and there—at
three a.m.'

It had been glorious fun. The Elliott sisters were exhausted,
but they loved so to laugh that they went to bed merry. For
George McClellan, Nat's long-suffering manager, who had
spent a peaceful evening free, it ended in irritation. He was
awakened by Nat, who had a brain wave to announce—he
wanted Miss Elliott for his company. Some minutes of argument went by before McClellan could push Nat off, having
persuaded him, he thought, that his company for Australia
was complete.

When Mr. Goodwin's card was sent up to the room in the
Baldwin where Maxine and Gertrude lived, it was late morning, but the girls were not yet dressed. Maxine told the page-
boy to beg Mr. Goodwin to wait a few minutes downstairs
while they made themselves presentable. A simple peignoir
would be perfectly suitable for receiving Mr. Goodwin, and
their hair could be loosely coiled for casual morning wear.
Neither of them ever had to think of the ravage that too much
drink the night before might have left, and they were young,
twenty-eight and twenty respectively, able to face the sun
without worry.

Nat knew he had to move quickly because George Mc-
Clellan had said sleepily and angrily during the night that if
he insisted he might engage Blanche Bates, 'who was playing
rings around' Maxine. He did not want Blanche Bates, he
wanted Maxine. Beautifully turned out and emanating a
ruddy glow (in the morning Nat could look ashen grey or
ebulliently pink, according to his mood) Nat presented his
proposal to Maxine; he wanted her to join his company at
once, and to take the first boat to Australia. He seemed to
think she could be ready to sail on the *Alameda* the next day,
but admitted in the end that it was only fair to give poor old
Tim some notice. He swept aside Maxine's commitments to
play in New York next season for Harry Miner and Joseph
Brooks; for him they became non-existent as soon as he learned
that nothing had actually been signed and no money had been
received. Maxine turned her great eyes on Gertrude, who
listened demurely and respectfully ('I recall the awe with
which she reviewed every act and speech of her beautiful

sister'), and said she could not leave her. Nat said he would
engage her whole family if she so desired. Maxine, who was
receiving seventy-five dollars a week from Tim Frawley while
Gertrude received forty, asked a salary of no less than a
hundred and fifty dollars a week with seventy-five dollars for
Gertrude.

'Done,' said Nat. The whole business was completed in a
short time, Nat saying no to nothing. He then suggested he
should go immediately to square it with Tim and be back at
three o'clock with the contracts for both Elliott girls to sign.
After that, they could all go to the shipping office and see
when two bookings for Australia could be made.

Maxine was excited. Each moment of bargaining became
easier—this business of stating your wishes clearly, concisely,
showing no fear that you might not get what you asked. It
had been a major struggle to break away from Daly; it had
been a little easier to come to terms with Sydney Rosenfeld
and to arrange terms with Tim Frawley. But Frawley had
every right to refuse the release of two members of his company, and Nat Goodwin could easily change his mind. At
three o'clock he was back, however, with the contracts all
prepared. The money the girls were to be paid was only part
of the value Mr. Goodwin seemed to be putting on them; he
admitted he had agreed to pay Tim a large sum to recom-
pense him for their loss, gave Tim the rights to his play
A Gold Mine, and only seemed distressed that Tim had
demanded also that he should be allowed at least a few weeks.
There was a sailing for Australia on July 24, and he persuaded
Nat to let the girls travel on that. They would have a few
more weeks to play in San Francisco while others were re-
hearsed for their roles, and some publicity could be built up
about the departure of Maxine Elliott and her sister to join
Nat Goodwin, that could be of benefit to the Frawley company. Nat saw the reasonableness of the request—although
he had already pledged to pay for his whim. If Nat had money
anyone could get it out of him, and it seemed quite unim-
portant to him at the time. It was a nuisance that he would
have to open in Australia with Blanche Walsh in the parts
in which he was already visualizing Maxine, but perhaps
changes of bill would be required, now he came to think of it.

It was possible that Miss Walsh might be troublesome. Anyway, George McClellan would fix it all up. Now he had to go and pack, wresting promises from the Elliotts that they would be at the boat the next day—'Some fellows have promised to make a party of it.'

The contract for which they were engaged gave Maxine and Gertrude a good deal more than the Australian tour. It was a three-year engagement, with a tour of the United States scheduled after their return in November. (How would all this fit in with Maxine's divorce proceedings? Anyway, they were not worth mentioning.) The bill included the two plays Nat had performed in San Francisco—*A Gilded Fool* and *In Mizzoura*; there was a new play by Madeleine Lucette Ryley, called *An American Citizen*, which Nat thought he'd try on the Australians first; there were possible productions of *The Rivals* and *David Garrick*; he had the script of *The Prisoner of Zenda*, which had been so successfully performed in New York by Richard Mansfield. The salaries also were only starting sums; if Nat was able to build Maxine into the star he foresaw she could be, her salary would progress accordingly, with a share of the box-office take, as she contributed more and more to the drawing power of the Goodwin-Elliott combination. As for little Gertrude, her rise in salary was assured with Maxine taking a share in the book-keeping.

It must have been that same night that the word got around to the Frawley company. Maxine and Gertrude were more than capable of saying nothing, but Tim Frawley was not. He would have to re-schedule plays, call for more rehearsals; and he could hardly refrain from telling everyone of the bitter blow Nat Goodwin had dealt his season, and of the manner in which he had forced Nat to pay for his plundering action. An account has been passed down through members of the company that when the news was sprung upon Frank Worthing he fainted dead away. Admittedly, he was a frail man, who was to die of tuberculosis only fourteen years later at the age of forty-four, but strenuous working years still lay ahead of him then, and surely it was not ill health that had such a devastating effect, but the shock of seeing all his plans swept away from him overnight.

Maxine had remade her plans without giving him a thought.

She had little time to talk to him that night, because Nat
Goodwin was in front, come to see precisely what it was that
he had bought, and when he came around afterward, ecstatic,
he told both Maxine and Gertrude that he was totally bowled
over by their power as actresses—no need to mention the
beauty; that had already done its work.

Once more George McClellan was hauled out of sleep by
Nat's sudden entrance. Somehow during the course of the
day, he and Nat had failed to meet.

'You goddamn fool!' McClellan shouted when the truth
penetrated. He said that Maxine and Frank Worthing were
in love, and she would probably refuse to leave him in the
end. Nat said he would engage Frank, too. 'He's a good
actor.'

'Oh, go have your head examined,' were McClellan's final
words.

The send-off for Nat Goodwin on Thursday, June 25, 1896,
must have made the other passengers on board the *Alameda*
believe they were travelling with royalty. The Dutch skipper,
Captain van Otterndorf, observed contentedly that the familiar
four-week run across the Pacific was likely to be enlivened
for him by a willing and whimsical drinking companion. All
the guests of the Bohemian Club dinner, all members of the
Frawley company, several of John Drew's company, and other
assorted friends and acquaintances had assembled on the dock.
They pressed around Nat and grabbed for his hand, until he
had to be extricated and hauled on board as the gangplank
was about to lift and the whistles and hooters bellowed farewell. Tears rolled down his face. Maxine and Gertrude,
clutching their high feathered and beribboned hats in the
crush, felt cheated, as they so often did, when they found
that their sex excluded them from the last farewell prank of
all—a group of men on a chartered tug tailed the steamer as
she manœuvred her way out of the San Francisco dock, then
suddenly bobbed up on the port side of her, displaying a huge
canvas bearing the words 'Good Luck to Nat'.

There was a feeling of letdown on the dock. The groups
trailed off, back to the humdrum. Nat was someone who made
things happen; he changed the ordered course of events and
suggested a big, free world where things were not bounded by

limitations of money or convention. He was a clown, but in the grand manner. Frawley seemed unbearably vulgar, Frank earnest and colourless, John Drew so staid; Maxine could not wait for the next month to pass. She guessed that Captain Tom, disturbed by the sort of gossip Nat aroused, would offer wearisome admonitions, but had she not already shown herself capable of steering her course well, and taking care of Gertrude besides? Now she must go to work on suitable wardrobes for them both. The summer clothes that they were wearing now must not reappear in the strange summer they would find before they left Australia, and their winter clothes, which would be immediately necessary, were all stored in New York. There was plenty to do before they too sailed on the *Alameda*'s sister ship. Best now not to notice the tragic expression on Frank Worthing's face and get to work.

On July 31, a correspondent from Honolulu reported that Miss Maxine Elliott and her sister had passed through on the way to Australia and had said all the appropriate things about the beauties of the island. The press and the residents of Honolulu had waited hopefully for some of the high jinks that Nat had provided on his pause there a month ago, but the Elliott sisters were entirely decorous, took the prescribed drives, gasped at the flowers, loved the music, and retired back to their cabin.

Travelling on a liner as an honoured passenger, whom the captain desired at his table and fellow passengers eyed with admiration, was a different experience from travelling on the little barque *Will H. Case*. That was fourteen years before; strange to think that then she had spent weary hours in the cramped cabin studying her schoolwork, banging out her scales on the upright piano, to emerge later for air to find little space on the deck where she could stretch her legs. Here she lay on her cabin bunk, studying once more—this time parts in *A Gilded Fool* and *In Mizzoura*, Lydia Languish in *The Rivals*, and the plum of all, the role of Princess Flavia in *The Prisoner of Zenda*. When she emerged, she could stride around the promenade deck and with gracious amusement choose the lucky man who should be allowed to fold a steamer rug round her ankles. Gertrude, who had seen ships leave

8

from Rockland always carrying others, seldom herself, gloried
in every moment of it, constantly torn between the vigorous
gaiety that made her want to join any deck game offered and
her shyness with strangers, the fear that men who selected her
as the one whose steamer rug was the most tuckable might
not meet with the approval of little Dettie. They stopped at
Samoa, and heard that Nat had made the pilgrimage up the
hill to visit Mrs. Robert Louis Stevenson and to pay homage
at the grave high amid the rocks and seabirds.

They reached Melbourne on August 20. The Australian
audience had hated *The Rivals*, hated *A Gilded Fool*, but
consented to come, though in no overwhelming numbers, to
In Mizzoura. Only the musical shows were doing great business. Nat joyously welcomed Maxine as the saviour of his
season and decided to have her open in *The Nominee*, a farce
he had had in his repertory for several years. Blanche Walsh
did not care a rap about appearing in such foolish fare, but
she waited to see what Nat proposed to do about the part of
Lydia Languish and the excellent woman's part that was
available in the new play *An American Citizen*. It did not add
to her good will to hear all the talk about Maxine's coming to
bring in the public at last.

Maxine and Gertrude found Nat hilarious company. They
laughed to hear his account of arriving in Melbourne in late
July, in cold that was like 'a December blizzard without the
snow', without his winter overcoat or his long winter unmen-
tionables. They were full of admiration of him when work
began, observing how the scatterbrained, devil-may-care
clown gave way to a careful workman, concentrated and
patient, willing to re-do and re-do a scene until it was perfect.
Working under Nat's direction was a new experience; the
great stage effects that were the mark of a Daly production
were not a part of Nat's way; there was none of the helter-
skelter getting by of a repertory company such as Rose
Coghlan's, in which newcomers had to fit themselves rapidly
into the pattern of the old hands. Nat's rehearsals followed a
careful formula, starting with hours of work in which gestures,
facial expression, and moves were mapped out while the actors
still had their books in their hands, ready to make script
changes. The special quality of Nat was an inevitability and

ease in his business, something that frequently made people declare that the wonder of him was that he didn't 'do anything', but just came on and 'was himself', never realizing that this effect came from the most exact attention to timing— nothing too quick, nothing too slow—and a teamwork drilled into his actors that blended their timing exactly to his. Maxine and Gertrude were benefiting from training that went back to his vaudeville days, an ability that must stand on its own without the assistance of swanky scenery, dependent solely on the nimble interplay of the performers themselves. A tired old play like *The Nominee* was given as much attention as a new one, with the exception that with each revival it became a little more Nat's, and the rewriting on the stage was done without benefit of its author. He roared at actors he found muttering their lines in the wings; they must study when they were at home, no matter how much sleep they lost; here at rehearsal they must concentrate solely on getting each move into split-second exactness. The clarity and common sense with which he mapped a scene appealed immediately to both the newcomers.

The Melbourne audience enjoyed *The Nominee* when it opened, and there was a notable rise in business as they also piled in to see the new beauty who had joined the company. But where did this leave Blanche Walsh? Nat and George McClellan tried to work out some arrangement by which the ladies could alternate in the leading parts. Surely Miss Walsh had been happy about the arrangement originally discussed for *The Prisoner of Zenda*—the Princess Flavia was so obviously the part for Miss Elliott and Antoinette de Mauban really a finer acting part. A play for two leading ladies? Miss Walsh wondered if it was worth her while at all to study this role in which she shared honours with Miss Elliott if she was going to find herself only rarely appearing in the other parts already hers for two seasons with Nat.

And what of the new play? Who was going to get that? Nat was remarkably silent about *An American Citizen*. The trouble was that he had already shown it to Maxine; she had urged him to do it when he was only lukewarm, and her enthusiasm had warmed him. There was little or no question that her pleasure in the play was due partially to the excellence of the

woman's part, so how could he now ask her to share it with
Blanche Walsh? Maxine would become as angry as Blanche,
and at this point Maxine's anger was taken as justified whereas
Miss Walsh's had become a nuisance. The situation was
hardly new. Nat's enthusiasms and coolings off had a way
of colliding in the most awkward fashion; timing, of which
he was such a master on stage, inevitably tripped him in
the arrangement of his private affairs, both business and
personal. Finally Blanche Walsh's patience snapped. She flatly
refused to go on to Sydney with the company, claiming herself
frozen out and her contract violated. She demanded her immediate fare home and sailed for San Francisco. There was a
sigh of relief all around. The company ticked off George Mc-
Clellan as a killjoy and a bore for worrying about the talk
that her departure might cause. Had Nat also observed that
trouble might be brewing in another quarter? asked the unfortunate Mac. There were already two *ingénues* in his company, Misses Ethel Browning and Dorothy Usner, and now
there was Gertrude to be fitted in. Maxine certainly would
not stand for her little sister's being elbowed out. And what
did Nat propose to do with *The Prisoner of Zenda*? Could
any of his *ingénues* and his old ladies fill the part of Antoinette
de Mauban, which required a dramatic actress of the weight
of Blanche Walsh? Nat had an engagement at the race track
and preferred to shelve the discussion. Meanwhile the correspondents in Australia for American newspapers that carried
theatrical titbits happily cabled stories back to the United
States that Blanche Walsh had left the Goodwin company
in a huff.

The amount of admiration Maxine had received as a
beautiful woman in her six years in the theatre would match
the lifetime of many another woman's experience, so there was
nothing particularly new to her in the reception she got from
the Australian audiences and from Nat himself. The delighted
discovery of her effect upon others was long past; the fact
of accepting her own beauty had now become second nature.
There was, however, something refreshingly different in the
seriousness with which Nat treated her as an actress, nor did
she yet know that this was one of Nat's ways of wooing,
almost a necessity inside himself to claim for the woman of

the moment all the virtues, including talent. Maxine was neither the first nor the last woman to whom Nat talked of starring, of how great she'd be in this, in that, of how he could build her into a supreme actress so that all the world should recognize the amazing gifts that he had already seen. Women with far less to offer than Maxine had been told, and would be told in the future, that they were his equal as performers—and Nat was a genius. Many of them caused his career immeasurable harm by being, while his ardour lasted, the absolute condition for which he would sign up with a manager; many a manager decided to forgo Nat Goodwin to avoid having that appalling Miss X foisted upon him.

Maxine was by no means a liability as these others were, but she was certainly subjected to the same treatment, and loved it, and wanted to believe it, and in fact supremely benefited by it. Nat had at last changed for her the pattern of things; at Daly's there had been no chance to be anything but second woman with Ada Rehan in the company; with Frawley Blanche Bates had stolen the reviews; now, at least, a woman who was spoken of as one of the rising dramatic actresses of the moment, Blanche Walsh, had been obliged to capitulate. Instead of Maxine's being the beauty whom all the non-theatre people wished to invite out to supper, while the critics patronized her and the managers gave the acting chances to others, she was now queen of the situation, with no rival in the company for the parts that put her firmly in the position of opposite lead to the star. Blanche Walsh had the distinction of being the last woman to whom Maxine was professionally ruthless or unkind, and Blanche Walsh vitally affected the course of Maxine's life, because when she returned to the United States she talked. Before she left the Goodwin company, too, she had talked, and she left in her wake budding rebellion and more talk, so that events were set in motion that stretched far into the future.

The next result of Maxine's triumph over Blanche Walsh was the effort of one of the *ingénues* to lock horns with Gertrude. Precisely what happened has been lost to history. The Elliott sisters did not tell their story; Nat in his autobiography makes no mention of Dorothy Usner's objection over losing her roles to Gertrude Elliott, but declares he fired her from

the company for having posed for photographs in the nude.
Dorothy Usner returned to the United States and talked and
talked, far more shrilly than Blanche Walsh, and apparently
with some hope of stepping firmly into the limelight that
always surrounded the doings of Nat Goodwin. She talked
to the newspapers, and she talked to Mrs. Nat Goodwin the
Second.

Nat's fatal timing immediately joined the act. His claim for
divorce from Nella Pease Goodwin suddenly leaped into the
headlines. He had filed it in California, having been legally
separated from his wife four years earlier in 1892. At that
time the courts granted Mrs. Goodwin a cash settlement of
$15,000 and half the proceeds from the sale of furnishings
from the house they had shared at 226 West End Avenue in
New York City. That residence had figured vividly in the
news when Mrs. Goodwin barricaded herself inside it and
Nat, in a variety of disguises, had tried to gain entry, as usual
enchanting the readers of the scandal sheets by his pictur-
esquely confused affairs. Since then he had become involved
with his Kentucky heiress and had started the divorce proceedings in order to marry her, determined that Nella Pease
Goodwin should get no more out of him. He used grounds
admissible in California which if proved would give him his
liberty without further cost; he claimed that Mrs. Nella Pease
Goodwin was so habitually drunk that she had caused him
grave nervous distress and had been unable to fulfil her duties
as a wife. Nat claimed that he had suggested to his attorneys
in San Francisco that they could drop the divorce proceedings
when his plans to marry the Kentucky heiress had faded,
but out of deference to the hard work they had done in
preparation of their case he had consented to let them go
ahead, set off for Australia, and forgotten the whole thing.
Nella Pease Goodwin could not be found when the papers
were ready to be served upon her, so Nat's claims for divorce
were published in the newspapers in late August when Nat
was eagerly welcoming Maxine to Australia.

Joyfully the American press pounced upon this new episode
in the the career of Nat Goodwin. Mrs. Goodwin was found
and expressed stunned amazement; she was asked what she
thought of the latest titbit that a California newspaperman

had unearthed—that another divorce had been filed in California at almost the same time against George MacDermott by Jessie MacDermott, who was none other than Nat's new leading lady, Maxine Elliott. Mrs. Goodwin said she would file a countersuit and name Maxine Elliott, and the Kentucky heiress, and the notorious Lelia Farrell with whom she knew her husband had been carrying on before and during her marriage, and possibly many more. Her life had been utter misery with Nat (had there not been an incident in St. Louis when Nat was rushed to her hotel just in time to get her to a hospital, where she was revived from a suicidal overdose of sleeping pills?), and now he was being such an unutterable cad as to accuse her of insobriety. She would fight back with all she had. Her lawyers leaped at the returning Blanche Walsh and Dorothy Usner; they received nothing but a disdainful brush-off from Miss Walsh, but Miss Usner eagerly assented to sign affidavits affirming that the hotel rooms in Australia inhabited by Nat Goodwin and Maxine Elliott had a connecting door.

It was early October before the American newspapers reached Australia. Maxine and Gertrude, in their hotel room in Sydney, happily settled down to spend a morning devouring the news from home. The campaign of William McKinley versus William Jennings Bryan was just getting under way (it was just as well they were in Australia, as an election year meant trouble for the theatrical business). New cycling outfits figured much in the fashion news. Mrs. Potter Palmer was ending her first season in Newport with a ball. There were several important successes on Broadway; John Drew had a triumph in *Rosemary*, and it was nice to see that many of the papers gave his little niece, Ethel Barrymore, a mention; William Gillette had opened in *Secret Service*; Daniel Frohman's Lyceum company had started its season with E. H. Sothern in *An Enemy to the King*; and Edward Harrigan was back in *Marty Malone*. The roof gardens which featured summer vaudeville programmes were closing down for the autumn; the beach resorts were closing; the name of Mark Hanna occurred again and again; the *élite* of society had returned from the Czar's coronation in St. Petersburg; a Free-Silver-ite had tried to force his way into The Breakers on the eve of the Vanderbilt-Whitney wedding; beloved James Lewis of Daly's had died.

Then suddenly appeared the headline, 'Mrs. Nat Goodwin's Turn,' in the New York *Sun*. The article was long, giving the details of Nat's suit and Mrs. Goodwin's countersuit; it made much of Nat's recent brawls in saloons over 'a most conspicuous woman' whom he had forced upon the public in Texas, her first and last appearance on any stage; and right in the middle was a garbled account of Maxine's meeting with Nat at the Bohemian Club, her change of plans to join Nat after leaving Frawley's and cancelling her contract with Miner, who claimed to have released her because 'she would go whether he gave her leave or not'. Into this paragraph came the claim by Blanche Walsh that she had been 'frozen out of her position as leading lady' by Maxine.

Much more cruel was another article under 'Topics of the Theatre': 'Maxine Elliott, to marry whom N. C. Goodwin is seeking a divorce from his wife'—Maxine shrieked and Gertrude rushed to see what caused her such distress—'was not long legally separated from her husband. . . . When she came to New York and became an actress she employed an advertising agent to exploit her. She wore elaborate costumes on the stage and off, and she succeeded with her beauty and her money in becoming valuable while yet a novice in art. Blanche Walsh, whose stage career was equally remarkable in gaining headway at the very outset, Goodwin's leading lady in his present company, was crowded out of some roles by the sudden engagement of Miss Elliott.'

The tears were rolling down Maxine's face.

They read on appalled. The word 'plot' was used, a plot hatched between Maxine and Nat in San Francisco to obtain divorces and marry as soon as they both were free. Maxine was accused of callously pushing Blanche Walsh out of her position, and Nat was supposed to have tried to escape from his marriage to Nella free of cost, simultaneously abandoning a series of other ladies who felt they had claims on him, and all because he had fallen under the spell of the beautiful Maxine. It was suggested that the tour in Australia was a cover for a flagrant love affair which they planned to legalize as soon as the inconvenient obstacles were removed.

Both sisters erupted into Nat's hotel suite hysterically weeping, their arms loaded with newspapers. His cheerful greeting after a successful day at the race track was drowned in their lamentations. 'I shall never forget the day Max and Gertrude came to my room in the hotel in Sydney. . . . They pointed to the pictures and glaring headlines of a most sensational character.' The girls upbraided him for not mentioning his divorce, and when he asked Maxine why he had not been informed of her own, she answered that it was nobody's business.

To Maxine the sneering, laughing, peeping-Tom sort of publicity was a terrifying invasion. It seemed to undermine her in a manner that was surprising in view of her great strength. It was, however, precisely this strength that left her feeling so exposed and appalled. She had planned with the utmost care each move in her own secretive pattern, believing herself secure from observation except as she wished to be observed. Suddenly the serene, beautiful mask of Maxine Elliott was stripped away and people were poking and peeking at Jessie Dermot and her miserable marriage. The only way she could tolerate the failure and unhappiness of her life with George MacDermott was to wipe it out as if it had never happened, and here it was spewed in her face. She felt that everything she did was orderly, her life now a delightful round of social activities as the leading lady in a company, Nat an amusing companion whose more questionable activities were none of her concern. To be pointed at was intolerable to Maxine because it meant she had momentarily lost control of her environment. The tears she shed were suddenly those of a bewildered, infuriated child. Gertrude, recognizing immediately the depths of nervous irritation and melancholia into which such a situation could throw her sister, burned Nat with her great reproachful eyes, full of fear for little Dettie, full of tigerish protection of her.

As Nat and Maxine at last got onto sufficiently coherent terms to talk to each other they agreed they must set about writing denials to America immediately. Gertrude, keeping her head considerably better than the other two, suggested that it was wiser to refrain from denying what might happen in the future—'One never knows what may occur, and you two do certainly seem to get along together.' Suddenly they all laughed. Nat, happy to feel an easing of tension, suggested that they should have early supper there with him before the night's performance; he had a chicken that he had brought home on his way from the track and he had put it on a spit to roast in his grate fire. In the excitement of the girls' arrival he had forgotten it, and now when he rushed to salvage it, and with it everyone's good temper and good will, he found it a mass of charcoal.

Maxine hammered on. 'I'll never go back to that beastly country. Just see what they say about you and me.'

Nat tried to reassure her that the whole thing would be forgotten when they arrived in San Francisco at the end of November. Maxine was sure their return would bring a host of avid reporters to the boat and fresh scandal would burst out.

'But we haven't done any wrong, any harm, so why should we worry?' Nat said. 'We know our behaviour has been absolutely right.'

'We know,' said Maxine, 'but the world doesn't know.'

A table was brought with food from the hotel kitchen to replace the burned chicken. Nat upset a bottle of claret.

There is no way of knowing whether the shocked response of Maxine and Nat to the scandal-mongering was due to hurt innocence or distress at being found out. Much of Nat's autobiography is on a note of injured self-justification which, when the facts are examined, turns out to be not quite in agreement with the truth. His biography, which appeared first in serial form in newspapers in 1911 and was then published in book form in 1914, was the result of seventeen years of jotting down notes; it is disjointed, opinionated, and emotional, some parts written out in full with an excellent command of language, some suggesting scrawls upon an odd sheet of paper by his bedside set down in some moment of fevered wakefulness during the night. There are always the conflicting notes of high-minded conventionality, deploring the state of immorality of the world and its wicked ways, and the joyous, impudent reports of a man who laid down his own rules for living. Nat's attitude to women was totally formed by his attitude to his mother; never during his lifetime did she say a word of criticism of her boy. If things went wrong Mrs. Goodwin was always ready to believe that there was some good explanation, and thus Nat expected all women to behave well, to regard his sins as the mere nonsense of a boy and to understand that he did not really mean any harm. The only woman who totally fitted into this comfortable arrangement for him was his first wife, Eliza. The succession of wives and non-wives, managers, club friends, fellow actors, members of the public who ran afoul of Nat's waywardness, were more inclined to judge him in the subjective way and revolt against him because of the effect of his actions upon them, and always Nat was horrified and shocked that people should be so mean, so narrow, so dirty-minded.

It is entirely possible that Nat could have been having an intense love affair with Maxine and yet be shocked to death that anyone should accuse him of it; Maxine, with her belief that the non-admitted fact was the non-existent fact as far as the public was concerned, could have had precisely the same reaction. It is also more than likely that they were entirely innocent. Nat's life was lived far more with men, the congenial society of fellow drinkers, fellow gamblers, fellow larksters, or of beloved friends in the profession, such as Stuart Robson, William H. Crane, De Wolf Hopper, John Drew, who loved him in return, whereas women, whom he changed constantly, were never fully real to Nat as human beings. He lost his head about them, set them on impossible pedestals, knocked the pedestals down, and then turned away in revulsion from the earth-bound creature he had unmasked and went rushing away again in pursuit of some other dream woman. Maxine's life, particularly at this moment, when she had become leading lady in an important company, was lived as socially as possible; she was enjoying all the parties, being fêted, and the rough and tumble of a love affair would be an interruption to the teas at the governor-general's residence to be fitted in before the evening's performance, and to the supper parties afterward given by Australian bigwigs. It seems far more within the characters of the two people involved that Nat was working himself into the enjoyment of yearning over Maxine, romanticizing her, believing his greatest agony was her unattainability, but in truth gaining far more happiness from it than from attainment, while Maxine was appreciating the uncomplicated fact of a high-spending, high-living, vivid escort who loudly expressed his admiration for her but troubled her emotions little.

'It was the most inharmonious meal I ever ate,' said Nat, describing that dinner in his suite. 'I was rattled!' Maxine's nervous, dark misery could cast a total blight. Nat was nervously fussing, and Gertrude was silent until Nat spilled hot tea in her lap.

Suddenly Gertrude blazed at them. 'You two people are acting like a couple of fools. There's only one way out, and you've got to take it.'

They turned on the tense, upright figure of Gertrude and saw her mouth buttoned in determination. 'Cable America you're engaged and are to be married sometime next season,' she advised. It was a new experience for them to be ordered to behave by Gertrude.

Probably this was turned into a laugh again. It was time to go to the theatre, and nothing further was said then between Maxine and Nat. Nat tried to escape after the performance but Maxine caught him.

'What do you think of Gertrude's suggestion?' asked Max.
'What do you think of it?' Nat parried.
'I'm game,' said Max.
'You're on,' said Nat.

Thus Nat reports their engagement. Since neither had yet obtained freedom, any immediate change of status was out of the question, but Maxine could flash an engagement ring and the word 'fiancée' would preserve her respectability. They probably never would have married if the public had left them alone. But Maxine had been right about the reaction to their return to the United States; the papers roared with talk about them, and it continued as their tour led them across the country, from November 1896 to May 1897. It continued when they reopened their season in September and gave New York the first view of them in *An American Citizen*; it continued as they took the play on tour with others in Nat's repertory, and tried out a play called *Nathan Hale* in Chicago. While they were in Chicago, on January 19, 1898, Nat's divorce at last became final; his own charges were flung back in his face, and Nella Pease Goodwin gained from him a settlement of seventy-five dollars a week and an injunction that he could never marry again within New York state, where the divorce was obtained. Maxine had long since received her final decree, on November 21, 1896, a few days after the Goodwin company docked in San Francisco from Australia.

There was nothing now to keep them from marrying, unless they were in New York state. They baulked at marrying in Chicago because Nat had already married Nella there and preferred a different locale—it could not be Buffalo, because it was within the New York state ban—so they chose the next town where their tour took them, and on February 10, 1898, they became husband and wife at the Hollenden Hotel, Cleveland, with only Gertrude, the company manager George Appleton and his wife, and Mr. Hobst of the hotel present, with Dr. S. P. Sprecher of the Euclid Avenue Presbyterian Church officiating. They were entertained that evening at supper by Mr. and Mrs. William H. Boardman (nephew of the great leader for women's rights, Miss Margaret Boardman). Nat was a little the worse for wear after a bachelor night with Dick Golden and Walter Jones. ('It was a lucky thing that the marriage ceremony was only "recovery" for me! The boys had put me in no condition to learn a new part!') They left the next day for Pittsburgh, the next stop of the tour itinerary. Maxine wore a dark blue outfit, skirt and frogged jacket made of heavy satin with lace choker, and a large hat carrying a great wing that swept across her forehead. For her wedding she received from Nat a private railroad coach the 'Goodwin Special', which was hooked onto the regular train from Cleveland to Pittsburgh, and new diamonds flashed from her neck, hands, and wrist. In the grandeur of their departure the small, battered man at her side could be forgiven for his hangover.

7

JACKWOOD

Mr. and Mrs. Goodwin were unable to take a honeymoon immediately. Their tour of *An American Citizen* plunged off to the deep South and the South-west. Cowboys, Indians, and gold miners were no novelty to Nat nor he to them. Maxine knew the one-night stands of the North-east and Middle West by heart, but here she was travelling in new territory. The part she played was the kind most appealing to towns separated by deserts, rivers, and mountains from the centres of fashion; an elegant English lady with numerous changes of costume. There was a scene that caused delight when Nat with expressions of fearful agony tried to hook up the back of her ball dress. Word began to fly ahead that 'our Nat' was bringing his wife with him, a real elegant dame and a beauty. The story was told that somewhere—perhaps San Antonio, Texas—the company manager, stepping into a saloon before the performance to get a quick drink, saw a party of enormous men with guns, mighty hats, and dainty high-heeled boots heave their way through the swinging doors to the bar, to shout for attention. He moved away to give them respectful elbow room but listened to them talk and returned white-faced to the theatre to report what he had heard.

'If this here Max-hiney Elliott ain't all she's cracked up to be, there's going to be some shooting around town tonight.'

There was no need to worry. The audience (including Indian women carrying papooses seated in a special section) was delighted. They whooped, whistled, and also expressed their pleasure by throwing gold nuggets upon the stage.

Nat was in his element. He had friends wherever they went,

and the rougher the place the more he gloried in it, as being the real America, his kind of America, the America that only he, Mark Twain, and Bret Harte understood.

Finally, on May 21, 1898, the tour was over. Nat did not yet have a home he could offer Maxine. His house at 226 West End Avenue had been stripped of its furnishings by his divorced wife. His bachelor apartment at Worth House on Broadway and 58th Street was not designed to accommodate a woman, lavish though it was. The maroon-plush-covered walls, divans strewn with tasselled cushions, mantel of green tile, Japanese lamps, dark oil landscapes (summarily described by Nat as of 'the French School'), enormous oil portraits of himself by Mr. Bunn of Philadelphia—all added up to the sort of masculine mess which Nat could create around him in no time at all. Rodney, the worshipful valet, could cope with Nat's confusion, unpunctuality, and disorder, but was thrown into a panic at the thought of serving a lady. They moved into the Hotel Grenoble on 56th Street, and Nat proceeded to entertain the whole of New York. Late hours and haphazard engagements caused the first friction between Maxine and Nat. She closed her door on him, and he wandered off, disconsolate, to find solace with the boys down at the Lambs Club. Striking an attitude in the doorway of the bar, he was obliged by his nature to make a joke out of his miseries.

'Boys,' he announced, 'I thought I'd married the most beautiful woman in the world, and I find my wife is a Roman senator.'

But he was contrite, she was forgiving. They decided they owed it to themselves to have a proper honeymoon. They agreed they both loved England, and there they would go and rent a house for the summer months.

'Rent a house? Hell, Max, I'll buy you one.' Overjoyed at the pleasure he could give his beautiful wife, Nat insisted they must sail at once, pack up all the fancy pipes, pictures, and knick-knacks from his apartment, and ship it all, including a great ugly stallion, Kentucky, bought in a moment of exuberance from Charles Thorne and left stabled somewhere on Long Island. With little sister Gertrude and trunks enough to stagger the baggage master on board, they sailed away in June for London. They settled temporarily in a

London hotel, and before Maxine had done her hair in the morning and selected a dress to wear at lunch, Nat was out bombarding real-estate agents. Without any question, he declared on his return, Jackwood Hall, the house of Lord Penzance, was the ticket. The Gilbert-and-Sullivan name of its owner amused them. It was black and white, half-timbered, Elizabethan, built on the model of Haddon Hall by a Victorian architect—an ancestral mansion not yet thirty years old. Jackwood had stood empty for some time and the real-estate agents were delighted. The Goodwins bought it immediately for fifty thousand dollars, undoubtedly far too much.

It was a charming, comfortable house in the London suburb of Shooters Hill only eight and a half miles from London Bridge. It was set in grounds which combined rolling meadow and woodland with formal gardens and a small shady walk beside a natural spring which Nat christened 'Little Carlsbad'. There would be no problem at all in getting friends to visit them and passing a congenial summer. At a later date Maxine learned that anything as stridently olde English as Jackwood was slightly comic, but at that moment she was delighted.

It has been suggested that the marriage of Maxine Elliott and Nat Goodwin was a working partnership only; that Maxine married Nat to further her career and he married her because he had the marrying habit. There is a small element of truth in both accusations, but also there is no doubt that both intended this as a real marriage and did their best according to their different temperaments. Nat was touchingly proud of Max's beauty and manners. He loved her formal and almost quaint mode of expression, which seemed to him truly lady-like. The tone of voice can be faintly heard in some letters Maxine wrote at this time to newspapermen friends, chiefly Melville Stone of the Associated Press, and Mr. Freiberger of the *Saturday Evening Herald*, Boston. They are small, gracious notes. Enclosing a picture of herself and Sport and another Boston bull called Miss Muffin, she wrote, 'What do you think of the new Boston bulls. Nat gave them to me for Christmas. They are prize winners and the darlingest things in the world, *I* think . . . Sport! Miss Muffins! This is Mr. Freiberger. They are making their bow

HIGH JINKS AT JACKWOOD
(*left to right*) Melba, Nat Goodwin, Maxine, M. Moorehouse,
Haddon Chambers, H. Melville

ON TOUR IN CHICAGO; MAXINE WITH GRACE WASSALL

JOHNSTON FORBES-ROBERTSON IN *HAMLET*

to you.' 'Jackwood will feel very much honoured to be allowed a corner in "House Beautiful" some time.' 'Thank you for the beautiful roses—I think you have kissed that famous Blarney stone. Trembling in anticipation of tonight [the *Nathan Hale* try-out in Chicago]. Turn in your thumbs for us—that means good luck, you know.' 'You may expect us to materialize at Rector's at 11.30.' 'All send regards and "all" includes Clyde Fitch who materializes today.' 'I wanted from Sarony *one of each position* of the "cabinets" in evening-dress—not one sample has materialized.' 'Thank you [the Forty Club, Chicago] for changing the date of your invitation for us—we are bowing low in acknowledgement of your graciousness.'

Maxine did not marry Nat with any illusion that this was Romeo and Juliet; at the age of thirty, and with one failed marriage behind her, she was not seeking romance. She admired Nat's gifts whole-heartedly. Respect for a man's performance in the world was absolutely necessary to her. The dark and melancholy side of her was reassured by a man who could make her laugh. They were enormously good friends. She was well aware that Nat was a heavy drinker, but she made the human and female mistake of feeling sure she could cope with this perfectly. It was easy to believe that some of the more distressing incidents of the past would never have happened if Nat had had a good woman at home.

No impermanence in the marriage was expressed by the furnishing in which they indulged. Maxine ordered linen by the dozen and dozen and dozen again, all heavily embroidered with the initials M.E.G. The glassware, wine glasses of all sizes, tumblers, and finger bowls—all bore the same M.E.G. in gold. Crates of importations came from America to astonish the station master at Shooters Hill. The Goodwins had definitely moved in.

It was Nat's house, with Maxine its châtelaine and his con-sort. He paid the bills, and many a headache they gave him when he found he had taken on tenantry and a market garden besides. Since Nat never minded studying a new role, the first summers at Jackwood, only two months in the year, were a source of great amusement to him. He was now Nat Good-win, the country squire, and he would play it with the

inimitable Goodwin touch. He bought shooting jackets, shooting caps, gaiters, high boots, checked jacket. The interior
crawled with dogs, and there were prize hounds in the
kennels and riding horses in the stable, to which was added
the snorting stallion, Kentucky. There were traps and wagons
and carriages and a buggy from America, fascinating the
inhabitants of Shooters Hill as it shot through the village
street, with Nat in barest control of the flying horse that drew
it. Max Beerbohm has most eloquently described his vision of
the Goodwin invasion of the English country:

> . . . One of the horses I remember especially: an enormous brown
> creature with a flashing eye, driven by Nat Goodwin in a fear-
> some little vehicle whose name I forget. It was a vehicle which
> Goodwin had brought over from America, and I think he regarded
> it as a rather false note in the English scene: he used to say,
> with a note of apology, that it was 'vurry handy'. It was appal-
> lingly handy. It consisted of nothing but two very large thin
> wheels with a sort of little basket slung low between for Goodwin
> and one friend to sit in. I was sometimes that friend. The gigantic
> horse I regarded as our common enemy. There was nothing
> between him and the basket, and I think that had he dared he
> would have killed us both with a couple of well-directed kicks.
> But he dared not. He was a coward of cowards. There were few
> things he did not shy at, and from them he bolted. But who am
> I that I should sneer at him? He at least had the courage of his
> cowardice; not I of mine. I pretended to be enjoying those
> rides.

While Nat played his games, Maxine created for him the
background that was his ideal. She was a charming, gracious
hostess to his friends and took her life at Jackwood seriously.
She did comfortable, reassuring, domestic things such as
create for herself a little upstairs boudoir. She found her own
corner in the garden where she could be regularly found
serving afternoon tea. She wore simple, filmy country clothes
all summer long. Maxine was play-acting a little, too. Nat's
friends told her of another summer some years ago when Nat
had tried living in England as a bachelor host and had then
been so appallingly imposed upon by hangers-on and all sorts
of riffraff that it was a joy now to see her there protecting his
interests. These friends and admirers were people worth

listening to. They included Sir Henry Irving, Herbert Beerbohm Tree, Max Beerbohm, W. S. Gilbert, John Hare,
Haddon Chambers, actors, writers, musicians, painters of
prominence. Americans flowed to Jackwood. Ethel Barrymore
came to debate whether she should marry Irving's son Laurence. The theatre managers Charles and Daniel Frohman
both came, and their colleague Charles Dillingham, the playwright Clyde Fitch, and William Gillette, who was delighting
London in *Secret Service*. Nat had the gift of attracting
around him creative people of a convivial kind. During the
first and second summers at Jackwood, Maxine enjoyed life
as the lovely wife of a man of genius. She learned the ropes
of being a hostess, and she learned well.

*

When the summer of 1898 ended Jackwood was left to care-
takers, stablemen, kennelmen, and gardeners. The Goodwins
returned to America for another six months' tour preceding
a new opening in New York. Tryouts on the road were carried
out under difficulties. In South Bend, Indiana, on October 1,
where the autumn tour began, Nat was still obliged to walk
with a cane because during the last week at Jackwood Kentucky had managed to throw him, and he was still carrying
the scars of a country squire as he took up the role of actor.
Whereas Maxine's instinct was always to try to duck away
from the press—she described the attentions of newsmen as
'the third degree of the Fourth Estate'—Nat had cheerfully
said it was only fair to give a full account of his fall to the
boys who came aboard the s.s. *Lucania*. Maxine saw the
reasonableness of giving interviews connected with professional work, but she loathed the invasion of private life, and
would go to any length to conceal a physical injury (an
indignity) or any details that applied to emotional life (worse
indignity still). She winced when Nat merrily described how
he had turned to close a gate, touching Kentucky with his
spur, so the horse bolted and was only stopped from smashing
his rider into a wall by Nat's managing to throw them both.
Nat's leg had been caught under the body of the horse, and a
bone in his foot was broken where the stirrup cut it. Nat
could have won Maxine's complete respect if he had gritted

his teeth and walked off the boat without a limp, no matter what the pain, telling no one.

In their repertory the Goodwins were playing *An American Citizen*, *A Gilded Fool*, and *David Garrick*, but the new play *Nathan Hale* was the most important item. They had briefly tried it out just before they were married, and now were polishing it on tour for the New York opening. It was by Clyde Fitch, a triumph of persistence on his part. As early as December 1895 Fitch had written to his fellow playwright Marguerite Merington to say, 'I am going to write *Nathan Hale* for Goodwin! I hope you like the idea.' But Clyde Fitch had found Nat hard to pin down, and petulantly complained that it seemed as if Goodwin were avoiding him, which he was. It was Maxine who persuaded Nat to take a look at the script, and in November 1897 Marguerite Merington received the report that Goodwin had been nabbed:

> My *dear* Marguerite, *how* sorry I am not to have been in when you called—I was with Goodwin . . . Goodwin said to me today (don't mind my repeating it to YOU, will you?) 'Fitch, I never heard anyone read a play so well as you. I thought I was the best, but you can read better than I.' He said 'than *me*', really. Well, he loves *Hale*! I read it through this afternoon. Often, he laughed aloud. Several times his eyes got full and his cheeks took the tears and loved them dry. And once he said, 'Hell! They don't say a word, eh?' and put his two arms on the table and his head on his arms, and cried! And I don't care if he buys the play or not, all the same he's a dear! And he's kind and he's sympathetic.*

Clyde had succeeded in getting both Nat and Maxine to his elegant apartments above Carnegie Hall. He settled them among the furnishings he had earnestly sought out in trips to Europe, put a decanter at Nat's elbow, and thoughtfully arranged a comfortable place on the divan where Maxine could lie in a becoming light. The moment was of extreme importance to him with a list of recent failures and his longing to buy a house in the country. He needed Nat and Maxine badly. He had cleverly rushed his designer friend Virginia Gerson into making some sketches for the costumes to submit

---

* *Clyde Fitch and His Letters*: by Montrose J. Moses and Virginia Garson. (Little, Brown & Co., Boston, 1924.)

to them on the same evening. He was well informed about the personal situation of the actors he was wooing, including the fact that to please Miss Maxine Elliott you must also take good care of her little sister Gertrude. The costumes for Angelica Knowlton, the part proposed for Gertrude, were particularly adorable, a pert panniered eighteenth-century dress of ankle length, a becomingly folded fichu at the neck, with powdered locks topped by a sort of tilted basket trimmed with flowers.

> . . . They did *just* what I wanted them to do! Angelica made a hit and Miss Elliott *jumped* at her hair!! . . .
>
> They seemed staggered by the rooms and raved breathlessly about them every other minute. Miss Elliott was handsome and charming. Becky [Clyde Fitch's dog] tumbled right *over!!* Hale made a good impression and *Goodwin bought it*—but oh they stayed so long! . . . till 4.30 and Goodwin drank enough W&S to put his hand on his heart and say he had from that spot a true and lasting affection for me! And that I was GREAT! . . . Oh! They stayed so late! Till every candle had burned out in its socket, and the electric light had heard the Sun coming, and sneaked away!

When the Goodwins' tour brought them to Chicago, Clyde Fitch dashed to see them, and dashed away again. Both Goodwins were delighted with him; his gifts as a playwright were those of a tailor always ready to remodel and refit according to the requirements of the individuals he was serving. He worked at lightning speed, never fearing to rewrite and capable of doing it overnight. Nat's enthusiasm for Clyde's professional workmanship was such that he forgot his usual resentment of effeminacy and was blind to the characteristics that the writer Amy Leslie noted—Fitch's 'airy manner, prettily coifed locks, and curly moustache'. Maxine found him supremely comfortable. With him she could discuss her beauty and her clothes in an impersonal way with no man-woman fencing.

The title role of *Nathan Hale*, the Revolutionary hero, a twenty-one-year-old Boston schoolmaster caught by the British and shot as a spy, was a curious one for a plump, short, red-headed ex-vaudeville comedian. When Nat's arms were roped behind him for the final scene ('I regret that I have but one life to give for my country') his waistcoated stomach protruded in a definite bow; in knee breeches and stockings, he had a tendency to look knock-kneed. Nevertheless, Clyde Fitch's determination to get Nat for his Nathan had good sense in it, because Nat's gifts had pathos and even nobility. The critic Alan Dale, one of those who had blamed Nat for wasting his talent in slapstick farce and then blamed him for daring to be anything else but funny, remarked that he was always attracted to 'golden heroes'. Jim Redburn, the sheriff in *In Mizzoura*, was a heroic part, and there were pathos and self-sacrifice in his part in *An American Citizen*. Nat Goodwin's audiences confidently expected to laugh, but they also liked to shed a tear and feel pleasantly elevated.

Maxine's part was Alice Adams, Nathan Hale's pupil in school. It seemed strange also to put such a buxom womanly woman, over thirty, into the part of a teen-age schoolgirl, but again it was right. Clyde Fitch wrote a part calling for precisely what she could do. She started with flirtatious banter and ended in grief expressed in silence and dignity—no melodramatics.

Thirdly Gertrude was the comic but enchanting *ingénue*. Her part as Angelica Knowlton allowed her to make a character-comedy vignette as a lisping young lady of the Lydia Languish type. Clyde knew precisely what he was doing in pleasing Maxine (and therefore Nat) by allowing Gertrude her brief moment of show-stealing. Woven into the play was a small part for a handsome man in uniform with few lines, played by a certain S. M. Hall, none other than little brother Sam Dermot, who needed work. Big sister Jessie was ready to take care of him, and Nat had been well used to a Weathersby sister or two when he and Eliza ran the *Froliques*. He was flattered and pleased to feel like the father of the tribe that belonged to his Max.

Nathan Hale opened at the Knickerbocker Theatre on Monday, January 2, 1899, to a brilliant first-night audience. After the first act they called for Nat to speak, but he begged to be allowed to remain in character until the end of the play. During the silent scene when the eyes of Nathan Hale and Alice Adams met for the last time without a word passing between them, the total silence on stage was broken by snuffles from the audience; later there was a gasp when the volley offstage told that Nathan had fallen. The curtain fell, handkerchiefs made hurried repairs, and applause crashed over the house.

Most reviews were kind. Maxine, said the *Times*, acted 'with more facility of expression and a larger share of emotional force than before', her comic, sentimental and tragic scenes 'positively a little triumph of virtuosity'. The *Mail and Express* noted that Nat was quiet and earnest but Maxine 'the most affecting player upon the stage', and the *Herald* agreed in giving major attention to Maxine and admiring her 'exuberant vitality and her restrained tragedy', describing her 'a delightful creature who has steadily advanced'. The *World* found Maxine 'arch, winning, attractive, dignified and impressive'. By and large Maxine stole the reviews from Nat, although Alan Dale was rude to them both on their appearance; Nat's shape, he said, was 'a bitter blow' and Maxine was 'somewhat mature'; he exhorted them both to be careful—'Life is evidently pleasant, and *embonpoint's* fatal clutches are evident.' Clyde Fitch wrote to Marguerite Merington:

> there were 27 calls the first night and your little pal made a *long* speech! Miss Elliotts, 1 & 2, both were very fine and made unusual personal successes. Nat was *splendid* in parts, and showed absolute power to grow into the part. His whole last act was *perfect* . . . it was a lovely production, and I felt repaid.

The Goodwins had an enormous success on their hands. They played to packed houses nightly for the nine weeks in New York, and had they not been booked to continue a tour they could have gone on till the end of the season. Everyone was in high spirits and Clyde was writing them another play. By mid-March they interrupted *Nathan Hale* to give Clyde's *The Cowboy and the Lady* a week's tryout in Philadelphia. They closed in April in Buffalo and were London bound.

*

It was not a quiet retreat at once to the dogs and horses of Jackwood. They had decided to invade the London theatre, booking Daniel Frohman's Duke of York's Theatre through

June into July. They felt it impolite to English friends to
reopen the American War of Independence by putting on
Nathan Hale, but they wished to be clearly Americans, not
trying to rival English drawing-room comedy. They chose
The Cowboy and the Lady, with *An American Citizen* ready
if a change of bill should be required. Clyde Fitch's second
play for them, a Western romance, had Nat in 'dude' clothes;
he played a gentleman rancher misunderstood by the lovely
Eastern lady he worshipped, who considered him an idler and
a playboy until he nobly proved otherwise. It followed the
perfect formula: a dramatic second-act curtain with Nat
dragged off accused of murder; the third and final act a court-
room scene, with a last-minute reprieve and love rewarded.
Gertrude played Midge, a wildflower of the West, an orphaned
girl who had been adopted by a whole group of rugged men.
Teddy North, otherwise Nat, kept a box into which each
man must drop a quarter if he used bad language in front of
Midge.

The London critics heartily loathed the show. They found
it silly, unreal, and crude. Hurriedly, after two weeks of poor
business, *An American Citizen* was put into the bill. This was
more popular. It ran for five weeks, until London society
left the city in a body to visit one another's country estates,
and the theatre season followed suit. Maxine and Nat had had
sufficient success to plan to reopen at the Duke of York's in
September after their six weeks of country entertaining.

They had more friends than ever now to invite to Jackwood. Nat had become one of the first American members of
the Garrick Club. They were a popular pair, and Jackwood's
ease and good living brought down droves. There was a difference, however. For the first time, theatrical London had seen
little sister Gertrude, and her personal success had been huge.
She was no longer just an adorable shadow who demurely
conducted William Gillette to see the flowers when he tired
of conversation round the tea table. Maxine was amazed and
excited when she found a letter from the Duke of Manchester
asking if he could come because he would like to see more of
Miss Gertrude. The Goodwins' genial friend, the ex-soldier
playwright Captain Robert Marshall, a favourite bachelor
among the hostesses, came with a professional offer for Ger-

trude. He had written a charming romance of love in high places called *A Royal Family*, and wanted Gertrude's combination of dewy innocence and spunk for his young princess. There was a family conference which decided it would be a good part for her, and she was allowed to accept.

Maxine and Nat were curiously blind about their own lives when they launched Gertrude on a separate course. Clyde Fitch had exactly observed the power of Gertrude's position in Maxine's and Nat's life. He had made Midge in *The Cowboy and the Lady* the gentle go-between, the little sister who reassured 'big brother' that the lady had a warm and loving heart beneath a marble surface, and who pleaded with her big sister that the man had meant no harm and should be forgiven and cherished. Clyde was observing from life. He had watched how Gertrude's presence had smoothed out difficulties and acted as a sort of safety valve between Maxine and Nat. She was Maxine's child, but Nat's affection for her was also obvious. They shared jokes, and Nat lovingly called Gertrude—a long, slim thing—'Appetite Cora' because of the hearty meals she could tuck into. The scene in *The Cowboy and the Lady* that won her such praise and stopped the show was when she eased Teddy's bruised and bewildered emotions by singing in her pure voice his favourite song, 'I Love a Lovely Girl, I Do'. Clyde surely guessed that many times Nat wanted to use such simple, sentimental words to Max, and Max had found the moment inappropriate and brushed him off—'Nat's being a bore.' Maxine had plenty of reasons to complain of Nat. He not only drank too much, but had begun to repeat the pattern of life he had lived with Eliza: he felt himself free to indulge his constantly roving eye now that his wife was safely won. He expected Maxine to be all-forgiving, but she felt humiliated and unwilling to be lulled into good will when he turned to her for love. Her pride was great and she exposed her feelings only to Gertrude. In the future, the confidantes Maxine was to have would not be so charitable.

Amid the horses, dogs, flowers, and guests, there was a flurry of dressmaking to get Gertrude's costumes right. The Goodwins reopened in September, but closed before October 14; thus they could be present at Gertrude's first night at the Court Theatre. The play was a charming bouquet of roses and a great success. When the Goodwins sailed for America to fulfil their touring engagement they had to leave Gertrude behind, assured of a run in *A Royal Family* for some months. Somehow, none of them had quite foreseen that this enormous separation would come so soon. Madeleine Lucette Ryley, the playwright, and her actor husband, John H. Ryley, took Gertrude to live with them, assuring Maxine that they would treat her as their daughter and protect her every moment of her waking day. Mr. Hammond, stage carpenter at the Court, father of a family of girls who all became theatrical dressers, volunteered his daughter Nellie as special watchdog within the theatre, always ready to chaperone Gertrude home and see that no unsuitable gentleman got through the stage door. Good-byes were said amid floods of tears from everybody.

The pattern of Maxine's and Nat's personal life and their professional life had become reversed since their marriage. In the theatre he had been boss, guide, and teacher, but a shy man personally who approached the beautiful Maxine hesitantly. Now at home, at Jackwood at least, they lived Nat's life. Maxine objected to prolonged conviviality but she acted as wife and ran the house according to his wishes. It was not at all her way of doing things, this casual, open-handed hospitality that Nat loved to dispense. She would have preferred a clearly defined guest list and menus thought out in advance. She wanted time to get into the right costume and not be taken by surprise by impromptu lunches, or by guests who came to dinner and stayed so late they had to be found a bed.

On returning to America and to work Nat deferred more and more to Maxine's desires and opinions. In the very first play that they had picked together, Clyde Fitch's *Nathan Hale* (it was Maxine who had hammered at Nat to read it in the first place) an actor had walked out during the Chicago tryout claiming he could not even read the part for Nat Goodwin without criticism and advice not only from Miss Maxine Elliott but also from Miss Gertrude Elliott. If the two men who engaged him, Nat Goodwin and Clyde Fitch, were to have nothing to say he was not going to tolerate being picked on by a couple of women. Since that time, Maxine's authority

had steadily grown. Nat considered her a brilliant judge of
a script, and in this he was perfectly right. Every business
arrangement was discussed between them. At the time of their
marriage Nat was supposed to have been worth about a hundred thousand dollars. Maxine may have had a few savings,
but she depended largely upon her salary. Very soon after
the Australian tour, Nat had made good his word to put her
on a percentage basis, so that her earnings now were a third of
whatever the Goodwin company earned. Since they had become a team their earnings were steadily rising.

Maxine's influence was constantly pushing the Goodwin-
Elliott combination away from farce and into high comedy,
without opposition from Nat. He was no exception to the
rule that a comedian in his heart always longs to play Hamlet.
He had joyfully embraced the pathos and nobility of Nathan
Hale, and now the longing to be taken more seriously was
growing stronger; the magic name of Shakespeare had entered
the long professional debates of the Goodwins. There were
rumours now that they were considering *The Taming of the
Shrew*, but the ferocious Katherine was not for Maxine.
Sensibly, she had denied any dreams of Juliet, though she
played a little with the thought of Rosalind or Viola. But
Nat Goodwin was a star, his name in heavier type than hers;
he could not be asked to give a production so completely for
her and accept a melancholy Jaques or a Malvolio—even the
mad dreams of Nat could not turn him into a young Orsino
or Orlando. *The Merchant of Venice* would give them both
opportunities as Portia and Shylock, but Daly had a new production of it with Ada Rehan and Sidney Herbert, so they
must wait awhile. Crossing the Atlantic they read scripts. The
most promising seemed one by the young London actor
Henry V. Esmond, with the provisional titles of *The Trinity*
or *Pals*. As they toured through the autumn this play took
shape and emerged eventually as *When We Were Twenty-
One*, the greatest success they had together.

They both felt it a shock to be parted from Gertrude. They
talked less; often their social engagements were separate.
There was a flurry of anxiety when Captain Marshall wrote
to say he was closing *A Royal Family* but wished Gertrude
to stay on for his new play, *His Excellency, the Governor*.

Maxine and Nat examined the script and found no fault with
it, so they abandoned the happy dream that Gertrude might
be home for Christmas. Gertrude in London was torn between the longing to be with her sister and excitement at her
developing career. From Mrs. Ryley's house at No. 3 Clem-
ents Inn, she wrote a letter to Mr. Melville Stone, an old
friend of her sister's and general manager of the Associated
Press.

November 26, 1899

Dear Mr. Stone,

What a very nice note and how kind you are to write me
all that distance away. It is very pleasant to hear from home
and I do feel lonely sometimes, not that I have time to do anything but rush rush rush. Through all the dashing about though
I miss my sister *all the time*, and I shall never get used to being
away from her.

London is Transvaal mad. One spends all one's time playing
extra matinees or selling programmes at them for the 'widows
and orphans' of the 'Tommy Atkins' at the front.

The 'Royal Family' is going very well, for which we are all
very thankful and they have been very kind to me for which
I am duly grateful, in fact I am very happy in the theatre. I
love the part and like all the people and the theatre is charmingly run.

I am living here with Mrs. Ryley, author of the 'Citizen'. She
is a dear and we are as comfy and congenial as never was.

If I should wait until I am a star, to return to America I fear
me sore I should never see my native land again. However, I
thank you for your friendly exaggeration of the *pleasant* possi-
bilities of the future and believe me I remain

Yours sincerely,
Gertrude Elliott

Undoubtedly letters from London which have not been
preserved followed Maxine to Cincinnati, Chicago, St. Louis,
Pittsburgh. Amid the hotel living and the long train journeys
perhaps Maxine had a flash of envy for her little sister in
London in the midst of its Boer War excitement and the
glitter and bustle of Christmas shopping. The Goodwins got
to New York for Christmas Day, but with no sense of home-
coming. The family feeling of the season would have meant
more if Gertrude had been there.

'Nothing ever happens on Christmas,' Maxine told an interviewer who had asked her for some words upon the happy season, 'nothing, at least, but recurrent "blues". The monotony of our end-of-the-year holidays never varies. To me it is rather a depressing day, with an extra performance to worry through. That's all.'

When We Were Twenty-One opened in New York at the Knickerbocker Theatre on February 5, 1900, Maxine's thirty-second birthday. She had evidently taken Alan Dale's rude remarks about her figure very seriously, for she was slim, lovely, and radiant. The play was a modern comedy allowing her to wear fashionable clothes designed for the individual style that she had begun to work out for herself. Ysobel Haskins as a showy lady called 'the Firefly' was given the brilliant colours; Maxine contrasted herself with Ysobel's beauty by her new style, one of moderation and quiet elegance. Gone was all the flamboyance; her clothes now were of rich material and workmanship but extreme simplicity of line. Instead of rich reds and blues, which she had once believed a dark-haired beauty should wear, she now allowed her own colouring to be the most brilliant note in the ensemble, set off by pale cream colours and greys, with white predominating. She told an interviewer that French dressmakers were putting sashes on everything, but it spoiled the line so she removed them all. M. Worth and M. Poiret were already beginning to learn that they could not tell their American client Miss Elliott precisely what to wear. Their great names failed to impress her. The fact that she was willing to pay the price of a thousand dollars or more for a dress gave her every right to pick it apart as she saw fit.

The Goodwins stayed two months in New York that winter —a month of *Nathan Hale* in January before a month of the new play. They lived at the Hoffman House. On many evenings Nat went to the Lambs or took some pretty young lady with stage aspirations to supper. More and more, he and Maxine tended to seek different friends. Nat loved an evening of hilarity with De Wolf Hopper or William H. Crane. He kept a New York cabby called 'Red' constantly in attendance, and paid him in advance to see him home when the dawn broke. He liked to go to the expensive gambling clubs and

play for heavy stakes late into the night. He could afford to
do it, with *When We Were Twenty-One* proving to be, as
he described it, 'a gold mine', but it was best to conceal his
losses from Max. Often Maxine's evenings consisted of a late
supper of sweet biscuits and milk, but this was from choice,
to preserve her figure and have a little peace and quiet. By
no means a grieving grass widow, she had become more and
more involved in the personal affairs of two friends. Mrs.
Grace Wassall had become her most constant female companion, closer now than Ysobel Haskins, as Maxine separated
her work from her private life more and more. Mrs. Wassall
was from Chicago, a woman of great charm and elegance who
played the piano beautifully and had once had hopes of
becoming a concert pianist. Now her marriage to a dentist,
which had originally interrupted her career, had begun to
fail. The two women could talk with frankness and intimacy,
both knowing professional life, both unafraid of the word
divorce, both attracted to social life and luxury. Grace Wassall
was deeply in love with another man, and Maxine became
passionately absorbed in long conferences with her about the
future, the children, the finances; their voices dropped, their
sentences were left unfinished if Nat came into the room. The
man Grace Wassall loved was precisely the kind Maxine most
liked and admired (the kind she never married). He was
Thomas L. Chadbourne, a tough fighting lawyer originally
from the Middle West with a drive and a gift for money-
making which had already turned his night-school law education into a career as investment consultant to numerous large
corporations, with the interested eye of J. P. Morgan already
upon him. Tom was six feet six, a yachtsman, an athlete with
the build of a god and humorous pale blue eyes. He also had
to obtain a divorce, and Maxine was in the thick of the
romance.

Four months of touring were left after New York, with a
brief engagement in San Francisco (where Captain Tom, now
skipper of the square-rigger *A. J. Fuller*, could admire the
new elegance and grandeur of his daughter); then *When We
Were Twenty-One* was closed for the season on June 30 in
Minneapolis. The 'Goodwin Special' was put onto the sidings
and the Goodwins returned to England. Gertrude had moved

to a third role, supporting Miss Compton (as that actress was always billed) in a play by her husband, R. C. Carton, *Lady Huntworth's Experiment*, under the dual management of Arthur Bourchier and 'Dot' Boucicault, son of Maxine's old teacher, Dion Boucicault. The Goodwins saw the play and were delighted. Then the London season closed for the summer, and they were all back together for their third year at Jackwood, the family threesome reunited.

8

FORBES-ROBERTSON

ERTRUDE was still 'little sister' to Maxine, doing what she was told and trying desperately to please, but to the London world she was something quite different, with a positive personality of her own. Her picture was appearing in the same magazines that had pounced on Maxine in her Daly period. She was described as the most interesting new personality in London, with a sparkle, a freshness and a lightness of style that made English comedy *ingénues* seem heavy-handed by comparison.

Nellie Hammond, her dresser, who had become Mrs. Sam T. Pearce, was keeping admirers at bay. One was the son of King Chulalong, who is familiar now to readers or theatregoers as the monarch in *Anna and the King of Siam* or *The King and I*. Another was the Duke of Manchester, known to everybody as 'Kim' from his secondary title Kimbolton. Maxine was pleased to find that Gertrude had fiercely clung to Nellie when the young Siamese prince's card was sent round to her dressing room, but felt she ought to try to be a little more gracious to the young duke. Gertrude didn't like either of them. A third suitor, and one of great danger, was added to the public discovery of herself as a woman. Her old colleague from San Francisco, Frank Worthing, remembering her as 'little sister', had looked her up in London and discovered that in the past he had been bedazzled by one sister and failed to notice the one who could really understand him. Maxine was appalled to learn that Frank was whispering in Gertrude's ear inducements to return with him to the United States so that they could set Broadway aflame as a new young acting couple. Maxine was relieved to learn of a legitimate way to break the plan: Ian Robertson was looking for a new

GERTRUDE ELLIOTT IN *NATHAN HALE*

THE MERCHANT OF VENICE

(*left to right*) ANTONIO (Maclyn Arbuckle), BASSANIO (Aubrey Boucicault), GRATIANO (Vincent Serrano), SHYLOCK (Nat Goodwin) and PORTIA (Maxine)

leading lady for his brother, Johnston Forbes-Robertson, and
had made an offer to Gertrude.

Since the time that Maxine had seen Forbes-Robertson at
the Lyceum Theatre ceremony honouring Sir Henry Irving,
he had gone ahead and fulfilled the promise predicted for
him. Forced by Sir Henry's kindness to accept the Lyceum
while the resident company toured the United States, Forbes-
Robertson had gone into management for himself and in his
second season of 1897 had appeared as Hamlet. Few Hamlets
had been seen for years in England except Sir Henry's. Fully
conscious that he was making an act of abdication, Sir Henry
leased his theatre at cost, lent scenery, costumes, and props,
and remained in London long enough to witness for himself
the triumph of a younger man. The day after a brilliant first
night, Forbes-Robertson re-entered the Lyceum and found
Sir Henry in his own office surrounded by all the morning
newspapers. As he opened the door the old man peered
fiercely up at him from under his beetling eyebrows, spread
his spidery fingers across the words of praise from all the
critics, and said, 'You've done it, m'boy, you've done it.'
George Bernard Shaw loudly rejoiced that at last London was
hearing *Hamlet* as Shakespeare wrote it, and Forbes-Robertson
became the leading romantic and classical actor of his day,
at the age of forty-four replacing fifty-nine-year-old Sir Henry,
who rejoiced with true generosity of spirit.

Forbes-Robertson over the past three years had produced
many plays, including Maurice Maeterlinck's *Pelléas and
Mélisande* (in which he played Golaud, the one human being
of the fantasy, husband of the moon-drenched Mélisande),
For the Crown (a translation from the French of François
Coppée), *Magda* by Hermann Sudermann (translated by
Louis Napoleon Parker), *Romeo and Juliet*, *Macbeth*, and *The
School for Scandal*. He had taken his company to Berlin and
been graciously received by Kaiser Wilhelm II.

During those years of management (1896–99) his leading
lady had been Mrs. Patrick Campbell. They were a fascinating
pair of personalities, both possessing something that suggested
intellect, a fineness of spirit that was new at a time when
the blustering, ranting, uncontrolled actor of the melodramatic
school was by no means past. Sometimes they were berated

for being too nice (Shaw scolded them for creating a Macbeth family that was altogether too well-mannered), but the general opinion of the team by both critics and audience was the highest. The words of Shakespeare were being clearly heard, and the productions were beautiful to behold. Forbes-Robertson had the most resonant, musical voice on the English stage, one that he never used to play tricks with, never intoning, never committing the sin of wallowing in its beauty or listening to himself; he wore costumes of any period as if born to them; and his straight, slim figure, his grace of movement, and his classic head which suggested a young poet gave nobility to any part he played. Mrs. Pat had fluid grace, a fascinating mobile face, lambent eyes, tip-tilted nose, and a lovely young body that she dared to use.

The association had come abruptly to an end in the autumn of 1899. Ian Robertson informed everyone that his brother was seriously affected by ill health and must leave the stage for many months, perhaps forever. Johnston disappeared, fleeing to the Continent with another brother, Norman Forbes.

Johnston had had the misfortune to love Stella, Mrs. Patrick Campbell. With her destructive temperament, she needed only to know that a man was in love with her to begin her games and wiles and subtle art of torture. She mocked him, she played with him, she committed sins of such professional enormity as to make him shrivel in shame. When Ellen Terry came to see *Romeo and Juliet*, Stella changed from a dark to a blonde wig in the middle of the performance because, she declared later, she wanted Miss Terry's opinion as to which suited her best. It was the sort of defiance of theatre manners that most shocked Forbes-Robertson. Any close friend of Ian Robertson's, Johnston's devoted brother and manager and a fine comedian, knew that Ian left the theatre daily in a burning rage, incensed with some new whim of Stella's, utterly exhausted by his own efforts to keep some of her nonsense from Johnston. By correspondence, she played off Forbes-Robertson against Shaw; she loved to keep both of them dancing, and she damaged Forbes-Robertson far more profoundly because she was trifling with a man whose love was not given lightly, but with devotion, with idealism, with a devouring passion. Years ago, as a very young man, he had loved Ellen Terry, but when she became the special property of his beloved Irving, he withdrew entirely. He had later fallen in love with the beautiful blonde American actress, Mary Anderson. They had been formally engaged to be married, until her intense Catholicism and his ethical free-thinking, with which the Forbes-Robertsons had all been raised under the influence of William Morris and John Ruskin, came to a fatal clash, and the engagement was broken. His serious spirit had remained uninvolved until the invasion by Stella Campbell. He reacted to her flippancies with violence and suffering. He did indeed become physically ill and could stand it no more. Stella, all injured innocence, claimed she could not understand what was the matter with him, and wailed, 'Betrayal, betrayal!' She took the script of a play they were going to do called *The Sacrament of Judas* and sent it back to him with the word 'Judas' underlined. When the unfortunate, banished Patrick Campbell, who had spent years abroad trying to make a living to support himself and his wife, was finally reported killed in the Boer War, an uncle of Stella's arrived at the Forbes-Robertson home, 22 Bedford Square, to claim that her name had been much damaged when coupled with Johnston's and demand that he now do the right thing by Stella. Fortunately, Johnston was far away in Sicily, and the uncle had to face Johnston's mother, cool, contemptuous, and adamant, who sent him packing.

Undoubtedly Maxine had missed none of the gossip. It seemed as if emotional involvement for Gertrude with a man of Forbes-Robertson's age and temperament were out of the question. Judging by the qualities of Ellen Terry, Mary Anderson, and Stella Campbell—all positive, developed women—it would seem that the type that attracted Forbes-Robertson was quite different from little Gertrude. He would be something of a father to her, a man over twenty years her senior, who, no matter what his emotional upheavals may have been, had the highest reputation for propriety and could be trusted to take care of her. He was also offering her some splendid acting opportunities; she was to play Ophelia, and there was a fine short play called *Carrots*, adapted from the French of Jules Renard by Alfred Sutro, in which the woman's part was a little French peasant boy. Gertrude's slim daintiness—her lack of bosom and hips often distressed Maxine when she had to plague Gertrude with heavy, stuffy padding to make her look like an elegant, contemporary lady—could be ideally adapted to boy's costume. There was Shaw's *The Devil's Disciple*, too, in Forbes-Robertson's repertory, and Louis Tierclin's exquisite short play *The Sacrament of Judas*, forfeited by Stella Campbell.

Ian Robertson submitted to Johnston a list of actresses as possible leading ladies, the result of a spring season of theatregoing done by himself and their sister Ida, Mrs. Buchanan. The two had examined all young actresses with the thought in mind that they must fit the professional requirements of the plays Johnston planned but must also be girls of quiet, gentle, lady-like temperament as unlike Stella Campbell as possible. It was a mission they undertook with joy, for Johnston's interest in a new season showed that his spirits must be improving under the influence of the Grecian temples and theatres of Sicily and loving friends wherever he went. The closely united, clannish family pounced upon Norman when he returned to report on their brother's emotional health. It seemed Johnston had returned to his early love—his palette and brushes—was sightseeing with delighted interest, and now had begun to write long letters home about the activities of the Mafia. His hearty, easy laugh was to be heard again, and he was not coughing any more. Studiously Ian and Ida examined the girls the London stage offered and made out a list with comments. Against Gertrude Elliott's name they put nothing but praise, with merely a query, 'Can she play Shakespeare?' When Johnston received the list, he thought it over and wrote back to Ian, putting the name of another actress, not Gertrude, at the head of it. Then as he was walking the streets of Palermo, Johnston suddenly found himself in a telegraph office in a fever of worry. He wrote out the message to Ian: 'If not too late engage Miss Elliott.'

'The question was,' he says in his autobiography, 'which would win, the letter or the telegram. As the hours and days passed, I found that I was not taking the matter with that philosophic calm proper in an actor-manager, and the fact disturbed me. Suddenly to want a certain young lady, with whom I was but very slightly acquainted, to be of my company seemed unreasonable under the circumstances. What was the meaning of it? At long last my brother telegraphed: "Have engaged Miss Elliott." '

The Elliott sisters had met Forbes-Robertson once at a supper party at Captain Robert Marshall's. They had both found him charming and good-looking, and Nat was vociferous about his supreme qualities as an actor. The engagement in his company seemed a splendid opportunity for Gertrude that would show her to the best advantage, and it was obvious that Forbes-Robertson was a tractable man who would listen to any of Maxine's strictures before she was obliged to sail away to America and leave little sister in his hands. Gertrude would remain in England, in a respectable management, safely away from Frank Worthing, but still accessible to the young Duke of Manchester. Before the summer was over, Maxine insisted they should accept an invitation for a Saturday-to-Monday visit at one of the young duke's estates. Gertrude was less impressed than ever on finding that she was obliged to walk miles to a bathroom, and when she got there she caught her foot in a hole in the floorboards. Maxine was annoyed with her criticisms of the ducal mansion, and Nat laughed heartily.

Johnston Forbes-Robertson and his sister Ida Buchanan on a visit to Jackwood brought along the designs for Gertrude's costumes. Everyone was delighted; the black dress for Ophelia's mad scene was particularly interesting. Nat, a little overwhelmed by Forbes-Robertson's old-fashioned courtesy, felt him to be more saintly and gentle than he could cope with, and only under protest was pushed off alone with him to the golf course on Sunday afternoon. He came back, however, aglow with blue-eyed, beaming joy. Johnston had taken a swing at the ball, missed it, and sent up a shower of grass and earth, accompanied by a lusty 'Goddamn it to hell'. 'Thank God he's human,' said Nat. Ida, a woman of enormous character, had observed Maxine, and Maxine had observed her; they did not like each other, two tigerishly protective sisters, but they felt mutual respect. Gertrude and Johnston hardly addressed a word directly one to the other, but amid the discussions their eyes often met. When Maxine accompanied Johnston and Ida to the Shooters Hill station on Sunday evening, she flirted lightly with him—he was so remarkably handsome—and Ida reported herself as thinking at the time, 'It's no good, my girl, you setting your cap at Johnston. It's the little one he's after.'

Mr. and Mrs. Ryley, Ida Buchanan, Ian Robertson and his wife, and Johnston himself all promised to take good care of Gertrude when the Goodwins left for America. Maxine was further reassured, once home, by a letter from Gertrude saying that, owing to her dissatisfaction with a housemaid from Jackwood who had been engaged to tour with her as dresser and personal maid, she had sent an S O S to Nellie Pearce at the Court Theatre, who had immediately joined her on tour at Southport. Typical of Forbes-Robertson's gracious manners was the fact that he had turned out on a Sunday to meet Nellie at the train after the first long journey the young woman had ever taken. In joining Gertrude Elliott on that Sunday she began a lifetime with the Forbes-Robertson family and company.

Gertrude was now well looked after—so well that as Johnston felt more and more the desire to talk intimately with his young leading lady he was unable to find her alone. Everything sounded decorous and cheerful in the letters that Gertrude wrote to her sister as the Goodwins toured the provinces of America and the Forbes-Robertson company toured the provinces of England. There came a day, however, when a whole group of the Forbes-Robertson company, playing in Liverpool, hired bicycles and set off for an outing in the country. It was early November, often one of England's most benign and sunny months before the winter cold sets in. They rode gaily away in the autumnal landscape, Nellie left behind with her mending and ironing, and soon Johnston and Gertrude had drawn far ahead of the party. He seized his opportunity to propose marriage, and Gertrude accepted him.

Gertrude's letter telling Maxine about the engagement arrived at the same time as rumours of it, which had come out in the English press, were cabled to America. Maxine and Nat both denied it, Maxine lightly disguising her distress—'Engaged to Forbes-Robertson? I'm not at liberty to tell,' she told an interviewer with a teasing laugh. 'Let's talk of gowns, that's such a safe topic.' To Gertrude she wrote in quite a different manner. She absolutely forbade the marriage. She said that Forbes-Robertson was far too old, that Gertrude was far too young, that to marry an actor promised an unstable life; perhaps she even pointed to her own experience with Nat, asking Gertrude if she wanted a lifetime of slavery, railroad carriages, and hotel bedrooms. If she married an Englishman, why not marry at the top and become the lady of a medieval castle? Could she not count on her big sister to go to work on improving the bathrooms?

Gertrude had obeyed her sister in everything; every detail of her life was designed to try to please Maxine. But when it came to a big decision, Gertrude worried herself to death, chewed her nails to the quick, and did precisely what she wanted. The Forbes-Robertson company finished the tour in the London suburb of Streatham in December, and Gertrude returned to Mr. and Mrs. Ryley's house. There she was dressed for her wedding by Nellie Pearce. She married Johnston Forbes-Robertson on December 22, 1900. Those present at the church were Johnston's father, John Forbes-Robertson, an art critic now totally blind, with a great black beard and a strong Scottish accent; his mother, Frances Forbes-Robertson, with the thin, fine features of her son; several of Johnston's ten brothers and sisters; and some members of his company. Mr. Ryley gave Gertrude away. She married without the blessing of her beloved older sister, but in total calm. She was even able to prompt the minister, Canon Borradaile; he, seeing his beloved Johnston, whom he had known since he was a little boy, now entering into holy matrimony at the age of forty-seven, got confused in the ceremony and forgot his lines. A hilarious wedding breakfast took place at the Ryleys' house, nearly causing the Forbes-Robertsons to miss their train for Folkestone. They left for a honeymoon in Biarritz.

Maxine and Nat were playing *When We Were Twenty-One* in Cincinnati. Maxine was so upset that she merely played her part at night and would speak to no one. They spent a miserable Christmas.

*

If Maxine had enjoyed work in the theatre more, she might

have understood Gertrude's marriage better. It meant that
Gertrude had dedicated herself to a life in the theatre. Proud
though Maxine was of all Gertrude's successes, she believed
that Gertrude should use them to meet the right kind of man
outside the theatrical world, who would take her from it, to
enjoy those ultimate blessings, money and leisure. She felt she
had dedicated much of her own work to easing life for Gertrude, so that her young sister would not be obliged to go
through the grind that Maxine was willing to accept for herself. Now Gertrude had turned aside everything she had
offered her. Maxine made the mistake of those who think
they can see the pattern of another's life clearly, and she cried
out in her heart, 'Ingratitude!' No matter how much Nat
emphasized Gertrude's undeniable gifts as an actress, for the
moment it remained impossible for Maxine to understand
that Gertrude, apart from loving Johnston, had found through
him precisely the life and work she wanted, and would have
shrivelled up in unfulfilment and boredom if asked to spend
a lifetime as a lady of the manor.

As the Goodwin tour continued, a young lady of the company, Miss Irvine Sidley, remarked in some private letters
that the door of Maxine's special coach remained constantly
closed. If she appeared, Miss Elliott was gracious but entirely
withdrawn. Often Nat wandered down the public coach to
seek companionship among the lesser members of the company, brightening immediately when he found himself able
to produce a roar of laughter. Once, Miss Sidley was dining
in a restaurant in Boston and saw Nat in rapt conversation
at a table for two with a very pretty young lady who was not
Miss Elliott. Miss Sidley said nothing at the time, not even
to her best friend in the company, Suzanne Perry, Maxine's
own first cousin, but she felt concern for the Goodwins. The
scene distressed her, because she was engaged, and when Nat
and Maxine had given a party for her on stage after a performance, presenting her with a silver dressing-table set, she
wished sincerely that their marriage could be as happy as hers
promised to be. Undoubtedly, over these weeks when Maxine's closest friend in the company, Ysobel Haskins, had left
to join Amelia Bingham's company in still another Clyde
Fitch play, *The Climbers*, it was Suzanne Perry who bore the

brunt of Maxine's distress, expressed probably not in words but in small outbursts of temper over trivialities. But Suzanne, too, said nothing to anybody; she was grateful to her cousin Maxine, who had persuaded Nat to take her out of a book-binding business in Boston, where her eyesight was being seriously impaired, and give her a job in the Goodwin company. She also was from Rockland, Maine, where personal affairs were not for public discussion.

Nat was able to provide a total change of subject. They were going to try their first excursion into Shakespeare. The choice was *The Merchant of Venice*, which seemed to combine ideal parts for them both—the dignity and humour of Portia for Maxine and a strong character role for Nat as Shylock. He had become far too chubby now to play any leading role that was at all romantic, but if he could succeed as Shylock he might try *Richard III* and possibly even *Macbeth* or *King Lear*. Leave Hamlet and Ophelia, Othello and Desdemona to the Forbes-Robertsons and let the Goodwins take over Shakespeare's heavier couples. They planned a lavish show with an all-star cast. No Shakespeare production as splendid as this had been seen since Augustin Daly's last offering to the American theatre. (Daly had fallen dead a year before in a Paris hotel, and Ada Rehan retired from the stage at that time for several years.)

The Merchant of Venice was for a limited run only. Nat wanted to see if he could defeat all those voices that cried out that Nat Goodwin must only be funny. They played it in New York and several major Eastern cities, and only Boston was kind. Shakespeare seemed to have diminished the authority of Nat. The most charitable critic said only that his Shylock was intelligent, sober, quiet, in good taste, showing an absence of pedantry. He seemed to be without force, his voice too light. He was accused of falling between two stools.

Maxine was harshly handled by the critics also. She was damned by such adjectives as 'neat, correct, efficient, and superficial', it was noted that in the 'mercy' speech she had no bravura. One critic scolded her for not bringing to her Portia precisely the quality that it would have been expected Maxine Elliott could give, that of 'court ladyhood', and protested that in Portia's light and humorous scenes she giggled

—and surely Portia was above giggling. Of course, no one
failed to remark that she looked beautiful in her black court
robes lined with red and in the brocaded and bejewelled
dresses she wore with a blonde wig to differentiate her lady of
Belmont from the Portia masquerading as a young lawyer,
played in her own black hair.

The scenery and costumes, the music and songs and dancing ('Hark, hark, the Lark' to Schubert's setting somehow
crept in, out of the text of *Cymbeline*), and fine actors such
as Harry Woodruff, Vincent Serrano, Frederick Perry, and
Maclyn Arbuckle all seemed drowned in a general atmosphere
of greyness. This gorgeously mounted, expensive *Merchant of
Venice*, so full of earnest endeavour, never came alive. In New
York, the May 24 opening was a brilliant occasion at which
ladies' outfits ranged from formal winter evening dress to
summer muslins with beribboned straw hats. It was a suffo-
cating night, with fans flapping annoyingly in the auditorium,
and a thunderstorm broke out just before curtain time, causing
many late arrivals. The gala twelve-dollar price for an orchestra
seat dropped to the usual two dollars. Many steady first-
nighters were unable to be present, having already departed
for the shore. Miss Ethel Barrymore, now a leading Broadway
actress, since her first starring performance in Clyde Fitch's
Captain Jinks of the Horse Marines, was seen to slip late into a
box.

Despite what the New York critics wrote, audiences everywhere seemed to enjoy it, especially in Boston. In Washington, it seemed as if the summer dispersal of Congress and the
Senate was months away, with Henry Cabot Lodge and a
party, Mr. and Mrs. Leiter, and Mrs. van Rensselaer Cruger
giving the evening a tone. To Nat it was a failure. His dreams
of invading London with Shakespeare faded away. He was
savagely angry with the critics, and Maxine was furious that
he gave interviews of self-justification, trying to argue his
critics into accepting his Shylock. Maxine loathed failure, but
felt that if it came it must be met with dignity and silence.
On June 1, the experiment was over. They sailed for England.
One magnificent quality Maxine always possessed. If she was
faced with an undeniable fact, she set about making the very
best of it. Her anger at Gertrude's marriage was pushed into

the past, and on her arrival she greeted Johnston as her beloved brother-in-law. From then on, if anyone dared to suggest that Forbes-Robertson was not the greatest actor ever
produced by the English theatre, Maxine promptly laid him
flat. He was her Gertrude's husband, he was her brother-in-
law, he was the best. Gertrude and Johnston found themselves overwhelmed with invitations to Jackwood and battered
with suggestions for plays for them to do in the future. It
was then that Gertrude, with much shy circumlocution, had
to admit that she was unable to make any plans for the
moment, for she had become pregnant within the first month
of her marriage, and a baby was expected in early October.
Maxine found it tiresome of them both.

She was relieved, however, that her plans would enable
her to be in England when the baby was born, for she and
Nat were going to open *When We Were Twenty-One* in September at the Comedy Theatre in London. 'Forbie', as she
began to call Johnston, would be obliged to resume a tour
also in September, without his wife; if he was out of town
when the baby arrived, at least Maxine would be present. All
preparations had been made at 22 Bedford Square, the
doctor waiting, a nurse ready to come immediately to the
house; Mrs. Forbes-Robertson, Senior, who had gone through
eleven pregnancies of her own, felt herself entirely capable of
dealing with the event.

Nevertheless, Maxine worried about Gertrude. There were
five flights of stairs at No. 22. There was also an atmosphere
in the house which Maxine thought profoundly depressing,
and she did not like to think of Gertrude waiting there day
after day in the uncomfortable six weeks before the baby's
birth. She felt the old people were no proper companions for
Gertrude. Mr. Forbes-Robertson, in his blindness, fumbled
his food and made Gertrude nervous by running his hands
over her face to learn the shape of her features. Mrs. Forbes-
Robertson seemed a sad and almost bitter personality. The
Forbes-Robertson sisters showed that since Johnston's marriage they did not consider 22 Bedford Square the exclusive
residence of the newly married couple and the old in-laws,
but felt free to run in and out any time they chose. Ida
Buchanan could always be counted on as a woman of sense,

but Daisy, who was stunted in growth to the size of a dwarf, and Frankie, who believed that free speaking denoted intellectual honesty, could send Gertrude into a dither of anxiety by comments that bordered on rudeness. They laughed at Gertrude's American phrases and showed they found her distinctly odd when she would nervously click her nails on her teeth and say, 'Oh, ginger!' Since Gertrude was unable to run a house and handle servants, Mrs. Forbes-Robertson, Senior, remained the lady of the house and Gertrude seemed like an awkward visiting youngster. On Saturday, September 21, although Gertrude's time was very close, Maxine came round after the performance at the Comedy and swept Gertrude away for a Sunday at Jackwood.

It was a beautiful day, and Gertrude suddenly felt wonderfully well. She called Maxine's two Boston bulls, Sport and Flossie—a Christmas present from Nat two years before—and went for a long walk. The dogs found some joyously muddy places to investigate along the borders of 'Little Carlsbad', and when Gertrude returned to the house she was worried that their dirty paws would ruin her sister's new carpets and upholstery. She got them inside up the back stairs and proceeded to give them a good bath. Her back ached as she leaned over the low tub. She was in labour.

Someone was sent flying to the village, but the doctor had been called elsewhere. Someone else thought he knew where the local midwife was. One guest was staying at Jackwood, an English actress who had a part in *When We Were Twenty-One*. This lovely young woman just rising to prominence, Constance Collier, had started at the Gaiety but was now graduating into dramatic roles.

'It was the most beautiful thing I had ever seen,' said Constance. 'Maxine had her arm round Gertrude, supporting her to the nearest bedroom, and their long black hair flowed down their backs and seemed to mingle. Nat was in his shirtsleeves and was terribly efficient and seemed to know what to do about things like hot water and towels. There was a procession along the corridor to the bedroom, and I followed them (silly goose that I am), streaming with tears and behind me came Sport and Flossie, both looking hideous and shaking themselves from their bath.'

The midwife arrived in the final moments of labour, and together she and Nat delivered the Forbes-Robertsons' first-born child. It was a girl, Maxine Frances Mary, later always called Blossom.

The same Saturday night that Gertrude had gone to Jack-wood, Johnston caught the overnight train from Edinburgh to London. He had a sense of urgency although the baby was not supposed to be due, and a fellow traveller, Sir Alexander MacKenzie, the composer, tried to distract him with tales of the musical world. At last he reached London, and dashed into 22 Bedford Square. 'All is well,' his mother told him, but her voice was filled with disappointment. Gertrude was not upstairs in the bedroom prepared for her. Cryptically, Johnston says in his autobiography: 'She told me my wife had been obliged to stay with her sister at Jackwood, on Shooters Hill. It had been settled that my wife should have been at our house, but the event came about sooner than was expected. To Jackwood I hurried, to find that both were well, and I was permitted to hold in my arms our firstborn.' There could of course have been no question of moving Gertrude, so the carriage was sent from Jackwood to 22 Bedford Square to pick up all the baby clothes that were neatly laid out await-ing the event.

Johnston had to leave early on Monday morning to play Hamlet in Glasgow. The train was late, and the curtain had to be held until he arrived. Brother Ian could be counted upon to calm his frenzied emotions with a deadpan comment, 'Well, I suppose you'll tell me it's the most wonderful infant that was ever seen.' Anxiety suddenly lifted, and joyously Johnston replied, 'There's no doubt about it.'

Johnston was deeply upset at Maxine's interference; in fact, he never quite forgave her. She was not entirely wrong in thinking that life in Bedford Square was difficult for Ger-trude. She was not wrong, either, when she faced Forbie with the situation and told him she believed Gertrude with a young baby should not return to a house dominated by his parents. It was by her doing that he found rooms nearby for his parents and moved them out of 22 Bedford Square, but it was her bad luck that neither of them survived the year. Always Johnston was haunted by the feeling that he had turned the old people out when they had very little time to live and that possibly the disruption in their lives had helped to kill them, and always he remembered that it was Maxine who had forced him to take this step. Silently, with enduring good manners, Maxine and Johnston took battle stations.

9

HER OWN WAY

ILENCE descended on the Goodwins after they left
England in January 1902 to tour once more. There was
nothing to say. Maxine rode the length and breadth of
the United States in her private car and wrote many letters
to friends in England. Sometimes Nat, attempting to entertain her, embarked on a story. 'Yes, you told me that in
Seattle,' she said, raising her eyes; 'her cruel, dreaming eyes,'
Nat said.

Maxine's love for her sister Gertrude was such that conscious
jealousy was unlikely, but comparison between the Forbes-
Robertson marriage and her own was unavoidable. Johnston
was a devoted husband, his career at its zenith, and within
a year of marriage there was a beautiful child. Maxine's plans
for Gertrude had indeed been grand, based on her belief
that she, the strong hard worker, could present her sister
with the gift of no work at all, but Gertrude had made her
choice of marriage combined with career. For Maxine, to
think of the Forbes-Robertsons meant to build, to plan, to
look forward; but to look across the car at Nat made her sure
that her future could not lie forever with him. He looked
much older than he should. He collapsed when he was not
buoyed by admiring laughter. He had already humiliated her
too many times by public drunken scenes or cheap flirtations
for personal communication between them—never strong—to
survive.

The pattern was depressingly like her former marriage. She
had experienced this disintegration before, rapider in its
development with George MacDermott because he lacked the
artistic gifts which had made Nat palatable a little longer.
She knew where drink had landed George; he had come to

borrow money from her, out of work and friendless, and was
fast approaching death in a rooming house in Harlem. Nat
had made disparaging jokes about him—'See that dent on
the bar top,' he had said to his nephew, Nat Burn, when he
had taken the boy with him to the Brunswick. 'That was
made by the elbow of my wife's former husband.' But now
it seemed as if a few more years would make the difference
between the two men negligible. Marriage seemed a state that
was doomed to failure for Maxine. Only her working association with Nat had made her second attempt last as long as it
had.

But now a professional problem had risen as well and was
becoming pressing. It was difficult to find plays that had suitable parts for them both. Constance Collier reported her
shock on seeing the Goodwins for the first time. Her acquaint-
ance (which developed into lifelong friendship with Maxine)
had begun a few weeks before she officiated at Blossom's
birth, when she presented herself at the Comedy Theatre to
try out for *When We Were Twenty-One*. Maxine and Nat
needed someone to play 'the Firefly' because Ysobel Haskins
had left the theatre forever to marry a rich stockbroker. Constance had made up her mind to turn down the part, which,
though showy and scene-stealing, appeared only in the second
act. The reputation of the Goodwins, a wonderfully beautiful
woman married to a fascinating comedian, was what had
made her go for the interview, to have a look; she expected
to thank them prettily and depart after satisfying her curiosity.
The manager took her to Miss Elliott's dressing room;
Maxine turned round from the desk where she was writing.

'I had hardly believed the legends of Helen of Troy and
Cleopatra,' Constance wrote later, 'but in that face I saw why
worlds had been lost and won.'

Constance, a beauty herself, gaped at Maxine, and found
that she was being complimented on her own looks ('She
took the wind out of my sails') in Maxine's direct, disconcerting way. She was advised to get a red wig because they
were both equally dark—'or you'll eclipse me,' said Maxine,
further enslaving the girl; her salary was discussed, along with
rehearsals and costume arrangements. So overwhelmed was
she by Maxine's beauty, allied to her kindly, matter-of-fact

way of doing business, that she walked out of the door engaged
to play the part.

Eagerly she awaited the meeting with this paragon's fascinating husband. 'I did not see Nat Goodwin that first day.
. . . I saw him for the first time . . . standing by the T-light,
that strange, mysterious light that only actors know, the only
light ever permitted at rehearsal in those days, dreary, hard
and fierce . . . it certainly did nothing for Nat. He was
nervous and tentative, and a little frightened . . . like a gold-
fish frozen in a block of ice . . . in a very loud check suit,
and the lights accentuated the pattern and took all colour
from his face. How could that gorgeous Maxine be his
wife?'

Nat was considerably shorter than Maxine, so tricks of
stage management had to keep them from standing side by
side—hardly convincing in their romantic passages, with Nat
a few feet upstage from Maxine. For curtain calls they were
always obliged to have another player between them and to
take their individual calls alone, never hand-in-hand as would
be expected of a married team. Here was a couple difficult
indeed to cast in a suitable play.

Nat was the star, and his name drew devoted crowds all
over the United States, but Maxine had risen steadily in
popularity in the six and a half years they had played together.
She had also bloomed into her full beauty. 'That beauty!
How can one describe that beauty!' Constance raved. 'Her
head was small and crowded with great braids of coal-black
hair. Her eyes were a sort of violet, and I have never seen such
big ones, or with such a soft, tender look in them.' (To Nat
they were cruel, dreaming.) '. . . the colour varied as she
talked, and gave a feeling of the sea. Her skin was cream-
coloured like a camellia, with a glow behind it, and her lips
very red . . . she was ivory, ebony, and roses.' And beside
her was the star; pinkish, greyish, older, fatter, less sure of
himself, more stridently ambitious. The failure of Shylock
made Nat more determined than ever to conquer Shakespeare; Maxine, however, repudiated all further attempts
after her own failure as Portia. She did not mean to fight the
fait accompli; if Portia was not for her, neither were any
other Shakespearian women. This statuesque Juno could not

play Viola, Rosalind, Imogen; she had no wish for Lady Macbeth or Queen Constance, and the time was long past when
she could have played Ophelia, Desdemona, Cordelia. Nat
hankered after Iago (and prodded Forbie to retain *Othello*
in his repertory, so he could play it with him, and with Gertrude as Desdemona), but no one could dare suggest Emilia
for the glorious woman rising to the height of her power.

Maxine thought much during the long train journeys. The
voice of Clyde Fitch whispered in her ear: 'I'll write a play
for you alone, Lady Max. . . . Nat's becoming impossible.'
The voice of her closest woman friend, Grace Wassall,
whispered, too: 'I can't bear to see Nat drag you down.'

At Butte, Montana, Nat got drunk after the performance,
took morphine to quiet his nerves, claimed he woke up feeling terrible, and forgot he had taken morphine and took
some more; the following day he could not be roused. A
doctor was sent for; Maxine and George Appleton, the manager, in agony as they saw the time pass, knew they had missed
the train for Helena. Nat was hauled out of his stupor, well
enough to travel the next day, but a fourteen-hundred-dollar
house at Helena had to be refunded. The horrors of marriage
to George MacDermott flooded over her. Drunkenness, un-
reliability, undignified behaviour in the face of the world
were intolerable . . . and she was now allied to a man whose
every move was reported by the newspapers; there was no
hiding. Her poise was perfect; publicly she was all tender concern for her sick husband. Inside she was full of horror. Nat
could ruin the wonderful world about to open.

Maxine knew her own growing power with a matter-of-fact
clarity. She never made the mistake of belittling herself; it
seemed to her stupid to do so. To Constance Collier she had
been explicit: 'Of course you're beautiful, and you know it,
you're far too intelligent not to. Beauty is like a talent and
you shouldn't underestimate it.' She viewed herself in the
same manner. She knew that she had reached a moment when
she could command attention on her own. She knew that
she wanted this profoundly, and it was not solely from weari-
ness of Nat's disorders. In England before she left she had
known herself to be on the threshold of great things. She
wanted freedom to enjoy them.

It had begun in the summer, when she had complained to Nat that too many odd race-track, theatre, and gambling friends of his were showing up. ('She pronounced all my friends, all Americans, vulgar.') She had undoubtedly complained to others, among these Grace Wassall. Grace told Tom Chadbourne, the man she hoped to marry, that Maxine's life at Jackwood was becoming more and more difficult and that she needed 'decent friends'. So Tom wrote to the Honourable George Keppel, a man who when visiting New York moved in the same circles as himself, and who was in the very heart of London society. In June 1901, Maxine had received a note from George Keppel saying he would like to call upon her. No man could open more doors for her if he wanted to; he was a friend of the Prince of Wales, now King at last, after the death of the old Queen; he was a man of exceptional charm and popularity, part of the exclusive inner set of London society by birth, by choice, and by manners. Beyond all his own attributes, he was married to a woman whose position was unique. When he presented his tall, handsome person, with splendid flowing moustache, to call upon the American actress, he probably gave little thought to his wife Alice at that moment. She allowed him to make such calls and expected him to keep them discreetly out of her sight; he allowed her to be a favourite of the King, knowing that her manners were impeccable. He was therefore surprised when he met a woman totally different from his conception of 'an American actress', which no doubt meant someone delightful, temporary, and amusing to take to supper, an excursion into a department of life different from the world of society that he inhabited with his wife and friends. In no time at all he realized he had met a new social asset, a woman who would delight his wife as much as she delighted him. George Keppel did not keep Maxine discreetly out of the drawing room but escorted her there with the certainty that he had a 'find'. Mrs. Keppel agreed and was charmed with her. Here was the precise opportunity that Maxine most wanted: to become part of the brilliant world that attracted her, and enter it 'the right way', with the support of a couple as well established as anyone in London. Too well she knew the pattern of New York society; at the American Theatre or Daly's she could

have known any of the men of the Four Hundred but could
never be received by their wives. In London, due to the
enthusiasm with which the Prince of Wales had welcomed
attractive newcomers to his 'Marlborough House set', the
barriers were far less rigid.

So the snowball had begun. She went to Mrs. Keppel's
house and met many of her friends—Lord and Lady Alington,
who lived across the street in Portman Square; the Wilsons,
whose daughter Muriel became a lifelong friend; Lady Colebrooke; the Honourable Mrs. Ronnie Greville. The fun
offered by this group could not be indulged immediately; the
time was brief, with Gertrude's baby arriving and *When We
Were Twenty-One* to play. Nat was a definite hindrance, but
fortunately was often unwilling to share the invitations that
came, happier at the men's clubs or with young vaudeville
ladies he found more relaxing company than Maxine. So, on
her return from America, the great world now beckoned her
to renew acquaintanceship. She wanted her own inde-
pendent money in that world, and no husband to embarrass
her. Regretfully she was preparing to bid it good-bye for
another season when the plum arrived: an invitation from
Lady Colebrooke to attend a dinner in honour of Lord
Rosebery.

In Maxine's eyes a special significance clung to the figure
of Archibald Primrose, fifth Earl of Rosebery. He had been
Prime Minister the year of her Daly triumph in London;
therefore, in spite of all successors, to her he was always 'the'
Prime Minister. Enhancing his fascination more was the aura
of aristocracy he carried about him, the man so rich, so
privileged that he constantly disdained the high offices others
sought. He turned away from leadership and called politics
'the malodorous swamp'. He could not be found when people
were begging him to resume an active part in the Liberal
Party. He was off on his yacht, or shut up in his private
retreat—Barnbougle, in Scotland—where no one set foot but
he. A romantic story was told that he was inconsolable since
the death of his wife, Hannah Rothschild, enough to put
another woman on her mettle. He was loaded with houses,
great pictures, rare books; he had combined his own racing
stable with Hannah's and emerged yearly from seclusion to

entertain lavishly at his house on Epsom Downs, the Durdans, when Derby Day came round. He was supposed to have a sudden, hilarious wit, strange abstractions, moments of crushing rudeness, and an overwhelming charm, boyish and appealing, when in the mood. Maxine had noted how Rosebery's name always came back into the conversation. He was a constant question mark in the thoughts of the Liberal Party, which had been divided and weakened since the resignation and death of Gladstone. Now that the British people had grown tired and distrustful of the three-year-old Boer War, and some consciences began to fear that this action against the 'wicked Boer' was not so glorious after all, Rosebery's name —proposed by his old adversary Salisbury—was bruited about as a possible negotiator. The efforts died; the war dragged on another six months. Then in December 1901 a curious excitement began to brew; Rosebery was going to speak at Chesterfield. In the speech, on December 15, Rosebery urged the Liberal Party toward greater unity, efficiency, and timeliness; he also suggested that peace be negotiated with the Boers 'at a wayside inn', in the spirit of magnanimity. This call for generosity appealed deeply to the country; in fact, when Lord Kitchener and General Botha hammered out peace terms six months later, they followed Rosebery's recommendations closely.

When Maxine received Lady Colebrooke's invitation 'to meet the Earl of Rosebery', the illustrated papers were filled with his pictures, and he was the hero of the hour. Maxine was aware that he was supposed to be terrifying if he felt so inclined, and that he was elusive, easily bored. She was determined to hold his attention. Those pale, dreamy eyes of Rosebery's must not be allowed to brush appraisingly over her beauty and pass on, while the man decided it was too much trouble to get to know the woman inside the lovely shell. She determinedly set about doing her homework in advance. She noted that in the famous speech he had used the example of Spanish oppression of the Netherlands to show how an ungenerous victor fails to win his battle. He had quoted from John Motley's *The Rise of the Dutch Republic*. Motley was a fellow New Englander, a historian whose name she knew from childhood; here was an excellent peg on which to hang a conversational beginning with Lord Rosebery. Granted, she had never read Motley's works, but she could start this minute. She sent out to a book dealer's, determined to be word-perfect on the passages Rosebery had quoted; she was a quick study and could manage this while seeing that a dressmaker turned out a gown of perfection for the evening. Her dismay was considerable when a messenger arrived with *The Rise of the Dutch Republic* and she saw that it comprised five heavy volumes. When the evening arrived she had not even found the passage she wanted. She made do with learning Rosebery's Chesterfield speech almost totally by heart.

In Lady Colebrooke's drawing room her turn arrived to be presented to the guest of honour. She addressed him in the fashionable drawl of the day accompanied by the smile of glowing eyes and brilliant white teeth that seldom failed.

'I'm so happy to meet you. Your speech at Chesterfield has impressed me most deeply. I declare I nearly know it by heart. I think——'

'Oh, really?' said Rosebery, his drawl surpassing hers, and went on to the next guest.

She raged with fury. He was insolent and intolerable. He might be a great aristocrat, a great statesman, 'the veiled prophet' from whom everyone awaited a pronouncement, he might have titles, land, and millions, but he possessed no common courtesy. She took her place at table, far down in rank from Rosebery, and could hardly eat from anger, although she gave no sign to either dinner partner.

After dinner, after separation and reunion of the ladies and gentlemen, the guests were given some entertainment in the drawing room. Lady Colebrooke had asked Maxine to recite, and she had laughingly refused—she was not that sort of actress. But inspiration hit her. She whispered to Lady Colebrooke that there was something she could do which might be amusing (their heads were close together). Solemnly Lady Colebrooke announced that Miss Maxine Elliott had agreed to oblige with an American ballad. Maxine could see Rosebery sunk low in a sofa, suffering his way through the evening till he could escape, still present only because he was a victim of insomnia and bed was useless as yet.

She rose, looking dignified and beautiful, her face a still, melancholy mask. Then she started, with large gestures and rolling eyes to perform the mockery of 'Lasca the Cowboy' which had so overjoyed her family years ago. Momentarily the guests were hesitant; then they shouted with laughter. A beautiful woman who dares behave like a clown is always a delight. She was surrounded with admirers. Rosebery slowly emerged from his sofa and crossed the floor. He planted himself in front of her and took her hand.

'Miss Elliott, that was a joy. What a wicked, clever woman you are. And how beautiful. I would be so delighted to take you to supper one night.'

'Oh, really?' said Maxine in precise imitation, and turned away to someone else.

Insolence did not infuriate Rosebery when performed with authority. He was more charmed than ever. A supper did take place, and there were flowers and notes. When she sailed shortly afterwards for the United States she knew she had made a solid conquest, someone bound to make her return to England next spring infinitely more interesting.

And Rosebery was not quite the end of it all in that fascinating Christmas season of 1901, when Gertrude was back at 22 Bedford Square with the baby and the final performances of *When We Were Twenty-One* were playing to full houses. Maxine managed to do the rounds of her new friends, bidding good-bye. When she arrived at Mrs. Keppel's there was a pause before the butler took her to the drawing room, an air of flurry. Then Mrs. Keppel herself emerged.

'My dear, His Majesty has stopped in for some tea with me and the children. I had to ask his permission, of course, to have you come in; that's why I had to keep you waiting. But come, he would love to meet you.'

The meeting was brief, entirely easy, in the adroit, kindly hands of Mrs. Keppel. The King made no attempt to conceal the fact that he found Maxine gorgeous and assured her that when she brought her next play to London he would insist on seeing it. Maxine felt that her curtsey was passable when tea was over.

*

So she had returned to the United States at the beginning of
1902 with much to plan for the future during the touring
months. The papers were equally interested. Somehow news
of her meeting with King Edward VII leaked out, in garbled
form; the report said she had been present at a private lunch
at Marlborough House, in the absence of Queen Alexandra,
and that the company had consisted of the King's intimate
men friends—Sir Ernest Cassel, Lord Marcus Beresford,
Alfred Rothschild, Reuben Sassoon, and Sir Thomas Lipton,
as well as some other actresses. Maxine, enraged at the implications of such a party, denied it hotly. She had in fact met
the King, she said, but by chance at a tea in the home of a
friend.

'Who was the friend?' she was eagerly asked.

'I cannot give her name,' she said. 'She is a society woman
and would object.'

She hoped her discretion and refusal to name names or
boast for her own aggrandizement had also reached London.
Undoubtedly some of the letters she wrote aboard the train
explained the incident. She gave an interview to the press
about London society and its difference from American
society, stressing the interest of political talk, the greater
generosity to people who came to it from the outside, the good
manners, the sense of fun and amusement based upon the
proper knowledge of how to do things—perfect rules which
created order and the firm rock on which cheerful social exchange could take place. She was asked if she did not feel
strange in a group in which everyone carried resounding titles
and where protocol must inevitably exclude her from a high
place at the table. She laughed. 'I may sit below the salt, but
I'm there.'

It was also reported that she would attend the King's
Coronation. The papers described a jewel that she had ordered
at Tiffany's to adorn the front of her dress—an American
flag in rubies, sapphires, and diamonds made so that it would
appear to ripple in the breeze at each breath from her bosom.
It was so exactly the sort of stunt that Maxine could not
countenance that she did not even bother to deny the story.

Maxine had now stuck her head far up above the crowd.
Her actions would be followed as passionately as Nat's, but

with a difference! She hated his public high jinks, the lack of decorum. She was associating now with people who demanded the privilege of acting as they chose, their private lives denied to the public; but she, meanwhile, was still allied to a man who would not hesitate to let the world see if he got drunk or found a new face alluring. The lack of a suitable play to accommodate them both was not altogether a misfortune. She let Clyde Fitch know that she would be interested in a play for herself alone.

The tour continued through the spring of 1902, and at its end came the public announcement of Maxine Elliott's future plans. Charles Dillingham, the manager who had started in the Frohman office and had since been Julia Marlowe's manager, told the press that he would be presenting Maxine Elliott as a star in her own right, separate from Nat Goodwin, in a new play by Clyde Fitch, as yet unnamed, to be opened some time the following season. Maxine sailed promptly for England, and then was reported on board the Peter Wideners' yacht *Josephine* leaving for a cruise of the Mediterranean, armed with contracts to study at her leisure. Nat was reported negotiating with Klaw and Erlanger for a production of *A Midsummer Night's Dream* in which he would appear as Bottom.

The split in management of Maxine and Nat could not happen that year, however. Clyde, who had earnestly pursued them in the past, was now so busy that Dillingham was beginning to despair of getting a finished script from him. There was a bare outline already: a beautiful woman with a gambler brother should be trapped by her brother's misfortunes into an obligation to an evil man who wants her; the evil man manages to deceive the man the woman really loves, and who loves her, so that love is crossed for two acts, in the proper formula. Clyde had been listening to Maxine's private life again; her brother Tom had fallen into evil company and was gambling and taking drugs. Clyde also read the newspapers, and decided to remove the hero, during the period of misunderstanding, to the war in the Philippines. The only trouble was that Clyde had not put one line of dialogue on paper. Nat's production of 'the Dream' was also obliged to wait; they still had some months of touring in which money could still be squeezed out of *When We Were Twenty-One*, and they decided to seek a script together for the Christmas of 1902 to tide them both over.

Mrs. Madeleine Lucette Ryley had always been as good a tailor of parts as Clyde. She had just fashioned for Gertrude and Johnston a gentle, touching drama, *Mice and Men*, at which audiences sobbed nightly after many months' run; in the past she could always tailor a play for Nat and Maxine— they laughed in a rare moment of communication (always on professional matters) at the memory of Mrs. Ryley's exchange with Nat over *An American Citizen*. 'Write me a play,' Nat had written her. Her reply came: 'What sort of part? Nat Goodwin or a wig?' Nat had answered, 'No wig,' and on that slight directive *An American Citizen* was written; it had served them for two seasons. But Mrs. Ryley had no ideas. She had turned away from the Goodwins, never quite forgetting Maxine's opposition to Gertrude's marriage to Johnston (whom Mrs. Ryley worshipped), uneasy at the social change she saw taking place. The old camaraderie was gone; hers was a simple, very American talent, with no will to write for ladies of such elegance as Maxine. She pointed out, how-ever, that her play *The Altar of Friendship*, with two good acting parts, had been tried out by an actor named John Mason in a few Eastern cities, and since shelved. They took the rights from Mason, planning to put it in their bill when the Christmas season approached. Meanwhile, Maxine waited word from Clyde Fitch.

Life that summer at Jackwood changed drastically. There were fewer week-end parties because Maxine was constantly invited elsewhere. Once Nat went with her to some big country house and threw up his hands in outraged Puritanical horror (they evidently did not find him funny). 'It is a sort of clearing house for the sale of souls and the ruin of women's morals,' he later fumed. 'I leave to your imagination what can be consummated in a week at these places—where states-men and financiers lend themselves to intrigues—on yachts, in closed stone castles and concealed hunting lodges.' With-out naming names but pointing a finger directly enough ('an ex-Prime Minister', 'an American millionaire'), he railed against Lord Rosebery, Mr. Widener, Lady Colebrooke, the

Honourable Mrs. Ronnie Greville, and Millicent, Duchess of Sutherland. His performance as an outraged husband grew so vehement that Maxine agreed to cancel an invitation once and stay home from Saturday to Monday, a grim session when they faced each other across an empty drawing room. He agreed that a party should come to Jackwood; private married bliss could not be tolerated by either again, and Nat refused to expose himself to another visit elsewhere. He claimed that his only companion was Luic the butler, with whom he wandered the gardens, discussing the expenditures upon guests he was determined to loathe; and beneath the library window he heard a 'saphead' saying to his wife, 'How could you possibly have married that vulgar little person?' No doubt Nat was unnerved by the enclosed society of the English upper classes, who can be cruel and ill-mannered to someone outside the circle, but his moralistic self-justification (in many pages of complaint in his autobiography) entirely ignored his own deficiencies.

All forms of shared social life were so frankly awful that Maxine and Nat temporarily abandoned them. Nat went off to Ostend to gamble, then to Trouville, and Maxine could accept invitations where she willed. They met again in the safer company of Gertrude and Forbie, who came to stay with little Blossom. Constance Collier was of the party, and met Nat early one morning picking flowers in the garden. The sight was so unusual that she exclaimed about it. 'These are for Gertrude's breakfast tray,' said Nat, holding out the nose-gay. 'You know, Constance, I married the wrong sister.' Ever a believer in his loves when they were unattainable (destroy-ing them when they were in reach), Nat mooned out the rest of the summer in the conviction that he was in love with his sister-in-law.

Maxine, if she had willed, could have delivered the final blow to his ego at this moment. Lord Rosebery, who had clearly observed the state of affairs in the Goodwin marriage, came rather passionlessly out of his role of inconsolable widower and asked Maxine to get a divorce to marry him. That was as great a triumph in its way as Maxine ever had: to have stirred this melancholic, hypochondriac, brilliant, hesitant, over-sensitive, feminine, Hamlet-like man sufficiently from his withdrawn preoccupations of commitment or non-commitment to contemplate allowing anyone into his life. He had mourned his wife, it is true, but in her lifetime, though he had accepted her intense, anxious devotion to him, he had seemed mild in his response. Perhaps Maxine was the only woman he knew who could offer the sort of impersonal relationship he desired of a woman; her practical, direct masculinity, cloaked in lovely looks, might have been a comfortable counterpart to his introspection. Perhaps he felt he need demand little of her and have little demanded of him, while she most certainly would be an adornment to his houses and treasures—a woman of supreme beauty, who knew the proper manners of a society perfectly, splendid at the head of his table, almost a male companion who would not vie with him in over-sensitivity. Maxine's refusal of Rosebery sets her apart from the ordinary woman who wishes to arrive in society (almost inevitably in the search of the right husband). No one could have been more right than Rosebery; he was one of the grandest aristocrats of his time, of ancient Scottish family, in a unique political position, one of the richest men in the country, with so many houses that any tiff could be easily resolved by a short trip from one property to another.

She did not like her work in the theatre and was going at it with grim determination for the sake of getting out when she could make money separately from Nat. Certainly her marriage bound her no more. To refuse Rosebery at this moment —to his vast astonishment—was a splendid act. She knew that she wanted precisely his kind of life, but never again was she going to do anything she wanted on a man's terms. He had helped instruct her directly in the manners of that world which, from the outside, she had desired, and now from the inside saw as her proven ideal. To become Countess of Rosebery was surely the simplest short-cut. But she wanted something with greater passion than the life he offered; she wanted that life to become hers as Maxine Elliott. She retained his respect and friendship—another of Maxine's gifts was that she seldom lost men who came to her as suitors and were rejected, but turned them deftly into friends—while she went on to renew two months' touring of *When We Were Twenty-One* with Nat and opened just before Christmas in the last play the Goodwins did together, *The Altar of Friendship*. The play was not distinguished, but critics and audiences noticed that Maxine delivered one speech with particular fire (sometimes lacking in her performances)—an indictment of all men and a sarcastic commentary on the double standard of morals: 'Once there was a man, and his name was Adam . . .'

Clyde Fitch at last was at work on the script. The leading man was cast; Maxine's announcement, made through Charles Dillingham's office, said that Charles Cherry was the actor selected—'young and dashing, if a trifle chubby' according to the New York *Tribune*. She beat Nat's announcement by a day; Nat told the press that after Miss Elliott left their seven-year association to start work on her new play he would complete the tour with Zeffie Tilbury as her replacement. Zeffie was the daughter of Lydia Thompson, whose 'British Blondes' had given Elizabeth Weathersby Goodwin her start in America. It was as if Nat were publicly telling Maxine that he was returning to his own sort. She was going to leave Nat and sail for Europe, where Clyde was; she still had not read the script, and Dillingham did not even have a title to announce. At the Euclid Avenue Opera House, Cleveland, not far from the spot where Maxine and Nat had married five years ago, on the same avenue where the Boardmans of Cleveland had given the Goodwins their wedding reception, Maxine left the company on May 9, 1903. The parting of Maxine and Nat was entirely amicable; they had arranged to take a percentage of each other's future productions and were at pains to tell the press of this arrangement and deny that anything but professional reasons was causing their separation of management. They had difficulty finding scripts to suit them both; they would make more money working separately. In San Francisco, Nat brandished a freshly arrived letter from Maxine before an interviewer, saying that he had asked her to print all proper names because her writing was impossible; he also pointed out (with some pride, at a distance) that most of the names were lords.

While Maxine was on the Atlantic (a series of luxurious staterooms over the years had expunged the memory of the *Will H. Case*), Clyde Fitch was in Italy, flitting from city to city in search of antiques. At last, at the Grand Hotel in

Florence, he finished the script of Maxine's new play. He arrived in London in June in time to meet her.

He came to her hotel on June 16 on an evening of unusual heat. The reading began. Clyde always prided himself on the dramatic quality of his readings, insistent that he should make each character so different by voice alone that any statement of character name before a speech was unnecessary. Suddenly it occurred to Maxine that her room, on a courtyard, gave out onto windows as widely open as her own on this sultry night. At any moment the manager might appear to inquire if some horrible altercation was taking place in Miss Elliott's suite, or a neighbour might hammer on the door with complaints. She tiptoed across the room and closed the windows. For the three acts, Clyde, so absorbed in the fervour of his reading, failed to notice that sweat was pouring down his face and neck, sticking his elegant shirt to his body. Maxine lay upon the chaise-longue and fanned herself weakly. To have survived this ordeal and liked the script made her believe it must be good. Charles Cherry liked his part; she sent a cable to Dillingham that she was satisfied, the script was on its way to him, and further casting could be done. Dillingham cabled back for the title; he wanted to make another press release. He ran into the deadlock that had happened in London; there was no title, because Maxine would not take Clyde's suggestions and Clyde would not take hers.

Finally, Clyde resigned to the fact that he would give in, came to her hotel.

'Max, do you still stand out against my title?' he asked.

'I certainly do.'

Suddenly he burst out laughing. He did not like any of hers, but he had an inspiration. He had found something that suited her to perfection. 'Well, then . . . the only thing we can do is call it *Her Own Way*.'

Maxine liked it.

*

She returned to New York in September 1903 aboard the *Prinz Wilhelm*, looking bronzed and slim but complaining of six weeks of neuritis. Nat, who met her at Hoboken, admonished her for going out yachting when she had a chill and thus worsening her condition.

'I told her not to, but she would,' he said to the ship reporters.

'But that's my way,' said Maxine. They hurried together to the Garrick Theatre, where Clyde already had the supporting players in rehearsal. No one was there when they arrived. They learned that Clyde had realized his old dream of a house in the country and was breaking rehearsals early so that he could tear out to Greenwich, Connecticut, to supervise the workers.

The Goodwins also had a new house, covered in reddening Virginia Creeper, at 326 West End Avenue. They went there, Maxine eager to superintend arrangements also. Gertrude and Forbie were due to arrive soon, in time to attend her own opening in Buffalo, then to open together themselves in New York for the first time in Kipling's *The Light That Failed* (adapted for the theatre by a George Feming, supposedly a woman, confidentially identified as Constant Fletcher). Nat's rehearsals as Bottom in *A Midsummer Night's Dream* would begin within the month. Everything was confusion and excitement; there were workmen in the house (this did not look like a breaking marriage, and the press was calmed down); there were fittings for Maxine's clothes—they would be especially gorgeous in the first and second acts, dramatically contrasted with the plain black-net-and-lace mourning dress of the last, when she believed her lover killed in the Philippines. She would first step upon the stage in a creation of heliotrope chiffon velvet with a chemisette and hanging undersleeves of lace, topped by a large black hat with sweeping ostrich plumes, a black fox stole round her shoulders, and a black fox muff carried lightly upon one forearm. A white satin ball dress draped in classic style with silver trimmings would be the high point in the second act. The clothes were fresh from Paris, but her loss of weight demanded refitting; frantic women ran back and forth to bring a freshly altered dress from ironing to be retried once more for fear of the slightest defect. Maxine was brutal and tireless with herself; the only way to get a dress exactly as you wanted it was to fuss and fuss and sit over the dressmaker till you approved it. The same applied to work done at a great dressmaking house, she told Blanche Yurka some years later; you must simply move in on them with your sandwiches in a bag and sit it out till you get what you want.

Photographers were put through the same painstaking ordeal. Those who knew were prepared for her method, but it came as a shock to a newcomer who thought he was going to arrange his subject as he saw fit and indulge his artistic knowledge. Maxine promptly took over; the camera must be set so that she could stand in front of a looking-glass and see the exact result herself, trying every pose until the line of dress and hair pleased her. She refused to vary her expression, one of consciously softened eyes, the eyelids a little lowered, the head tilted up so that glance fell downward (and pulled up the line of the neck); she gave her expression a final slight saddening, holding her mouth quite still (she refused to smile), and the photographer could count himself lucky if allowed to press the button of the camera. He must return with proofs at once and follow the lines she sketched where bosom, waistline, and hips must be pared down. This carefully worked out formula produced only a few pictures that ever did Maxine Elliott justice; the unposed, laughing snapshots taken with friends give something a little closer to her shining, ebullient beauty, which combined classic features with brilliant colouring—a kind of beauty that is found today only among some women of India and Greece.

Maxine opened in *Her Own Way* at the Star Theatre, Buffalo, on September 24, 1903. The play went well; the audience loved the children who opened the play with their guessing game of 'What's for dessert?' Maxine's entrance into the party, the benign and lovely woman greeted with yells of delight by the children, brought an ovation. There were some tears when Maxine (as Georgiana Carley) watched the departure of the troops for the Philippines from behind a curtain at the window, or when she sat sadly playing the piano, thinking her lover dead, and there was delight when he arrived, arm in sling, to declare himself alive and hers forever. Nat and the Forbes-Robertsons sat together in a box. No one could be quite sure of the reaction; a Buffalo audience gave little idea of what a New York audience would feel.

The New York opening followed almost at once, on Monday, September 28, at the Garrick Theatre. The first-night

LORD ROSEBERY

NAT GOODWIN,
MAXINE AND
THE HON. GEORGE
KEPPEL

Photo : New York Public Librar

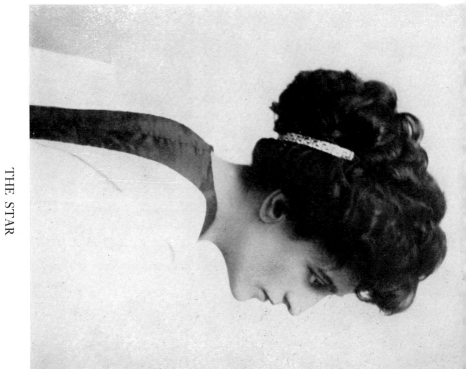

crowd came to see whether stardom would be conferred by acclaim as well as by Charles Dillingham's billing. A gasp went up at Maxine's first entrance, another when she appeared in the white ball dress. No one remembered her as ever having been so beautiful. She was charming, she was pathetic, she brought laughter and tears. The play, of Clyde Fitch's most pronounced cream-puff variety (he could do better), washed happily over the audience and they loved it.

In the stalls Ethel Barrymore turned to her neighbour after Maxine's first appearance in the white ball dress. 'It's the Venus de Milo,' she whispered, 'with arms.'

It was an enormous hit.

Maxine Elliott had proved that she could carry a play alone. Charles Cherry was charming, but he had none of Nat's authority, and was strictly a supporting player. The gloved hands clapped and clapped and clapped, but outside the stage door the massing gallery girls, quick to know a new idol, had pelted down from their high seats and awaited her arrival with autograph books and squeals of excitement, a far more permanent sign of stardom than the clapping hands of the social and professional audience who sat in the expensive seats but waited for the sound of success to carry them along with it as it poured forward from pit and gallery.

The girls at the stage door whooped and pushed as each well-known stage personality emerged after kissing 'darling Maxine' in the crowded dressing room banked with flowers. 'No, it's not Maxine yet,' the front ones shouted back to those on the edges of the crowd.

A maid, a butler, a stage hand emerged laden with flowers and began piling them in a carriage. They went in, to emerge again with more flowers and baskets of fruit. The carriage was piled to the roof, long boxes of American beauty roses taking up all seating space. The carriage drew away from the kerb, to be replaced by another. The maid came out alone in cloak and bonnet, leading Sport and Flossie, the Boston bulls, and climbed inside the carriage.

Nat appeared. He waved white gloves at the crowd, saying, 'Yes, it's great, it's great, it's great. . . .' Then his hand was extended and he led Maxine into view. The girls let out a howl. She signed what autographs she could, as the police

12

pushed and shoved a way for her to the carriage. She was dressed in white from top to toe, her white dress covered by a ruched white cape edged with fur and tied at the neck by an enormous white satin bow. Her ears and neck sparkled with diamonds; her shining black hair, plainly done with a centre parting, emerged from its setting of white. Finally she and Nat were in the carriage.

She waved a small hand from the window, and flashed glowing eyes and teeth at her admirers. They screamed in the wake of the carriage as it bore her away to supper.

10

THE STAR

MAXINE had become a star. She took her place among those whose names meant immediate consideration from backers; her name in lights would always guide a playgoer to the theatre where she played, and it would always top those of the other actors. It was a permanent status. Serious devotees of the drama might not be her most impassioned followers, because she was never identified with great roles, but they were forced to be aware of her.

Her appeal lay in the creation of glamour particularly attractive to women; she gave them a vision of themselves as they would like to be. The men who worshipped her were those who sought the great lady, the princess in women. The seeker after the cute or sexy would have to go elsewhere.

American beauty roses stood in their tall boxes outside her dressing room ('like rows of coffins' said Gertrude); babies were christened in her honour; she endorsed soap; any man of note seen with her was a possible romance. Her views were sought on all subjects . . . she declared she owned a White Incomparable motor car and found 'automobiling a stimulant and a sedative', and sales of the cars increased.

Critics claimed that Maxine Elliott in *Her Own Way* was a revelation, sure that they had observed a fast growth in her art. She answered that this was nonsense; she was no better than before. She crisply pointed out that critics and audiences insist on identifying the player with the part, and now as star rather than supporting leading lady she only seemed different. 'They just see more of me.'

Stardom had come after thirteen years in the theatre. She was thirty-five, slim, more beautiful than at any time in her life. She had evolved precisely the right style of clothes, depending on simplicity of cut and soft, gentle colours. She emerged totally at last a groomed and shining lady, splendid in her grandeur, all flamboyance discarded. She had learned to dress like a woman of society rather than an actress. There was no one quite like her. She seemed to step on to a stage as if into her own private drawing room, giving her audiences the delightful illusion that they were temporarily her honoured guests.

The work which lay in the past and had brought her to this position had been arduous. She had achieved the place at the top long after she had learned that there was no personal joy for her in acting. She had studied what she believed she could do, sternly put aside the old dreams of Rosalind, risked the destruction of her second marriage . . . and the professional success meant little in itself. Its rewards were paramount now. When she was interviewed shortly after the opening night of *Her Own Way* by *Theatre Magazine*, she expressed none of the breathless gratitude shown by many newly arrived stars. 'A reaction comes and with it a feeling akin to indifference,' she said.

She spoke of Richard Mansfield's description of an audience as a great monster that must be nightly fed. 'It's clever, isn't it? . . . An audience is something to be feared. No one who has not acted knows the exquisite torture, the positive bodily fear, of a first-night performance. I always feel like a child afraid of a steam engine.' It did not seem to fit the calm, dignified woman, whose manner grew in hauteur as she knew herself to be recognized wherever she went. She knew all the tricks of a star's behaviour and admonished Billie Burke for being too humble in demands on her manager, Mr. Charles Frohman: 'You must insist on your private car on the railroad. I wouldn't dream of riding from New York to Philadelphia except in my own car.' Nevertheless, the fear was genuine, rising from the deep self-consciousness that had gripped her since childhood.

In evaluating Maxine Elliott as an actress three facts about her are all-important; the self-consciousness that limited her, the major beauty that gave her opportunities, and the brains that told her to seize them. Her beauty demanded parts that would show her off; not to use it would have been foolish.

She possessed talent too; she could move well, create a pleasing stage presence, deliver comedy lines with lightness and
good timing, portray suffering of a muted rather than dramatic
kind. There was always the missing element, lack of which
stood in the way of greatness—the intangible quality of
temperament. She always stopped short of releasing the full
power within her, herself never quite carried away, therefore
never quite carrying her audiences to a peak of emotion. She
delighted thousands, but on a different level from the great
ones who provide the public with experience rather than
entertainment. She had become a true professional, always
able to give a good show. She approached herself and her
career in the role of an impresario, presenting herself with the
same businesslike attention to her assets and to public taste
that a non-performing, commercial manager would apply to
his performers. She avoided parts that would require her to
'tear a passion to tatters, to very rags'; a reviewer remarked,
'The great eyes blaze in anger, or sparkle with amusement,
but never glow with passion.'

The form most suitable for her use was light romantic
comedy, with a little pathos, a little suspense, some high senti-
ments, and a happy ending. Her estimate of the box-office was
correct, and she never varied the formula after the years of
her theatrical beginnings were over and she could, with Nat's
help, select her own vehicles. Several playwrights tailored such
plays for her year by year, and though they followed her own
directives she found the performance of their works intolerably boring. She condemned herself to play women she really
despised—sentimental, noble-spirited creatures who waited
out three acts to gain the men they loved. Such behaviour in
life would have seemed to her idiotic. The pattern was neat:
boy meets girl; boy loses girl; boy regains girl. She allowed
Clyde Fitch to fabricate tricks for her that were charming
stage business. Playing blind man's buff under the table at a
children's party, she grabbed a hand that was not, of course,
a child's but that of her undeclared lover; or she unpinned
and deftly repinned her cascade of black hair, which made
the audience gasp when it fell to her waist and then sigh with
pleasure when her strong white arms were lifted to pile it in
coils. She knew this was all presentation of herself and not

demands upon her emotional powers, and she was ready to perform these winsome tricks hard-headedly. The disappointments of past ambitions were long gone. The girl who had felt frustrated by Ada Rehan's position in the Daly company had shrugged her shoulders and departed; even the woman of only two years before who had been hurt by the critics' contemptuous reception of her Portia (but who never deigned to howl back imprecations, as Nat had done) had decided to forget the great classics and give the public what it wanted.

If there was an inexpressed element of disappointment, shown more clearly by Gertrude's flash of anger when she heard her sister brushed off as a 'society actress', Maxine had made her bargain with herself. She knew she could send away audiences bemused by her beauty, the men a little awed by the queenlike bearing, the women transported into efforts to imitate her hair, her little light laugh, her small shrugs. Her early struggles to avoid being classed only as a beauty had been useless, so beauty must be used to the hilt. Her ideas were practical and unvain. 'Beauty is of no help to a woman at the beginning of her career. . . . It challenges attention, but at best beauty is only a fifth wheel. You have but to look at successful women of the stage to prove this. They are plain, almost without exception! It is in the choruses of the extravaganzas that you find the real professional beauties . . . but their beauty alone without talent and determination and ambition and work will never get them out of the chorus.'

She had done with high art and become a money-making commodity. The public would pay to look at her, and this would bring her money. From money independence would result.

Between March and September, with three months away at Jackwood, Maxine completed her task of remodelling and furnishing the new house at 326 West End Avenue. Nat, who continued touring long after Maxine left his cast, took little interest in the project; it was entirely hers. The pattern she created over and over again of a conventional 'lady's' house came into full force; Nat was not entirely neglected and was given his 'den', but Maxine's dusty pinks, soft golds, and whites had taken over.

The household at West End Avenue in the autumn of 1903

was hardly harmonious, with Maxine playing to crowded houses at the Garrick Theatre while Nat was failing to fill the New Amsterdam as Bottom in *A Midsummer Night's Dream*. The newly installed telephone rang constantly for Maxine; the flowers, notes, and packages arrived at the door for Maxine. Added to the Goodwin family were the visiting Forbes-Robertsons. After seeing Maxine's opening in Buffalo they went into rehearsal at the Knickerbocker Theatre for their limited engagement of *The Light That Failed*, before going on tour. Maxine was rather annoyed with Forbie; he had a way of silently nodding at her suggestions for his and Gertrude's career and then making his own arrangements. He had politely not used Maxine's manager, Charles Dillingham, but, at the suggestion of a fellow actor, Arthur Lewis, had signed up with the Klaw and Erlanger management. Maxine was convinced that Forbie could not make an advantageous contract for himself.

The Light That Failed was not a success; its theme of the Boer War had little interest for an American audience. Maxine was even more disturbed by Forbie's impracticality when he sent his brother Ian dashing to London to get his *Hamlet* costume and sets out of the storehouse, a mission which Ian managed in thirteen days, missing only one of Hamlet's shoes. But Shakespeare, never a friend to either Maxine or Nat, saved the day for Forbie and Gertrude; he was acclaimed as the finest Hamlet seen in New York since Edwin Booth; Gertrude was called a tender and true Ophelia. A strange quartet of performers were all forced to live under one roof, their careers taking dissimilar routes. To make Nat's chagrin total, his management decided that losses over *A Midsummer Night's Dream* were too great to carry and sought a sure success with which to recover; at the same moment Charles Dillingham found that he could no longer keep *Her Own Way* at the Garrick because of a prior booking. Maxine and her resplendent success were just what the New Amsterdam needed. Nat's company left New York to play in Boston. The newspapers were anything but tactful; a drawing in the Sunday section of the New York *Tribune* showed Maxine in a nurse's uniform ready to bind up the wounds of the New Amsterdam box office; another column inquired whether

Maxine Elliott had run off with Nat Goodwin's lucky rabbit's foot.

The departure of Nat from 326 West End Avenue left only one person deeply grieved. The Forbes-Robertsons had brought their two-year-old Blossom to New York, and she had acquired a passion for Nat (as she remembers to this day). Even 'Nonny' felt a warmth for him when he wandered aimlessly to the nursery, though it alarmed her that he was often drunk, and gossip reported he had been rattling on the doors of the pretty Irish maids. Nat's career and personality were becoming unwieldy; he was more quarrelsome than before, his confidence frayed; he was even finding reasons to carp at Forbie and his beloved little Gertrude. There was no need for Maxine's success to be so injurious to Nat, but it seems to have been so. A perfectly reasonable decision had been reached when they agreed to act separately; it was indeed difficult to find scripts that would suit them together. The resentment felt by Nat came from deeper reasons. He could have had little doubts of his own genius; he was a total man of the theatre, often pretending to discard it forever but never able to exist without it. In Maxine he saw a woman who did not really like it and yet achieved enormous success; it made him feel that the public was fickle and without judgment. He could never take any of his emotional or professional upheavals calmly. He drank more and more; his capacity to carry liquor diminished.

Beyond the professional difficulties, the personal ones had become hopeless. Maxine and Nat no longer shared the same desires in life; their friends were different, their quarrels too harmful to be forgotten. Only the remnants of a working association remained—each held a percentage in the other's productions. They owned Jackwood and 326 West End Avenue jointly. From then on, the amount of time they spent together was negligible. Their tours took them on separate roads, and they hardly shared their holidays at all.

Her Own Way ran for two seasons. After its opening in New York it went out on the road. It reopened in New York in the autumn of 1904, and was off again to tour a different series of towns. Reportedly the play earned a hundred thousand dollars for Clyde Fitch; for Maxine the earnings must have been considerably greater, although shared with Charles Dillingham and Nat Goodwin. It produced a steady routine for her, with summers off in England. While working, she passed the time when not actually on stage playing bridge with her leading man, Charles Cherry. She brought *Her Own Way* to London and presented it at the Lyric Theatre (transferring to the Savoy) for a two months' run. It was her first appearance as an individual star in London, and her success was enormous. His Majesty King Edward VII attended a performance, ostentatiously leading the applause. It was delightful to be professionally acclaimed in London (after the mild reception there of *The Cowboy and the Lady* and *An American Citizen*), but the engagement book Maxine kept at that time makes no mention of her nightly appearances at the theatre. She was being socially lionized, and her entries are all teas, dinners, drives.

The routine was almost unbroken for two further years. After closing *Her Own Way* in London in early July 1905, Maxine had six weeks for yachting trips, country visits, and the purchase of a new wardrobe in Paris. Then she was back in America with a new play by Clyde Fitch called *Her Great Match*. It was the formula as before, with Charles Cherry as leading man. Clyde Fitch varied the theme but little—in *Her Own Way* Charles Cherry had gone to the Spanish-American War and for two acts the audience was fearful lest Maxine might be forced into marriage with another; in *Her Great Match* he was a royal prince and the audience must worry for two acts lest protocol prevent Maxine's love from being rewarded. Maxine was exquisite in a white lace dress and tiny tiara, Charles Cherry resplendent in a white Ruritanian uniform. The play opened in New York on April 9, 1906, toured, reopened in New York, toured again, and was presented in London.

Before the second season of *Her Great Match* Maxine had decided that sharing profits with a producer and an invisible husband was a foolish arrangement. A newspaper report remarked that Miss Elliott's theory was that fifty per cent of the profit should go to Miss Elliott and the other fifty per cent also to Miss Elliott. Charles Dillingham was no longer 'presenting' Miss Elliott by the early spring of 1907; he had been replaced by the dependable and experienced manager, George Appleton, who had arranged Nat Goodwin's tours all over the country for twenty years and now worked for Maxine on salary. She engaged her own personal representative, Mike Yack, to take care of publicity; he was also required to arrange temporary membership at country clubs for Miss Elliott, Mr. Charles Cherry, Miss Suzanne Perry, and himself so Maxine could be assured of a foursome at golf wherever she went. In closely booked engagements, frequently one-night stands, Maxine felt the need of exercise and air. She was working harder than any other star of the period, well known for her dependability, fulfilling engagements in spite of snow and sleet; she was driven by the incentive to accumulate her profits fast. There was hardly a city in the union with a hall that did not see Maxine Elliott during these years. Theatre managers sighed with relief when they had her company booked: she was bound to be there on time. This was the woman who had been the first important star to play in the wrecked city of San Francisco after the earthquake and fire; there without complaint she appeared in an old vaudeville house called the Novelty.

In September 1907 Maxine opened her next play in London instead of New York. It was *Under the Greenwood Tree*, not by Clyde Fitch but by Henry V. Esmond, author of the Goodwins' biggest money-maker, *When We Were Twenty-One*. Maxine had decided to discard lovely ball dresses of the latest fashion and appear in gipsy costume. The public did not like it. Later it opened in New York, where the reception was no better. Charles Cherry was missing—he had sprained his ankle. The play was abandoned after two months and replaced by *Myself—Bettina*, by Rachel Crothers, in October 1908. This was an even greater departure in style. It was an attempt at a serious drama about New England bigotry; Bettina was a woman who had fled to Paris to become a singer and now returned to shock and disturb her old neighbours with a Salome dance at a church social, and also to rescue her little sister from ruin. Perhaps Maxine's memory of Rockland attracted her to such an unsuitable script; she realized at once, however, that her next play must return to sophisticated dialogue and fashionable clothes.

The success or failure of individual plays of Maxine's after *Her Own Way* never changed her status as a star; she remained in that position until she left the theatre for good. As she reached the peak of attainment she was already laying her plan to get out. She suffered through the four years of Clyde Fitch successes as a man will go to his office with no real love of his work but the necessity to earn a living and fulfil his duties. She often said that no theatrical formula was as interesting as life. She informed Vincent Sheean wearily, 'You wouldn't find anything very interesting in the theatre after saying "I love you" night after night precisely at 10.28, plus the matinees.'

The drive to achieve was gone; now it was a chore, a round of getting the right clothes, the nuisance of finding a new script when a play had been performed beyond its money-making capacity or was a failure. It meant long journeys which only card-playing made tolerable. She was careful in her selection of casts and good to her company, but she shared none of the joyful post-mortems of the typical actor. She left the stage, removed her make-up, went home to her biscuits and milk (and a game of bridge), and wished to have no more thought of the performance just given or the one to come the next day. She often seemed strange and remote to the people who travelled with her across the continent. They believed that somewhere on a dusty station platform in the Corn Belt she was bound to reveal more of herself, but she remained a civil lady.

There were some moments when she was the very opposite of civil, behaving like a person annoyed at being awakened from a dream. A party of ladies from Rockland called at her hotel in Boston; she came hurrying into the lobby where they awaited her. 'Oh, I thought it was someone I knew,' she said. In Boston also an even odder incident took place, but this may be explained by the sudden welling up of forgotten resentments directed toward the White family of Rockland, once her father's associates, one the mother of her early romance, Art Hall. The Governor of Maine, a White, attended a performance of *Her Own Way*, and at intermission sent Bob Crockett from Rockland (now the debonair manager of Farwell's Opera House) with a note for Miss Elliott to say

Governor White and his party would be delighted to call upon her after the performance. From then on Maxine played her performance ostentatiously turned away from the governor's box; she never glanced his way during her curtain calls, and she never answered his note. She did not know this Governor White personally. She had no desire to hide her origins in Maine. It was said Maxine Elliott lacked passion, but this was an act of almost uncontrollable rage, coldly performed.

Maxine had taken that hard dedication to success almost like a drug. When the tours were over she would reawaken in England and her real life would be renewed. The companies who worked with her (with the probable exception of Charles Cherry, who was a visitor often at Jackwood and later houses she owned) seldom had the opportunity to see the vivid woman who was dazzling England. A young actress, Nellie Thorne, could be overwhelmed by the generosity of Miss Elliott, who brought her a brand-new dress from Worth in Paris (the measurements had been carefully taken with the assistance of the wardrobe mistress), yet Nellie felt unable to approach a step nearer. Maxine had put her life into compartments: she did her job, but her social life and her heart were elsewhere. The girl who had said with defiance that she would not let her brother actors bury her now wanted a good deal more than that. She wanted large money, important money, the kind that would get her out of the life of a working actress, but on her own terms.

Her earnings during 1907 sky-rocketed, even though individual plays were less successful than the two Clyde Fitch plays that created her popularity. She was investing all the time, constantly on the telephone to her broker in New York. Momentarily she flirted with a resumed relationship with a management to do the work for her, this time the Shuberts. They offered almost any arrangement she wished and promised bookings in all major theatres of any play she wanted, wincing as she pushed her percentage higher and higher. But she went home and thought it out. Someone said Maxine Elliott had been given an adding machine and with it spent a night computing profits; she observed that it had been possible for her to make considerably more money with her own gruelling round of smaller cities. She saw no reason for losing money

on a train fare (private car for her, and special coach for her
company) between Chicago and San Francisco when money
could be picked up at every city *en route*. But the work
involved had gone beyond endurance. As usual she put her
practical good sense to work; there must be some way to get
maximum profit and also stay in the same place. The answer
came quite easily; instead of enforced travel to theatres she
would have her own theatre. No theatre owner need be sought,
or paid either. She could become a stationary star in her own
theatre or, if she so willed, lease it to others. The goal was now
to be an actress-manager in New York City.

There is a story—a legend passed by word of mouth—that
somewhere on the road she telephoned her broker and learned
that a recent investment had proved successful, so she could
now boast a capital of one million dollars, and at that moment
gave the company two weeks' notice and planned her return
to New York. She was now in search of solid business associates to introduce her to corporation management and real-
estate control. Only people with titanic understanding of the
power of money were of interest to her. Nat, suddenly seeking
a reconciliation, wrote that a gold mine in Nevada would
make him a multi-millionaire. To Maxine this was just a
childish dream; she knew it was not to an artist she should
look for an understanding of the mystery and magic of
money.

11

MAXINE ELLIOTT'S THEATRE

THE STEP beyond stardom into management is always said to have been J. Pierpont Morgan's gift to Maxine Elliott. Very often it is the only titbit that anyone can dredge up if the name of Maxine Elliott is mentioned—'Oh, yes, she's the actress Morgan built a theatre for.' The story refuses to die long after the two people are gone and the theatre itself handed over to a demolition crew.

It has been firmly denied in print by Alexander Woollcott in *While Rome Burns*. He swore that Maxine had never even met Mr. Morgan. She probably told him so. I have heard her deny it; I have also heard her say, 'Oh, yes, I met him on a boat once,' and I have heard her say that she met Kaiser Wilhelm II when he visited Mr. Morgan on board the *Corsair III* in the Kiel Canal. The variations in the versions she gave suggest she knew him well; Maxine's statements were seldom unclear. I have no doubt that he played a part in her fortunes, but to what extent one can only conjecture. Two such worldly-wise people, under constant observation, were not going to hand information out to the curious. I do not, however, have any compunction in hazarding guesses because I also heard Maxine say, 'Let them write what they want after I'm dead.' She left behind her a challenge, with a twinkle in her eye.

Maxine had every opportunity to meet Mr. Morgan. She could have met him in innumerable London houses; she could have met him through Nat Goodwin, who had an enormous acquaintanceship outside the theatre, and loved to visit the grandest men's clubs at one moment and the lowest race-track touts the next. Charles M. Schwab was a neighbour and mutual friend. Above all, there was Maxine's good and trusted friend Tom Chadbourne (now married to Grace Wassall), who knew Mr. Morgan well in both the social and business worlds. With the opportunity offered it would not be likely that Maxine would have missed meeting a man who was champion in his field; with Mr. Morgan's admiration for beautiful and intelligent women he would hardly have missed the chance either. The extreme secretiveness of this friendship—when others between Maxine and men of distinction were not concealed—suggests that they arrived at an agreement to present to the world a deadpan picture of no acquaintanceship at all because it was more convenient so to do. Mr. Morgan would surely have subscribed to Lord Chesterfield's advice to his son, 'Never confess.'

Nat claims in his autobiography that long before he believed his marriage was failing he noticed that little lunches were taking place between his wife and 'financial friends' to whom he had introduced her. He complains that she received useful tips on the market which always paid off, while the same advisers might seem to offer him tips which always failed. He may have been trying to claim that his wife was receiving money as well as advice; she would use either one wisely.

Maxine was naturally gifted in the handling of money. She had been severely frightened in her early years and was ready to learn. Tom Chadbourne had become her legal adviser, probably from the moment she began to have a decent and separate bank balance after marriage to Nat. She listened to Tom's accounts of investments and paid attention, seizing the principles of which he spoke. Constance Collier sat at the dinner table of Charles M. Schwab and heard Charlie and Maxine talking for hours about the formation of United States Steel; Constance reacted like the romantic, impractical woman she was, noting mood, catching the light on Maxine's hair, seeing how Charlie moved his head as he talked, but not troubling to put her mind on the specifics of which they spoke. Most men at this period, if they talked business in mixed company, did not expect the womenfolk to understand or even listen, and usually would have kept any such discussion till a later hour in the evening over the cigars and brandy. The discovery of a brilliant financial brain behind the classic features and midnight eyes of Maxine Elliott was a startling experience. Tom Chadbourne was fascinated by her capacities all his life, and when asked once if his investments for her had produced her fortune had laughed and said, 'I take advice from Max as often as I give it.' It seems to fit with Tom's exuberant character and his admiration for power that he would urge J. P. Morgan to experience the extraordinary pleasure of meeting a lovely woman who knew exactly what he was talking about. The directness of friendship between Maxine and Tom made it quite unnecessary for him to be coy with her about the advantages of knowing Morgan.

Just as Maxine had learned to put her life in compartments (many of her English friends were only dimly aware of her theatrical career), so Morgan organized his life with the utmost care. Morgan was a secretive man, so quiet about his private life that he gave rise to a thousand rumours. He had strong opinions on the subject, and claimed for himself the full aristocratic privilege of ordering his own movements. He could be a national figure in finance, a great collector of art, a pillar of St. George's Church in Stuyvesant Square, an ideal husband when at home in the big brownstone mansion on 36th Street and Madison Avenue or the summer home on the Hudson, but he saw no reason to deny himself the company of whatever friends he chose on board his yacht. He believed in the sanctity of the home; he was a Victorian who protected his wife from all crudities of business, including the day-by-day actions which made him one of the major fortunes of the country. He never allowed that area of his life to conflict with his pleasure in the company of bright, intelligent women who conducted themselves with tact. Their names were protected as carefully as he protected his wife's honour. He was generous to those he liked and managed his gifts in such a way as never to cause embarrassment to anybody. His manners were princely. He did not expect his actions to be questioned, and arranged them accordingly.

Perhaps Mr. Morgan is concealed behind a story told by a saleswoman at B. Altman's. She was new to the job, excited to serve Miss Maxine Elliott with a beautiful brocaded evening coat trimmed in fur, but obliged to ask her whether this would be paid for in cash or charged. 'Just charge it,' said Maxine,

HER GREAT MATCH

MARIENBAD 1909 WITH EDWARD VII AND HIS PARTY

walking away without mentioning her address. The saleswoman asked the department manager if she had done right. 'Oh, my God, don't ever ask Miss Elliott anything,' said the manager, who had been out at lunch. 'All her bills come straight to me. You never enter them in your books. I send them through to Mr. Altman himself and he knows where they go.'

There were innumerable stories of houses that J. P. Morgan bought for Maxine where he could visit her unannoyed by the public. Not one of these houses can be traced on any record. There are stories of private railroad cars, shunted discreetly on to sidings, where someone saw Miss Elliott and Mr. Morgan arrive. None of these stories come closer than third or fourth hand. One story carried a little more weight because it had an element of description. A New York lady told a friend in Rockland that she had seen Mr. Morgan and Miss Elliott often arrive at a box in a theatre, usually just after the curtain had risen, with a maid always in shadowy attendance behind them. The lady who reported seeing them also said that they never addressed a word to each other.

Another strange legend says that Morgan endowed a hospital at Maxine Elliott's suggestion, and that it had a suite especially made for her. The story pertains to the Manhattan General Hospital on a corner of Stuyvesant Square, at Second Avenue, which at that time was the Lying-In Hospital. Morgan's connection with this hospital long predates the time when he could first have met Maxine. Where Maxine fits into this picture it is impossible to say, unless she needed care and Morgan recommended her to his friend, Dr. James Wright Markoe, a pioneer doctor of the hospital. Nevertheless, the legend persists.

By far the most impressive evidence of friendship between Maxine and Morgan was given by Maxine's friend and mine, Mrs. Jan Boissevain of Cap d'Antibes—Charlotte Ives on the stage—who reported a conversation she had with Maxine when they were driving together along Unter den Linden in Berlin. Maxine pointed to the Brandenberg Tor when they passed it and said, 'I drove under that once with the Kasier.' She told Charlotte she had met the Kaiser on Morgan's yacht, precisely as I had heard her say. Charlotte's report adds a characteristic detail: Maxine said, 'The arrangements on board Mr. Morgan's yacht were ridiculous. He had the cabins on a lower deck where there was no light, and the dining saloon on the upper deck. I had him change the whole thing so we could dine below, where we needed no outside light, and all the sleeping cabins could have proper portholes.'

During the period when Maxine Elliott announced her plans for a New York Theatre of her own, hints and even open statements appeared in the gossip columns, and in September 1908, when Maxine returned from her summer in Europe, a story appeared in newspapers that J. P. Morgan was travelling on the same boat. The stories even included dialogue; Miss Elliott was asked if it was true that Mr. Morgan had a financial interest in her theatre and she replied, 'Let's ask him about it, shall we?' When he was approached, Morgan's reported answer was, 'The only interest I have in Maxine Elliott's Theatre is that I'd like to get a free ticket on opening night.'

Finally there are two witnesses who have told me that they saw Mr. Morgan and Maxine together. One is Mrs. E. K. Baldwin of New York City, who, as a child, was on that same liner. She came aboard, she says, wearing a boater with long ribbons down her back and Mr. Morgan, strolling on deck, smiled at her and then told her mother, 'She's like a small Maxine Elliott.' Mrs. Baldwin does indeed have deep-set, glowing eyes. She remembers that there was much talk among the grown ups about Mr. Morgan and Miss Elliott taking their meals in a private dining room. The other witness is Miss Oza Waldrop, the actress, who joined Maxine Elliott's company. In Boston, she says, where they were playing prior to their New York opening in the new theatre, she chose what looked to her like a modest hotel—small and white, she remembers, on Boston Common—hoping it would be inexpensive. It was not; she had come upon a discreet, elegant, and exclusive place, and here, she found, the star herself had also registered. Several times she saw Mr. Morgan escorting Miss Elliott into the quiet, almost empty dining room.

Whatever meetings there may have been between Maxine and Mr. Morgan could only have been infrequent. Maxine was often away on tour for seven or eight months at a stretch, publicly appearing in the theatre; during the summer she was thoroughly observed at the house parties and spas of Europe. Any idea that Morgan 'kept' Maxine somewhere in a hide-away is ludicrous; she was not a commodity that could be hidden. If her fierce pride and independence had ever enabled her to accept the position of 'the woman on the side', tucked quietly away until her protector could visit her, she would have had no need to submit to months of theatrical tours which she heartily disliked. No important art treasures that could have been gifts from Morgan appeared in her houses; the fine Lawrence portrait she possessed was given her by Lord Curzon, and the Perroneau pastel was from Constant Coquelin; both gifts were publicly acknowledged. Maxine's private coach on the railroad, as we know, was a wedding present from Nat. No trophy from Morgan was ever in evidence.

The truth seems to be that she and Morgan met, liked each other, and continued to meet at widely spaced intervals, with an attraction of like to like. The complete organization of Morgan must have been a delight after Nat's disorderliness. In spite of his monstrous and famous nose, Morgan was said to be fascinating to women, with brilliant, compelling eyes and a smile that could suddenly be radiant. He had the beautiful manners and the aristocratic approach to life which Maxine admired. She may have found brief oases of peace with him, a father who did not shout, a lover who demanded no curtailment of her liberty. If she presented him with her proposal to build and manage a theatre for herself, she could talk freely and clearly. Her earnings as an actress, which she invested steadily, might still have been insufficient for a large advance of capital for purchase of land and for building costs; it could only have been his pleasure to advance what was needed with the knowledge that she was a sound investment herself. The arrangement would have been done with absolute discretion.

The idea of owning a theatre may have come to Maxine from Nat. He had spoken of it for years, even specifying the kind of intimate house which Maxine now decided to realize. 'Nearly all theatres are too big and everyone suffers,' he

said, 'the patrons because they can't hear, the manager because he has more rent to pay, and the actor because he can't
act so well. You can't be expected to talk clear across Broadway. . . . Ask a man to try and be funny in a ten-acre lot.'
Maxine may have given her version of these ideas to Morgan
as her dream, adding that she wanted a small, beautiful, high-
class house, devoted exclusively to drama and excluding large,
noisy musicals. Another story persists that when Mr. Morgan
inquired what her designs for such a theatre would be, she
replied, 'A theatre where the performers are decently treated,
with proper bathrooms and lavatories,' and he immediately
recognized this as the practical approach he liked.

Between the time that Maxine closed *Under the Greenwood
Tree* in London in 1907 and opened it in New York the
United States was swept by financial crisis. J. P. Morgan was
attending a convention of the Episcopal Church in Philadelphia as the news began to come that one bank after another
was closing down in New York. Frantic people were lined
up outside the doors of the city banks, anxious to get their
money out before it should all disappear. Couriers rushed
to Philadelphia to persuade Morgan to return at once. He
had about him the kind of magic that made everyone believe
that his very presence in New York would restore confidence. Morgan, however, knew that his every move was
observed. If he dashed away now from the Episcopal convention he could precipitate even worse panic. Everyone knew
his deep feeling for the church and his pleasure in the company of distinguished bishops; to leave the convention before
its scheduled time would make people say, 'Morgan's worried.' While his partners and friends begged him to come he
continued to sit in on the discussions of church matters and
eat long, rich dinners. Then quietly he took the train to New
York and went straight to his own house. Everyone brought
him details of the disaster. Men sat gazing into space in the
corner of the great room where Morgan sat behind his desk.
They awaited the miracle that he must produce. He listened
to everyone's story and then went into action. Every important financier was sent for and asked how much he would
put down to help save the banks that were tottering. Some
banks he considered necessary to let go; it was a military

action, abandoning one flank to consolidate the total position. Theodore Roosevelt, who disliked everything Morgan stood for and had waged bitter war upon him and all corporate financial power, sent him messages of gratitude. Gradually the pressure slackened. As panicked people found that they were able to draw out their money they began to relax their rush; some began to bring their money back. Morgan, through his control of brother financiers and insistence that they should all stand together and put their money into a joint effort to restore public confidence, had indeed saved the financial life of the country. It was this crisis, which left the country financially at the mercy of individuals, that eventually caused the creation of the Federal Reserve Bank, under President Wilson.

It may be entirely coincidental that two months after this crisis Maxine Elliott (after *Under the Greenwood Tree* had failed in both London and New York) had enough money to contribute her half share for the purchase of the property at 39th Street and Sixth Avenue, and her half share for the building of a theatre upon this site. Besides that, she also bought a new house on 81st Street, just off Fifth Avenue, and moved into the fashionable East Side, cheek by jowl with Harrimans and Astors. It would seem as if she ought to have been poorer at this moment when her play was not successful and her investments, like those of most other people, might have been expected to be reduced in value due to the crisis. But in fact she was much richer than before. Many people suggest that Mr. Morgan gave her outright the sum she needed to become a theatre owner. It seems far more likely that his guidance showed her how to profit from the crisis. Either she had learned so well that she could do it entirely herself (she certainly handled all her own transactions in old age) or she was at this moment learning the method from the greatest expert there was.

Maxine was always fascinated by the man of the moment, whether he was John Ward at bat for the New York Highlanders in 1887 or J. P. Morgan literally running the United States of America at a moment of crisis. One hopes that she did have the pleasure of having secret knowledge of the hour-by-hour transactions. She would have loved it. She could have had the strength to experience this tremendous moment of history without ever succumbing to the temptation of telling a few friends. If Morgan trusted her, as the men in political life in England trusted her, it was because she said nothing.

The agreement between Maxine Elliott and the Shubert Corporation for purchase of land and joint construction and management of a theatre was entered into on April 25, 1908. Lee Shubert, as party of the first part, and Maxine Elliott Goodwin, as party of the second part, each put forward at once the sum of $10,000 to be paid for title of the land to Eugene C. Potter for a property known as 107, 109, 111, 113 West 39th Street. A corporation was then organized under the laws of the state of New York, known as the Elliott Theatre Company, with a capital of $300,000 consisting of 3000 shares of a par value of $100 each. Each of the parties agreed to subscribe $125,000 to the capital stock. The agreed balance of capital stock, $50,000, was to remain in the company's treasury until the company required additional funds, at which time each should subscribe equal amounts; neither was entitled to subscribe or receive any balance of capital stock without the other. They agreed to mortgage the company's property and assets in order to borrow $250,000, or a sum advisable or obtainable. They would build a theatre according to plans and specifications mutually agreed, and the theatre should be run by the Shubert management subject to Maxine's approval. Maxine had the right at any time to play in any production in which she would personally appear with a notification to Shubert of her requirement sixty days in advance, and she had the right to remain as long as she wished, receiving fifty per cent of the first $4000 weekly gross box-office take, and sixty per cent on all sums exceeding that amount. Maxine had the right to have a representative of her own always in the theatre whose salary would be charged as an expense of the enterprise, and this representative should always be allowed access to the company's books. There was to be an annual meeting of the stockholders of the company held on the first Monday of every October, and special meetings could also be called. The company consisted of five people: Presidents Lee Shubert and Maxine

Elliott; Secretary J. J. Shubert, Director Thomas L. Chadbourne, and Treasurer George Appleton (for many years the manager of Nat Goodwin and Maxine Elliott).

During the negotiations that settled these financial and managerial arrangements there came a moment of near breakdown, caused by a tussle over the name of the new theatre. Maxine absolutely refused the name 'The Maxine Elliott Theatre'—it must be 'Maxine Elliott's Theatre'. That possessive apostrophe was of paramount importance. Like Clyde Fitch in the naming of her first star play, Lee Shubert eventually threw up his hands and said, 'Name it your own way.'

In June 1908 photographs were taken of Maxine Elliott wielding a shovel, breaking the first ground where the theatre would rise.

Maxine Elliott's Theatre (the name carved deep into the marble façade) was one of the prettiest theatres ever built. Its architects were Marshall and Fox, a Chicago firm, but the idea for its form came from Maxine herself, a close model of Le Petit Trianon at Versailles. Its front had four tall Corinthian columns; its top was finished in a classic balustrade. The whole was made of Vermont marble. It was pure, simple, austere, and the height of elegance, with no theatrical flourishes, nothing showy, nothing that did not suggest the small palace or temple of a goddess. Maxine told the newspapers that her theatre would be dedicated to the production of plays presented by herself or other leading actresses, a theatre suitable for women who needed a charming setting and the height of comfort. This was one theatre, she said, where the actress was not going to be treated as a second-class citizen, nor was any member of the audience. Its outside was dignified, and its interior fulfilled everything that Maxine had promised in comfort for both audience and actors. The Shuberts did not know what they were up against when they tried to squeeze in some extra seating by narrowing the dimensions of the seats; when Maxine found that her specifications, which allowed people to sit in comfort without cramped elbows and crushed knees, were not being followed, she simply ordered the seats ripped out and redone. When some lesser comfort (and therefore lesser expense) was sought in the cheaper galleries, Maxine did precisely the same thing. No one was going to enter her theatre and not spend a pleasant evening, able to see from any seat, to hear, to rise at the end of three acts without strained muscles.

Backstage the shock was even greater. For centuries actors and actresses had accepted poor quarters; they crammed themselves into the dressing rooms assigned them, desperately trying to find space to hang their clothes. They seldom had running water or a lavatory anywhere within comfortable distance; to wash they often had to climb flights of cold stone stairs, and sometimes even go across the street to a nearby boarding-house. Every dressing room in Maxine's theatre had a section which enclosed a wash basin and a lavatory. Her own dressing room had a full-sized bathroom. Every room had carpeting, gay chintz curtains at the windows (and there were windows), a dressing table with well-placed lights for making up and a full length looking-glass so that a player could see the full effect of the costume. There was sufficient hanging space for clothes and a comfortable armchair where a player could rest between the acts. Maxine herself had a chaise-longue. Sometimes a newly employed member of Maxine Elliott's company (or someone who worked in her theatre after Maxine herself had leased it to others) was reduced to tears of pure joy to find that such consideration had been shown for the comfort and dignity of the theatrical profession. Maxine may have disliked her life in the theatre; the company of actors bored her more and more (unless, like Charles Cherry, they could play bridge); but she passionately believed that actors had the right to be well treated and not housed like cattle.

In the weeks before it was ready she took infinite trouble, plaguing everyone with her attention to detail. She seemed to be constantly on everyone's back; her sudden bursts of anger over incompetence brought terror to many. No one quite understood what infuriated her and what did not (a petty question fumbled was her major irritation). The astonished house manager was quite shaken when he found her not angry at an incident he feared unpardonable. She swept into the almost perfect building with a party of friends, showed them all over, flung open her own bathroom door and exposed a large workman peacefully soaking in her tub. 'Excuse me,' she said politely, and shut the door. 'Another time,' she said to her friends. No one was berated later.

The opening night, December 30, 1908, was a brilliant affair. Some of the most beautiful or distinguished women of the time—Olga Nethersole, Nellie Melba, Geraldine Farrar —came to celebrate. Women of society were equally well represented. They all noticed with pleasure that the colours of the auditorium—soft creams, golds, light browns—and the lighting that played upon the faces of the audience during intermission were designed to show them off to their best advantage, to make skin glow, hair shine; and the generous spacing of seats allowed them to rise and promenade without fear that their best dresses had been crushed into a thousand wrinkles. It was remarkable at the time for a New York theatre to have only 725 seats, and in fact it was this modest seating capacity that made its life a comparatively short one. The play presented was a cheerful affair called *The Chaperon*, by Marian Fairfax. Maxine played the part of an American lady with a foreign title who was left in charge of a country house full of youngsters when the parents were obliged to leave on urgent business. There was the usual mix-up of a new romance in the lady's life, and an ex-husband who re-appeared, all neatly sorted out in the end. On the opening night, a mishap on stage led to a special *rapport* between the actors and an audience already warmly disposed toward the beautiful woman who entertained them so charmingly and had provided such an elegant setting. Oza Waldrop entered with a plate full of sandwiches for a picnic that Maxine was giving the young people in a sunken garden; Miss Waldrop's heel caught on one of the numerous steps, and sandwiches scattered over the stage. Bravely the actors went on while Miss Waldrop rushed to pick up the food. Suddenly Maxine observed her carefully dusting each sandwich off, then passing them around. Her eyes gleamed with amusement, her voice began to tremble, and she was seized by laughter. The whole audience responded with a roar, and for a few minutes actors and audience together shouted with laughter as Miss Waldrop's tragedy was turned into a memorable moment of good humour.

Maxine played *The Chaperon* till February; by April 1909
she had leased the theatre to others and had gone to London
to appear with Lewis Waller in *The Conquest*. She appeared
in her own theatre only once more, but she kept an office
in it always, and let it work for her in her absence, bringing
money to her bank account from numerous successes. One
of these was *The Passing of the Third Floor Back*, by Jerome K.
Jerome, in which Gertrude and Forbie began the New York
run of a play that became more popular than any other they
did together. Sam H. Harris produced *Rain* in her theatre, the
adaptation of Somerset Maugham's 'Miss Thompson', with
Jeanne Eagels; Ethel Barrymore appeared there in *The Constant Wife* and Helen Hayes in *Coquette*. Years later I heard
Maxine tell someone, 'The Communists are in my theatre in
New York'—it was the Federal Theatre Project. Another
time, I heard her say that she had a pantomime there. This
turned out to be Lillian Hellman's grim drama, *The Children's
Hour*. By then, Maxine was paying little attention to what
play was in the theatre, but she knew quite well whether it
was a success or failure.

By the time Broadway had moved uptown from 39th Street
and Maxine Elliott's Theatre had become a television studio
for Columbia Broadcasting, Maxine herself was dead. By
1959 the theatre was demolished. I arrived there as snow was
falling and saw the elegant façade almost entirely concealed
by the structures of a demolition crew. From inside there
came the noise of pneumatic drills and the shouts of workmen. Finally a helpful policeman found the boss of the work
crew for me and he led me inside, warning me to be careful
how I stepped, since the entire floor of the orchestra had been
removed and a sheer drop gaped beneath us to the cellars below where scenery had been stored. Only the front row of the
dress circle remained, hanging in mid-air, its seats all gone
and only a crossbeam or two holding the structure in place.
The air danced with particles of dust, and flashes of blow-
torches illumined the interior. The snow was beginning to
come in through the roof.

'I hate to see a theatre pulled down,' said the boss. 'It's
our job to pull things down, of course, and we don't think
anything about it. Somehow, though, I always think it's sad

when I see a theatre go. Somewhere where people have come
to enjoy themselves . . .'

His moment of sentiment about a passing theatre was much
more than Maxine herself would have felt. When the usefulness of something had passed, she let it go without a backward
look.

Even in the moment of triumph in December 1908, when
she had arrived at the peak of her career, a theatre-owner in
New York, she failed to be impressed with her own achieve-
ment. She had achieved the theatre, not for itself, but for the
added revenue it would bring her and always a greater freedom within her profession. She was asked by *Theatre Magazine*
to comment on a statement made by the great opera singer,
Emma Calvé. Madame Calvé had said that she did not believe
a public career was worthwhile—'The only life worth living
is the life of peace and quiet.' Maxine's words on Calvé's
statement are even stronger. 'Happiness someone defined as
the cessation of pain. We work so hard and so long to reach
success and happiness, to achieve that cessation of pain on
the stage, that I do not know whether it is worth while. I
seriously doubt it. Think of coming to the theatre every night
year after year for half or two thirds of your life! For me,
all that seems worth while is to have a home in the country,
where I will never be hurried or worried, where I can see
my sister and brother-in-law and their adorable children
as often as I like, to play with those children and have no
cares. . . .'

12

ROYAL PROGRESS

THE HOME in England (where Maxine was 'never hurried or worried') had changed since she and Nat became 'the Lord of Penzance' and 'the Lady Regent Max', as Clyde Fitch had christened them. After the opening of *Her Own Way* and the start of separate management, Maxine and Nat never had a full summer at Jackwood again. The story of Maxine's professional life has brought this chronicle to 1908, but it was in 1905 that her social life came nearer to her ideal than ever before. That year she presented *Her Own Way* in London, and Nat was no longer even a partial husband. Both Goodwins gladly accepted Herbert Beerbohm Tree's offer to rent Jackwood from them, and within a few years Nat sold it for twenty-five thousand dollars —half the price he had paid for it.

The friends of London society who had already seized upon Maxine delightedly ('but the husband is a bit of a bore') suddenly found her in blazing stardom and unattached. To these, more friends were added, and more and more. Maxine began a life of social brilliance in England hardly touched in her preceding six years. Names hardest to know in London society jammed her engagement book; three hostesses who looked upon themselves as specially privileged to entertain the Monarch (besides Mrs. Keppel) were suddenly there— Mrs. Arthur James, Mrs. William James (sisters-in-law), the Honourable Mrs. Ronnie Greville. Quickly crowding in their wake came Mrs. Potter Palmer of Chicago, unlikely to invite an American actress unless she was already very well received. There were Saturday-to-Monday visits to Lord Sandwich at Hinchingbrooke; to Rosebery at both Mentmore and The Durdans; there were suppers, garden parties, and balls at the houses of Lady Carnarvon, Lady Walter Gordon-Lennox, Lady Jersey, Lady Warwick, Baroness d'Erlanger, the Pagets, the Brasseys, Lady Alington, Lady Molesworth. Maxine had a supper engagement with Prince Francis of Teck (brother to Princess May, later Queen Mary); she went to tea at the House of Commons with Winston Churchill; the Marquess of Granby (later Duke of Rutland) fetched her for a drive; she was called upon by Mr. Harry Chapman, Sir Ernest Cassel, Captain Harry Graham, Alfred de Rothschild, all intimate friends of the King's, and spent a week-end with another of his set, Sir Reuben Sassoon, at Hatton. She broke engagement after engagement with Clyde Fitch, who was struggling to catch her free enough to listen to his reading of a new play. 'The quiet life with the family' received two mentions in her diary—a drive with Blossom one afternoon and the christening of the Forbes-Robertsons' second child, Jean. The energy involved in such a social life, with its almost continual change of costume, far surpasses the nervous expenditure of professional life, but Maxine was able to conduct the two simultaneously.

She made one last effort in the summer of 1906 to share an excursion with Nat. Reluctantly she went to Trouville. While they were there, Nat—through a mistake on the part of his valet, he claimed—saw a letter that Maxine had written to 'Lord ——' It was full of complaints: 'This place would bore you to death I think . . . the gaiety seems such a hollow, tinselly sort; if it were not for the golf I'd find it intolerable. . . . England is the place for me and my dolly is always stuffed with sawdust when I am away from it . . .' Explosions followed; Nat furiously claimed the letter as sufficient evidence to give him a divorce and walked out. The marriage had blown totally apart. To Maxine this was a relief rather than a disaster. Later Nat made attempts to approach her, suggesting a reconciliation. She refused to reply. He offered a ranch house he had bought in Nevada, proposing to retire from the theatre and mine gold, but Maxine was not prepared to join him. She had rented Combe Cottage, Surrey, from Lord Charles Beresford for the summer of 1907. Nat announced that he had bought a hotel in New York City and was making over a suite for them; Maxine never answered, but merely shipped him all his personal belongings. As Maxine worked on the construction of her new theatre in 1908 Nat had found a new interest; he no longer suggested reconciliation, intent now on marrying his fourth wife, Edna Goodrich. Shortly before Maxine Elliott's Theatre opened its doors its owner was divorced by her husband on the grounds of desertion, an uncontested case, taking seven minutes to make absolute in a court in Reno, Nevada. Gossip said that Nat had been dissuaded by his friends and lawyers from making vindictive claims of infidelity with a list of men which included J. P. Morgan, Peter Widener, Charles Cherry, Alfred de Rothschild, and Lord Rosebery. At the final moment he sent a regretful letter in his childish handwriting, wishing her well with her new theatre and warning her to beware of her 'new business associates'. With the exception of his memoirs, which shocked and hurt her when they appeared in 1911 ('That man will stoop to any money-making scheme, whether it's malice or mime'), Nat Goodwin had gone from her life for good.

The Forbes-Robertsons had become her only family. The Dermots had gone, with the exception of the yearly silver spoons sent at Christmas by Mrs. Dermot to the Forbes-Robertson children and an occasional glimpse Maxine got of her father when she was playing in San Francisco. Two brothers had died within a year of each other, barely in their early thirties. When she was still acting with Nat she had arrived at Denver in the winter of 1902 to be met by Federal agents come to tell her that her oldest brother Tom had been found shot by his own hand in a boarding house in San Francisco. It was Maxine who went to the San Francisco press and pleaded with them to keep quiet about Tom's short, tragic life of melancholia, instability in jobs, and a marriage in which a wife much older than himself had failed to help him fight the drug addiction that had seized him. Only a year later came the news that her second brother, Lew, who had long been absent as a seaman, had been washed overboard in a storm in the Indian Ocean from the deck of a British barque. He had never had the ambition of his father to rise to master of a vessel, but Captain Tom sadly claimed that few boys had the opportunity to be their own bosses in the merchant navy any more. 'The sea's for the fishes now,' he said.

Finally there was the baby brother, Sam, three years younger than Gertrude. He had joined the Goodwin company at about the time of his brother Tom's suicide in 1902. He also had been living on the West Coast, and showed no great signs of coming to grips with life, so probably Maxine and Captain Tom decided that she would try to give Sam a profession in the theatre and keep an eye on him. Few members of the company knew that 'S. M. Hall' was Miss Elliott's brother, and he made no attempt to ride with her in her private car or separate himself from the other supporting members of the cast. It was noticed, however, that Nat Goodwin included him in evenings of cards and drinks with the boys when safely away from Maxine's controlling eye. But Sam could not manage his alcohol. His companions were delighted with the immediate change from taciturnity, and without realizing the dangers egged him on to more stories, imitations, and songs, with Nat behaving like a proud father. An evening of this sort often made Sam incapable of appearing in the theatre next day; he took to vanishing, with sudden contrite returns; in the end Maxine had to fire him. Now he had gone into the real-estate business in San Franciso, and was receiving endless mothering from Belle Dermot. Maxine never tried to lure him back to her company or her household. She had struggled with enough drunks.

One last Rockland relative remained attached to Maxine's entourage for a few years. Her cousin Sue Perry played small parts and helped her in the general housekeeping of her homes. It could not last long; Sue was a woman who wanted a life of her own.

All Maxine's desires to have a family of her own perforce centred on Gertrude. She had always been the special one, but she had become a married woman and a mother. Wherever Maxine settled, at Jackwood, in New York, at Combe Cottage, she took it for granted that here was also a home for Gertrude and her family. Even if Maxine had scolded Gertrude roundly for becoming pregnant with her second child just as her acting career was in full bloom, she must have had some regrets that she herself never had children. She intended to do everything she could for those of her sister. Another obstacle barred her way; in Forbie she found a strong family man, who not only insisted upon his own separate house but was amply able and proud to provide for the upbringing and education of his children. The family made visits to Maxine's house, but in time Forbie would graciously declare that he must go home.

The professional commitments of the Forbes-Robertsons made them often unavailable. They had become enormous favourites in the United States, and toured as many months as Maxine herself. America had delighted in *Hamlet* and *Mice and Men*, and had been proud to be the place where George Bernard Shaw's new play for Forbie, *Caesar and Cleopatra*, opened for the first time in 1906 (one performance had been given long before in England for copyright purposes); Gertrude created the part of Cleopatra, which Shaw had written for Mrs. Patrick Campbell. Little Gertrude might nervously worry whether she had put on the right dress to see 'Dettie', but when it came to work she knew what she wanted. She roundly supported Forbie when he tried out a play by Henry James, *The High Bid*, which Maxine was sure was far too literary for success, and accepted with pride a new part in a play that Maxine told them not to touch with a ten-foot pole. They opened *The Passing of the Third Floor Back* by Jerome K. Jerome, deeply aware that its theme of a sort of Christ visiting a London boarding house might be too serious, even offensive, and found themselves with a success that ran relentlessly on and on. Gertrude, the little girl from Rockland, Maine, triumphed in it as a Cockney 'slavey' with dirty face and slatternly uniform. The Forbes-Robertsons were a beloved stage couple in England and America, and constantly had to set aside the claims of an elder sister.

It is difficult to guess whether Maxine was lonely and companionless during these years of her greatest success and greatest beauty. Perhaps the very abundance of her social life indicates that she was; she jammed the hours with brilliant names and cheerful people who played games well and filled the time with activity. She lavished kindnesses upon her friends, often in a thoroughly dictatorial manner. When Constance Collier became ill, Maxine carted her off to a

LADY DROGHEDA AND GARRETT AT HARTSBOURNE

GRAHAM WHITE GREETED BY DALTON, THE BUTLER

THE DUKE OF RUTLAND
WITH JEAN AND
BLOSSOM

MAXINE AND
LADY DIANA
MANNERS

hospital with a good scolding; she gave Renée Kelly, just beginning in the theatre, a rise in salary long before Renée would have dared ask for it. Maxine's manner was that of the strongly generous and bossy father of a tribe, inclined to think everyone around him a little incapable and silly. Among the six children born to Captain Thomas Dermot, that most masculine of men, the only true son he ever had was his daughter Jessie.

After *The Chaperon* had opened the Maxine Elliott's Theatre and played there successfully in the early months of 1909, Maxine abandoned it for another London venture. She joined the English matinee idol Lewis Waller in a play called *The Conquest*, an adaptation of Balzac's *La Duchesse de Langeais* by George Fleming (the mysterious incognito for the same female writer who had adapted Rudyard Kipling's *The Light That Failed*). It was perhaps flamboyantly romantic, with a dénouement that would have to be brilliant to avoid being banal (a loved lady apparently dead, who comes immediately to life on hearing the tragic parting speech of a man who had once spurned her), but it was not perceptibly sillier than any of the contrived romantic plays which were generally acceptable still in 1909. The reaction of the London audience, however, was startlingly savage. They refused to take the play seriously at all, causing one of the most unpleasant and disorderly first nights ever known. They laughed rudely, they mimicked the voices of Maxine and Lewis Waller. When the agonized actors at last got through to the final curtain, hideous boos drowned out the efforts of some part of the audience to applaud. The play closed after eight performances.

London audiences were notoriously more outspoken than American ones at this period. Every American actor who came to London felt the difference, delighted by openly expressed warmth or appalled at being booed. Londoners believed they had a right to shout their disapproval as well as their pleasure. 'If we had been a couple of murderers Mr. Waller and I could not have received such brutal treatment . . . From the moment the curtain rose the hostile spirit of the entire audience was apparent. I never went through such a night of agony in my life. Act after act things grew worse

14

and worse and then came that awful pitiless booing at the
end. . . .' Thus Maxine wrote to George Appleton, who was
managing her theatre in New York.

The entire company signed a letter on Mr. Waller's station-
ery apologizing to Maxine for the inexplicable bad manners
of the audience and equally savage attack by the press:
'During your stay in the theatre you have so endeared yourself
to us both as woman and artist that we were impelled to take
this step, unusual tho' it is.'

Momentarily Maxine believed she would never step on a
stage again—and certainly never in England—but her cour-
age was too great to stick to this resolve. The failure of *The
Conquest* was her only setback in these triumphant years; she
brushed it aside with her admirable ability to recover.

Three more plays followed, in the United States: *Deborah
of Tod's* (not a success); *Sayonara*, a play about Japan that was
tried out at matinees in Boston and dropped; and *The Inferior
Sex*, which opened her season of 1909 with excellent reviews.
This play, by Frank Stayton, seemed to have some of the
solid quality of success that had been so dependable in the
plays of Clyde Fitch. (He had burned himself out in a frenzy
of writing—once he boasted seven plays running simultaneously on Broadway—and died suddenly in 1909 at the
age of forty-four.) Maxine played *The Inferior Sex* till the
time for her usual summer break and revived it for the
autumn season of 1910-11, but she did not force it on too long
a tour. Maxine Elliott's Theatre, presenting other actresses,
other plays, was bringing in an excellent income; the investments in the bank were doing even better. She made no
announcements of retirement, but she had little intention of
returning to the theatre. She had reached her forties, still with
ravishing looks. On one summer day in 1908, her life in England had gone into still another phase, which would receive
her full attention.

*

From 1905, when Maxine's life in England had seemed based
upon some special favour not usually accorded visiting actresses, there had been whispers that it was King Edward VII
who had turned the eyes of society upon her and invited her

in. The rumour may have caused the effect, but it was a rumour only; true, she had met the Monarch briefly at tea at Mrs. Keppel's; he had come to her play and had announced she was the most beautiful woman in the world—acclaim enough, but the suggestion that she was a constant guest and companion of the King, happily reported by the newspapers, was not true.

In the summer of 1908, when Maxine returned to London after breaking ground for her theatre, she still found, of course, that hostesses such as the two Mrs. James and Mrs. Ronnie Greville invited her to their parties, but never on the same night that they had the honour to receive His Majesty. If she had achieved all else, including her own theatre in New York and the special friendship of Mr. Morgan, it unquestionably irritated Maxine that the final step into the private world of the King of England was being denied her by people who declared themselves her dear friends. The King could do much to command his own social life, but was nevertheless hedged around by royal position when in his own kingdom. Maxine had no intention of meeting him at any intimate little arrangement with no other woman present. At Marienbad in summer-time, his life was more relaxed. She decided to circumnavigate the plans of her friends in the London drawing rooms and meet him on foreign territory. A free American woman had the right to travel where she pleased, especially if she arranged her chaperonage with tact. Maxine was well aware that ladies who liked to arrange his dinners would be present in Marienbad, but Marienbad was not London.

That summer she decided she too needed to take the waters at Marienbad. She travelled with Mrs. Lee Eleanor Graham of Santa Barbara, a woman of wealth and elegance, who had taken a house in London for the last season and lavishly entertained. The company was perfect—a married woman of means, socially correct, who had the added advantage of not being a professional actress. Mrs. Graham, too, may have been thwarted in her attempts to secure the King for dinner, so here was also an ally, a fellow American ready to storm the fortress.

They stopped in Paris for their clothes. Maxine chose her

wardrobe with a perfect combination of good taste and the certainty of attracting attention. She had scarcely a piece of clothing with her which was not pure white. She had white Irish linen dresses, crisp white muslins, beautifully draped and twisted white skirts to go with shirt-waists of white frills and embroidery. The evening dresses she brought were demure in cut, with tiny sleeves that just covered the top of the shoulders, softly draped necklines, every one of them white, in chiffon, satin, brocade, silk. The only accent she allowed herself was a black feather upon a hat, or a simple all-black cartwheel. Her gloves, her shoes, her bags, and any little bit of filmy nonsense that she might require to cover her shoulders on the August nights were all white.

Maxine and Mrs. Graham had reserved rooms in the hotel directly across from the Weimar, where the King and his party were staying. A courtyard separated the two buildings. The two women immediately joined the life of a spa town; Maxine, in her practicality, was determined to get all possible physical benefit out of it for her face and figure, as well as to bring about a meeting with the King. Enthusiastically she sent a post card to Gertrude (with a picture of herself on it, snapped by one of the professional photographers that roamed the gardens) which said: 'Aug. 9, 1908: 7 o'clock in the morning. Already I feel so exhilarated that I could jump over houses. I wish you and Forbie were here. I feel sure it would do you both so much good. "I am so busy all the day I haven't any time to play." Ha. Ha.'

Within a day they learned that the royal routine was to walk slowly down the hill from the hotel through the Kurgarten, pause at the Kurhaus for a sip of the beneficial waters, and toil dutifully up the hill again. Some trouble had been caused by tourists who refused to respect the King's incognito, but now they were held back from flowing through the gardens as the King strolled down. A resident of the neighbouring hotel, however, could go where she pleased. Maxine, afterward, never concealed her careful plan for the meeting; in fact, she took an amused pleasure in telling the story.

In one of her most exquisite ensembles, Maxine, a book in hand, wandered slowly from her hotel. She could not fail to draw eyes, a strikingly beautiful woman going for her morning sip of the waters, who then changed her mind and decided to rest for a while on a garden bench, taking the sun, while she read her book. The King's party emerged. Maxine knew several of them already—Colonel Fritz Ponsonby, the Honourable Sidney Greville, and Captain Seymour Fortescue—accompanying their 'friend' on a morning walk. Her eyes were bent on her book. As the party drew level she merely lifted them, offering the full velvet impact of the midnight eyes which seemed to combine depths of melancholy with a sunny sparkle. The King spoke to one of the gentlemen; heads were drawn together; the party continued down the hill, but one of the number had detached himself and stood doffing his hat in front of Maxine.

'His Majesty believes you are the Miss Elliott he admired so much in your play.' Maxine bowed graciously. 'His Majesty would be delighted with your presence tonight for dinner. Mrs. Arthur James is giving a dinner in His Majesty's honour. Seven-forty-five at the Weimar Hotel. Your invitation will of course be delivered at your hotel.'

It seemed almost too easy. Maxine went home, rested, dressed her hair, put on her most lovely dress. Across the courtyard she could watch the arrivals of the carriages. The invitation had not arrived. She sat perfectly dressed, brushed, and discreetly made up, concealed behind the curtain, watching and waiting. At last the hour had passed when the King must have entered Mrs. James's suite. Maxine continued to sit without moving.

Inside the suite the new-fashioned cocktails were passed. The butler bowed to Mrs. James. She asked His Majesty to be kind enough to lead her guests in to dinner.

'But I'm waiting for Miss Elliott,' he said.

Maxine saw the footman dashing across the courtyard with a large white envelope. Mrs. James was tragically crying that the invitation to Miss Elliott must have dropped behind her desk. Without hurry Maxine accepted the card, drew on her wrap, and walked behind the escorting footman to the Weimar Hotel. She was graciousness itself; she never allowed it to show for a second that she was perfectly aware that Mrs. James had attempted to defy the King by diplomatically forgetting the invitation. She was charming; utterly at ease, she

chatted with His Majesty, who insisted that dinner should
wait while Miss Elliott was allowed her cocktail. He did not
sit down, nor could she. Nor could anyone else. For twenty
minutes the party was held on its feet, nervously watching a
sign from the King.

'My feet were killing me,' said Maxine later. 'But I sus-
pected everyone else's were, too.'

In later years my sister Blossom asked Aunt Maxine how
she could have tolerated the humiliation of waiting fully
dressed for an invitation that did not come. The Forbes-
Robertson girls hotly agreed they would rather have died—
we would have torn off our dresses and firmly set about washing our hair. Maxine's answer was simple.

'But I wanted to be there.'

This whole account is Maxine's own. It may betray some
of her capacity to romanticize her life, but thus she liked to
tell of her meeting with the King. Meet him indeed she did
that summer in Marienbad—a charming faded photograph
shows them together, in a party, the King in a Tyrolean hat,
Maxine leaning upon her folded parasol.

There was no possibility of hostesses' excluding Miss
Elliott now. She attended dinners; she went for drives in the
dark Bavarian woods. Everyone noticed that she had the
power to make the King laugh. It was decided that 'darling
Maxine' was definitely an asset. The interlude ended. The
King begged for exact information about her new theatre—
like Mr. Morgan, he enjoyed hearing about the quantities of
bathrooms. He returned to the affairs of state, and Maxine
returned to her theatre, her tour, then England again. Proudly
she returned in the summer of 1909, not as a woman awaiting
the King's pleasure, but as an actress, to appear in London in
The Conquest; she seemed to be asserting her right as a professional woman.

After its failure she returned to Marienbad in August, and
once more was seen as the constant companion of the Monarch.

Perhaps the King hinted that he might be denied the
pleasure of her company on returning to England if she was
in a hotel or too conspicuous in a London house. The time
had come for another English country home. She quickly

bought one; it was Lord Poltimore's estate, Hartsbourne
Manor, at Bushey Heath, Hertfordshire, less than an hour
from the heart of London. After getting the workmen busy on
a winter's project of alterations, she returned to New York
and touring till her first successful season in *The Inferior Sex*
(1909–10) could be closed. The house progressed well. Her
deft, clear planning of precisely what she wanted was becoming a practised art. Even the Forbes-Robertson nurseries (not
requested by either Forbie or Gertrude and reluctantly submitted to by Nonny) were ready long before any exodus to
country visiting could be expected from London society.

The house was pleasing and unpretentious, its large veran-
das hung with wisteria; Maxine had learned a great deal since
the days when she and Nat had indulged in manorial décor.
It was exquisitely comfortable, light, and airy; the furniture
was of the type Maxine always preferred—of the modern,
fashionable, but tastefully modified. The guest rooms were
well provided with bathrooms. There was central heating,
American comfort of a kind rare in England; no one was
going to freeze to death going to the bathroom, there would
be enough for everyone; there would be no period quaintness.
Her builders had a delightful time running up bills on all the
alterations she required for widened cupboards, fitted shelves,
and enough light, but decorators and sellers of rare antiques
were disappointed.

One feature at Hartsbourne was remarkable. Maxine's own
bedroom, boudoir, and bathroom opened onto a discreet side
corridor on the ground floor, and also through a door from
the formal white and gold drawing room, seldom used. It gave
Maxine completely private quarters, with a view onto rolling
lawns and meadows beyond. Near the door that led to her
bedroom was a very small stairway, easily overlooked by the
guests who used the generously curving main staircase that
led to the floor above; the private staircase led to her maid's
room immediately above Maxine's bathroom, or could be
used equally well by the occupant of the large corner bedroom over the area of Maxine's bedroom and boudoir. This
upper suite was referred to as 'the King's'.

Early in April the King sent word that he would like to
be shown Miss Elliott's new house and was coming down

privately, accompanied simply by a valet and one equerry—a
visit that could be called entirely secret, since it excluded
social companions. Constance Collier was staying alone with
Maxine; they were having a comfortable woman's party,
relaxed in old wrappers, while the finishing touches to the
house were being supervised. In consternation Maxine showed
the King's letter to Constance.

'He can't do this to me,' she raged. 'He'll ruin my reputation.'

'You can't say no to the King,' said Constance.

'But I'm going to.'

With the utmost care Maxine worded a letter of respectful
reproach that he should consider compromising her position
by arriving alone. She begged him to send her a list of friends
and it would be her honour to entertain them.

The days went by and no answer came from the King.
Constance felt that Maxine had risked being thrown into the
Tower of London; Maxine shrugged her shoulders and said
that if the gamble lost she would return to the United States.
She had no doubt of her own rights. He was seeking to treat
her like a clandestine mistress after she had been publicly
entertained by him and his friends. She refused now to be
shoved aside as a convenience. Either she was an accepted
member of the society in which he moved or she would leave
England forever. As time passed it seemed impossible that the
King would forgive a woman who had openly turned him
down. Maxine's rooms were filled with open trunks and tissue
paper, while her maid fussed from cupboard to cupboard. She
reserved passage on a steamer to New York.

Then the answer came. Without comment the King accepted
her terms; he named a week-end and enclosed a list of friends
he considered pleasant company for a Saturday-to-Monday
visit. If his temper had first overwhelmed him, admiration for
Maxine's good sense made him admit that she had roundly
caught him out on his own well-known insistence on correct
protocol. If people were fooled into believing the Monarch
was so relaxed in the intimacy of his own group that he would
forget proper behaviour, there was usually an instantaneous
reprimand and sometimes an irreparable dismissal. An evening could be gay and casual, but the man who came incorrectly

dressed was pounced on at once; anyone who had received a number of honorary decorations and dared to pick and choose among them on a formal occasion was scolded for discourtesy to a people, and their Monarch, who had offered those recognitions. At one impromptu Sunday night party in London the King accosted the Duchess of Marlborough for failing to wear a tiara—'Queen Alexandra has taken the trouble to do so, and why couldn't you?' Only grudgingly did he accept the Duchess's explanation that her tiaras were locked in the bank on a Sunday, and that she had rushed from Blenheim at his command hoping that an arrangement of diamond pins that decked her hair would cover her nakedness.

Maxine had, in fact, behaved like a perfect lady who knew the rules precisely. She had shown herself proud and jealous of her position, and courageous enough to defend it. Her letter had been couched in the right language. She had followed the Monarch's rule, 'Do it the right way'—a phrase that had become usual when she spoke of how to conduct oneself in the eyes of the world.

Hartsbourne was put into a turmoil of preparation. Maxine selected menus and wines, briefed the servants, loaded the house with flowers; guest rooms were prepared, with rooms for valets and ladies' maids and special detectives. During the week a rumour came that the King had a bad bronchial attack; a last-minute postponement was thought possible, because his excess weight did not allow him to take risks. Further rumours came that the King was up again and at work in his private office. A week-end in the country might be precisely what was needed to restore him to good health, especially in congenial company and the glorious month of May.

Early one morning in May 1910, as Nonny was giving the children their breakfast, in the nursery (there were three Forbes-Robertson girls now, since Chloe had been born the spring before) she heard running feet in the passage. One of the maids came bursting through the door.

'Nurse, Nurse,' she said, goggle-eyed, 'the King's dead. He died last night. The news's just came.'

'Well,' said Nonny, always dry and unexcited, 'that'll put an end to *her* plans.'

So King Edward VII never occupied the royal suite at
Hartsbourne Manor. The party was cancelled, of course, but
the friends who had been invited remained her friends. The
social blessing given by him when he accepted her invitation
assured her position. She wore deep black for him, as did
all women in England; in her case, the gesture was probably
more than the correct thing to do, because the King had fulfilled completely her dreams of what a royal personage should
be like. He appealed to her, as he did to the mass of the
British people, a man with cheerful, big appetites and complete dignity, a touch of Renaissance grandeur left in the
modern world. In later years if Maxine said 'the King', there
was no doubt which monarch she meant, although three more
succeeded him during her lifetime. His photograph in a silver
frame was always upon the piano, and when much later his
grandson, the Duke of Windsor, cried, 'Oh, do come and
look, Wallis, here's a terribly funny picture of Grandpapa,'
Maxine's face darkened with disapproval. Even a member of
the royal house could be allowed no word of disparagement
of the Monarch.

13

HARTSBOURNE

K ING EDWARD VII died in 1910, but the Edwardian
world continued until the outbreak of war in 1914.
He left his friends as a legacy to Maxine, and a great
life began in the house he never saw. Maxine made no
deliberate attempt to be a political hostess. The pretensions of
Hartsbourne were not those of the great houses devoted to the
meeting of the governing classes in private surroundings for
the purpose of government; it even came as a surprise to
her friends that she made public appearances for women's
suffrage. Maxine enjoyed the company of intelligent, well-
bred, positive men who could talk well. She enjoyed the
company of good-looking women. She loved to combine personalities—the special pleasure of the pure hostess; the
knowledge that a successful party had resulted was the only
reward. If some understanding took place between two men
in power, and a law was passed, a question asked in the
House, a job passed on to the right man, and she knew that
it had come about under her roof, it was a special pride to her.
It was not done from conviction; she made no attempt to
play politics. What she cared about was the interplay of people
served by the comforts she offered.

Maxine found her level in the world among people who
enjoyed politics, business, and the social life. She felt safer
in the clear-cut lines of these worlds; the climate of the artist
made her uncomfortable. The artist would often be included,
but he was always an additional and passing element. Mr.
Henry James sauntered in and out of that world, observing,
never part of it; because Mr. James dealt in words, and their
subtleties, in the end Maxine pronounced him a bore. He
probed too deeply, he deliberated, he refused to skim. The

world which Maxine adopted, and which adopted her, always
looked upon artists as interesting specimens, collector's items,
and they were never truly accepted. Neither did the artist
care to dally too long. Two divergent types of people viewed
each other and saw what temporary amusement could be
gained, and then returned to their own.

Maxine adored intellect but loathed intellectuals who did
not conform to her ideal of dress and behaviour. The crumpled
knees on Sir James Barrie's trousers were as irritating to her
as his long silences when he failed to 'pull his weight' at the
dinner table. The artist or intellectual who brooded upon the
state of the world and let his anxiety show was not 'amusing';
the man who ran things, who talked vividly about great events,
was the one who made a party go. There must be lively, lovely
women as well to stimulate the men to compete with one
another in wit. The solid rocks on which a successful party
was based were the purely social people, the ones who could
be counted on to dress right, keep it all going, while the high
points were provided by the men of special brilliance. Because
of her preferences for men of action, and because of the people
she had met in the King's group, and the men who urged
political leadership on Lord Rosebery, her chief lions were
men of governmental power, or those in opposition. Thus
Hartsbourne had some semblance of a political salon without
being planned for that reason. The purpose of week-ends at
Hartsbourne was to have fun.

It must be admitted there was also plain, simple, classic
snobbery. Maxine's was on a childish level. She liked the
sound of titles; my father's remark, 'Your aunt dearly loves a
lord,' was a simple statement of the truth. So at Hartsbourne
the titles abounded; they were carried sometimes by men who
bore the responsibility of the country on their shoulders and
sometimes by playboys. Maxine believed profoundly in the
mystique of privilege—'It opens doors.' If a doorman was
more attentive to someone he addressed as 'my lord' than to
someone whose name meant nothing to him, she felt that there
was obvious advantage in the fact of lordship. She was not so
foolish as to think titles the only bringers of privilege; she
knew that Mr. J. P. Morgan's name spelled more concentrated
power than the entire British aristocracy put together; she

knew that a tall New Zealander with the simple name of Tony
Wilding was a personage the world sought because that year
he had won the men's singles in tennis at Wimbledon; she
knew that Claude Grahame-White, a rough man with none
of the shiny table manners she demanded of those invited for
the purpose of employing them, gave her house prestige
because he landed on her meadow in his cracker-barrel aero-
plane. People must make some offering to the gaiety of things.

No house party at Hartsbourne was without a properly
matched bridge four, and tennis players who could give each
other a game. The order of the day was playing games, no
sitting around in endless world-planning discussions. The
tennis courts must be used, and those who wanted golf could
go over to the club and play it, and those who wanted walks
could walk, and those who wanted to drive or ride or swim
could do so; then, when the changing bell had rung, everyone must disappear and adorn themselves beautifully to make
the dining table glitter. And at table let the men talk. Let them
be witty; let them fight with words; let them be funny (and
they had better be as funny as Nat had been) . . . and after
dinner there was bridge.

The pattern suited a quantity of people. The mid-weeks,
when Maxine stayed comfortably on her own (or with a
woman companion for cards), were kept busy with the making
out of lists to fit in all the people who wanted to come, to
juggle dates, to put the right ingredients together during the
June, July, or August week-ends. There were fewer house rules
at Hartsbourne than at other established week-end houses.
Maxine herself was appalled when she was forced to play intellectual paper-and-pencil games at The Wharf, the house of
the Prime Minister, Mr. Asquith, and his wife, Margot Ten-
nant. She equally resented being forced to listen to chamber
music, being sent to bed too early or kept up too late, or being
prevented from smoking when and where she wanted. Within
reason, people could do what they liked at Hartsbourne. She
did not encourage excessive drinking, but if F. E. Smith (later
Lord Birkenhead) had been on the wagon too long and was
disgruntled and unamusing on a diet of ginger ale, she preferred to avert her eyes when Doulton, the butler, took extra
supplies of liquor to his room. She had little use for acting

games or charades, but if they happened from time to time they must be amusing and everyone must behave like sports— no shynesses, no 'Oh, no, I couldn't possibly'. Winston Churchill was permitted to disrupt a charade in the large central hall, where the party usually gathered after dinner, because his impersonation of a bear underneath a bear rug was so hilarious (especially as it had nothing to do with the syllable to be acted). She liked positive fun—no one getting too earnest or wanting to talk too much; no one misbehaving publicly; no one being stuffy, either. Pomposity was permitted Lord Curzon, but he had the magical right of privilege, even if some people were stifling yawns; melancholia was permitted Lord Rosebery, who had been her first mentor in the privileges of aristocracy. People could come to Hartsbourne and feel they were permitted to do as they pleased (if they did not fit the Hartsbourne pattern they simply were not invited), in comfort that seemed casual (carefully planned and prepared); no wonder it was a house of popularity.

Maxine later always referred to the years from 1910 to 1914 as 'the great days at Hartsbourne'. She meant by this the time when certain people were available—the leaders of Government and Opposition, and younger men such as Sir Robert Vansittart and Sir Archibald Sinclair; there were foreign diplomats, especially the Portuguese Ambassador, M. de Soveral, who was the chief favourite in London society for many years; there were the great aristocrat the Duke of Rutland and his brilliant artist wife, with their daughters, Ladies Lettice, Marjorie, and Diana Manners, still quite young, but beautiful; there were the Earl of Drogheda and his dashing wife Kathleen, a pioneer aviatrix. Among these people were some exceptional social triumphs for Maxine; to have got the Duke of Rutland from Belvoir was looked upon as a major miracle; to catch Lord Rosebery on one of his lonely hops from estate to estate was a coup. To mix the ageing and distinguished and powerful with the young, vivid, and active was her special gift.

Maxine was now totally sure of herself. She had learned and watched and knew all the ways of the world. Within this knowledge she could relax. She allowed her original directness to return, and her friends found it an added delight. She could startle with a quick, frank comment. As an American learning to get into this society she had muted herself; now she gave herself full play. The accepted person can be as different as he pleases, and everyone only appreciates him more. It was the lady-like grandeur and the blunt tongue which gave her a special vintage tang, especially attractive to the men of ancient aristocracy who could feel that here was the very embodiment of the vigorous young world, who also knew and respected their rules.

With due thought, and conscious of the honour he was conferring, Lord Curzon, recently a widower and ex-Viceroy of India, a man who confidently expected to be Prime Minister when his party returned to power, decided that this splendidly beautiful foreigner had all the manners of the ruling classes and would be a most fitting consort. (His first wife had been an American, so the thought was acceptable.) He offered her his hand in marriage. He was astonished to be politely refused. The rumour spread and even reached the newspapers; Gertrude, on tour in America, cabled Maxine to ask if the engagement was true. Maxine cabled back, 'I would not marry God.' Melville Stone of the Associated Press begged for confirmation or denial, and in her cable to him she said, 'I have honourable intentions towards no man.'

Her refusal to marry Lord Curzon at a time when her divorce from Nat was two years behind, when she believed she had abandoned the theatre for good, shows Maxine in a very special light. It means that her fascination with titles, or the great estates of Lord Curzon and his possible political power, was not her determining motive. She did not want any of the privileges of life handed to her. She had worked hard enough to become a person in her own right, not needing dependence on male privilege, and she would give it to nobody. She had made a similar decision when she was far less sure of herself, with Lord Rosebery. George Nathaniel Curzon (was she put off because he carried the names of both her husbands?) was a man of such overwhelming self-esteem that marriage to him would not have been ideal, but Maxine undoubtedly had long since stopped believing in an ideal marriage. She wished to live as if she were a man.

Maxine returned to America once during the pre-war years

to finish her engagement in *The Inferior Sex*. She was in England again by the spring of 1911 and remained with Hartsbourne as her base, often leaving it to go jaunting on the Continent with friends, but not again to New York. Maxine Elliott's Theatre ran smoothly. Inquiries made on Broadway about the star's own plans for next season received a non-committal reply from her manager, George Appleton. 'I don't know when she's coming back. I don't think she's found a play that suits her.' She had made no final decision; perhaps some fascinating play might lure her back, that was all she would say. Her interest in theatrical doings was absorbed by Gertrude's career, and by the box-office take of her own theatre.

Considerable thought had to be given to Gertrude's future, because Forbie had firmly announced that he was mortally tired and wanted retirement. He saw his sixtieth birthday looming ahead of him, in January 1913. This was the date he wished to set himself. An outcry came from his London and American managers and he compromised; he would announce his retirement and play for the last time in England during 1913, and then would consent to devote two more years to a farewell tour of the whole United States. Letters came begging him to come to this city, not to forget that city, so in gratitude to the public of America he promised to go to as many as he could and say his personal good-byes. By that time he would be sixty-two, with a career of forty-two years in the theatre behind him; he felt it was enough. He had never loved acting passionately enough to feel he could not bear to let it go. His thoughts were not unlike Maxine's. 'Never at any time have I gone on the stage without longing for the moment when the curtain would come down on the last act. Rarely, very rarely have I enjoyed myself in acting. This cannot be the proper mental attitude for an actor, and I am persuaded, as I look back on my career, that I was not temperamentally suited for my calling.' He was proud enough, too, to wish to give up with his powers still unimpaired; ahead he saw a time when he could sit at home, enjoy his children, read, read, read, and return to his first love, painting pictures.

Forbie was entirely aware that this withdrawal into private

Photo : Radio Times Hulton Picture Library

LORD CURZON

life was coming much too soon for his wife. Before the precise plans were laid for his farewell to England and then to America, while all was still in the discussion stage, a suggestion came from Maxine that she and Lee Shubert should back Gertrude for a trial run by herself. Some interesting plays were available; *Rebellion* by Joseph Medill Patterson (later creator of the New York *Daily News*); *The Dawn of To-morrow* by Frances Hodgson Burnett and *Preserving Mr. Panmure* by Arthur Wing Pinero. Gertrude split off from the Forbes-Robertson company for the first time since 1900 and tried her luck alone in 1910, 1911, and 1912. Her success was respectable, but other plays would have to be sought. She would join Forbie for his farewell appearance, and later she must follow her career alone.

Perhaps Maxine did not want to find a play for herself. Perhaps the unknown element which prevented playwrights from offering her plays and which may have also defeated Lord Curzon, was the New Zealand tennis champion, Anthony Wilding. He was as much a fixture at Hartsbourne as the political and social guests during the summer months of 1910 to 1914—a tall, blond young man whom Maxine watched when he won in 1910 and promptly asked to meet. The 'man of the hour' was always fascinating to Maxine, and there in the sunlight on the Centre Court at Wimbledon Tony was the focal point of all eyes; he had won the men's doubles with Norman Brookes; he had won the mixed doubles with Mrs. Lambert Chambers; and now he had the final title for himself alone. She invited him to come to Hartsbourne and give some advice on her courts.

It would be easy for the world to laugh and say of course a wealthy woman of forty-two might like having a handsome athlete as her constant escort, and for a while he too might find the arrangement convenient. But it seems there was no element in Tony Wilding's character which could possibly be twisted into the attitude of a gigolo; he was, on the accounts of many men and women who knew him, a person they can find only one word to fit: a pure man. He was clean, he was innocent, he was knightly. He moved about in a highly sophisticated society and smiled benignly upon it, neither adopting its ways nor censuring them. There is always a slight note of

15

wonder in people's voices when they remember Tony Wilding. There must have been wonder in Maxine, too, when she
found a man who looked straight through her veneer. He
never used her; he never abused her or turned on her. It
seems he loved her deeply. His capacity for love had not been
damaged and he gave it simply. Maxine, who had been
through so many disappointments, may never have quite
dared love him as much as he loved her. If Tony Wilding had
been George MacDermott (but Jessie Dermot might not have
been content with a simple man), perhaps no such person as
Maxine Elliott would ever have been invented. Whatever
existed between Maxine at forty-two and Tony at twenty-
seven, it was the best she had during her lifetime.

Tony's presence at Hartsbourne was, of course, remarked
and commented upon. Society thrived on gossip. Nothing
that Maxine allowed herself in this most worldly aspect of
her life was done in an untidy or unbecoming manner; if
Maxine and Tony were lovers, as the world supposed, there
would never be concrete proof. Tony was one of the men who
came to stay in the house, and he had a room on the floor
above Maxine's suite; nothing more could be said. 'Mr. Wilding's room' was, however, the charming, dormered room next
in line down the corridor from 'the King's room'; the small
private staircase was not too many steps away. Beyond him
was the Forbes-Robertsons' suite; they were not going to
sneak open their doors at night to see if anyone had walked
down the corridor. The rest of the guest rooms continued
down a long passage on the opposite side of the house from
Maxine's own. It was convenient, but it was not obvious.

In public they were affectionate; Tony made no secret of
his admiration for Maxine's beauty nor she of her wonder at
his brilliance on the tennis court. He laughed at the way she
showed him off, always wanting him to be admired, and he
obliged with grace, never crumbling into shyness at having to
make an exhibition. Maxine always did this to her own—Nat
must tell his funny stories; Gertrude must sing her 'coon'
songs. If Maxine could she would have made Forbie recite,
but she never broke his resistance. Tony had confidence because his gifts were those produced by co-ordination and training and did not depend upon the nervous system, except in

championship tennis. If it pleased Maxine to have him go
on to her tennis court to be admired by her guests, he did it
willingly; anyway, he enjoyed playing tennis. He also asserted
his authority; determined that she should not let herself get
fat, he relentlessly prodded her onto the court, never without
some admonition about her smoking. He admitted her fore-
hand drive was a demon but remarked that the opponent's
ball was not always going to land obligingly in its range—
'Max, you must *run*.' So notably did he improve her game
that they sometimes played in amateur championships together. In a match at Muswell Hill, where Tony 'carried' his
partner Maxine against Mrs. Lambert Chambers (women's
singles champion), who 'carried' the Honourable Arthur Balfour, it was the Wilding-Elliott combination that triumphed.

Tony Wilding was the healthiest man for Maxine in every
way. He was busy about his own life, so he never tried to
force himself on her. Sometimes he would be away for long
periods, when he and Norman Brookes went to Australia to
defend the Davis Cup against the American team. He played
in matches all over the Continent, whizzing off on his motor
bike. There were times when Maxine went to watch; she was
present when he won the men's singles on hard court in Paris;
she watched him through a week of matches at Nice. When
they travelled, it was not as a pair; she would turn up with a
bunch of tennis enthusiasts to watch him play, and after the
matches spectators and players joined parties wherever special
friendships lay. The only thing noticeable to the public eye
was that Tony Wilding always joined Maxine and her friends,
although he had friends everywhere eager to snare him. The
freedom that his power gave him seemed to release him altogether from resentment of Maxine's extreme sociability; the
men who admired her, of far greater worldly distinction than
himself, never caused Tony to make scenes. Of course, the
world watched them and speculated. Was this a relationship
that did not run very deep, a convenience that happened
to be charming just for that particular week? Was there a
confidence between them so total that they trusted each other
without question? The reports of observers to whom I have
been able to talk all said precisely the same thing: between
Maxine and Tony Wilding there was real devotion. The most

eagerly malicious of women, who shall be nameless, was unable to add a single sly suggestion. Lady Churchill said, 'Tony
Wilding was always so very good to Maxine, and he took
such care of her'—not the sort of thing said about a handsome
man who is attached to a woman fifteen years his senior and
a thousand times wealthier. Lady Portarlington said, 'Tony
simply adored Maxine,' and Lady Drogheda said, 'Maxine
simply adored Tony.' Gertrude, who would never have said
anything of an intimate nature about Maxine to me of the
younger generation, simply smiled and said, 'Oh, what a dear
Tony was,' and Forbes-Robertson said, 'Tony Wilding was a
great gentleman.' My sister Blossom, who was a small girl in
those Hartsbourne days, frankly worshipped him and remembers his hours of patient coaching on the tennis court, as he
bent his great height to adjust her grip on the racquet.

Whatever this romance meant to Maxine emotionally, it
did not change the pattern of her living. She gave her parties,
she went to parties. Tony was simply part of it on his own
terms. Perhaps the echo he set up in her was of a competent
and loving brother, the kind she never had. Tony was like
a young American; when the motor cars went wrong and
Gwatkin, the perspiring chauffeur in splendid sergeant's moustache, puffed over the snorts from the De Dion's engine, it
was Tony who lay on his back underneath the car and adjusted
it. Maxine loved this physical ability to cope with a situation
(her other men had been the kind who crippled themselves
if they touched a hammer). There was an expression of
contentment on her face, and a serene pleasure in 'leaving it
to Tony', when she and Tony, driving with Frank Myers
(a tennis expert) and his wife, found the Gerald du Mauriers
in a stalled taxi on the road to Hartsbourne where they were
bound for the week-end. Maxine's car stopped when she
spotted her guests in trouble, the ladies moved over to make
room for the du Mauriers while Tony got out on the dark road,
to fix the trouble. He and the hapless driver followed them
down later. Tony refused supper in the dining room, arranged
by Maxine after midnight, to spend another hour with the
driver, making sure the car was in running order.

*

The year 1913 brought some changes. (There was no change in Tony's pattern; he won the singles championship again, as he had in 1910, 1911, and 1912. Maxine, however, had allowed herself to be lured back into the theatre. It did not mean leaving England, and this was probably the reason she accepted the offer. Sir Herbert Beerbohm Tree (another new theatrical knight) was going to present a play already performed in New York, *Joseph and His Brethren*, by Louis Napoleon Parker, and he wanted Maxine to appear as the sensuous, vengeful Zuleika, wife to the Pharaoh Potiphar. Tree's theatre, His Majesty's, was one of the finest in London (when Sir Squire Bancroft saw it he shook his head—'A great many windows to wash'); his productions were always the most lavish. Possibly Tony talked her into it; she had sat in the spectators' seats so often to watch him perform, now why couldn't he have a chance to applaud her from the audience? The fussing on costumes began. Hartsbourne had professional visitors again; Brandon Tynan, who had played 'Joseph' in New York, came to give her some tips on Oriental seduction, although in London his part was to be played by George Relph; dressmakers came and went.

The Forbes-Robertsons were playing at the Drury Lane. For a limited season they would give all Forbie's most beloved plays and then say good-bye to London. Articles appeared in the papers demanding to know why this splendid actor had to withdraw from the scene so soon. The houses were packed every night, and there were always tears. Finally official public tribute came to Forbes-Robertson. A knighthood was to be conferred upon him in the 'Birthday Honours', always announced in June. Little Gertrude had brought home to Maxine a title for her own family; as the wife of Sir Johnston she would now be Lady Forbes-Robertson. Doulton, Maxine's butler, usually so suave that he seemed embalmed, stuttered with pleasure as he piled on the 'ladyships', dangerous for Gertrude with her tendency to giggle. On the final night at Drury Lane Maxine, gorgeous in a box, threw all control to the winds and openly sobbed as Forbie was drawn by a weeping, cheering audience to walk up and down the aisles of the auditorium, clasping the hands of old friends. Gertrude was buried in flowers, and the make-up streamed from her face. Whatever ducal honours Maxine may have wanted in the past for Gertrude, nothing better than this could have crowned her marriage and working career; Maxine's laughter and tears for her little sister on this night of triumph gave her one of the moments of pure joy in her life. With maternal pride she swept the Forbes-Robertsons and their friends away to supper, where demonstrations in the restaurant continued until they all went home exhausted and joyously united.

Maxine kissed Gertrude and Forbie good-bye for their departure to New York, and prepared for rehearsals on *Joseph and His Brethren*.

Tony had to play a match in Sweden, but he got back on the opening night. 'Maxine is acting in *Joseph* and I arrived in London just in time to see some of the first night, and am going to see it all through in a few minutes again,' he wrote to a friend, on September 3, 1913.

On September 8 Maxine wrote to George Tyler, the theatrical manager: "Apparently the play is a colossal success and we are all delighted, of course, but I can't help a sneaking feeling of regret for the lost peace and quiet of my country life. I am told they are having a record sale at His Majesty's, so we are in for a run and I shall have to move into town as soon as the rain sets in for a steady diet, but I think I should be perfectly happy never to see a city again. What demon is it that will never let us vegetate long in peace?'

Joseph and His Brethren ran for a hundred and fifty-four performances. Maxine looked splendid in the shimmering draperies and chunks of barbaric jewellery, but she did not feel happy in the semi-poetic style of the drama. Even when rehearsing in her library at Hartsbourne with Brandon Tynan, she had been embarrassed when he dramatically recoiled from her, crying, 'Away, my senses reel.' Such goings-on struck the funny bone of a girl from Rockland. The production was full of the usual hazards of a Tree presentation; a camel had to be cut out because the girth of its saddle never seemed secure enough to make Maxine feel happy perched on its back. (The animal is also reported to have bitten her and was therefore fired, but I know she liked the camel a good deal better than some of the actors.) There was a herd of goats—the Israelites' flock—which rushed madly onto the stage, often leaving hard pellet-like droppings on which the barefoot actors slipped and slid. It was a production of such opulence that disasters were bound to happen, causing hysterical giggles in the cast. Maxine was glad when it closed, but for her it had been a dignified and splendid appearance, something good to remember after the fiasco of *The Conquest*.

She returned happily to Hartsbourne, relieved that the public notice was over. She was not left alone for long, however, because suddenly now the newspapers took notice of her frequent appearances in the same places as Tony Wilding. Announcements appeared that they had been secretly married in Nice. 'Nonsense,' they both declared roundly.

Fat tears of despair rolled down Maxine's face as she saw Tony beaten for the first time in the men's singles at Wimbledon in 1914. It did not seem possible. Lady Drogheda, who was seated beside her, clutching her hand, said Maxine shook with sobs and before the dreadful final point was scored grunted deep inside herself with each ball hit. Tony was badly off his game. No one was worried at first, because he was a notably slow starter who often let slip the early games in a set, only to catch up and destroy his opponent when he had found his right rhythm. His friend and doubles partner, Norman Brookes, now his opponent, was so surprised at winning the first set 'that his racquet shook like a butterfly net' reported *The Times*. Tony lost the second set, and a muffed hit by Brookes half off the wood of his racquet somehow got past Tony onto the back line and gave Brookes also the final set. Tony was the only calm person at the Centre Court as he walked back, his arm round Brookes' shoulder, laughing with him over that rotten last stroke, and went to have tea in the pavilion with Arthur Balfour while Maxine put her tear-stained face back in order.

Perhaps Tony's concentration had been wandering and his earnest seriousness about the game shattered by all the talk he heard in the political circles that gathered at Maxine's house. There was grave fear of the warlike intention of the German Kaiser, which only a small incident could puff up into an opportunity to fight England. Then on the day Wimbledon opened came the news of the Archduke Ferdinand's assassination at Sarajevo. Some said it would all blow over. . . . A serious man such as Tony, who had adopted England as his home since the days when he had come over from New Zealand to enter Cambridge, would be deeply aware that perhaps ahead of him lay the urgent necessity to bear arms. He was booked to sail for America, where the Davis Cup tournament was to be played that year. Should he or should he not go? There were anxious consultations with all the friends. What did Winston think? What did F.E. think? Everyone advised that the best thing to do was the normal thing . . . go on with what you were going to do as planned. Perhaps this was like the Agadir Crisis in 1911 . . . a moment of intense danger which would pass.

Weeks of agonized rumour went by in glorious weather. Maxine's most faithful week-end guests were largely unavailable. There was not a man who was not part of the frantic efforts during the month of July either to prevent war or to plan war. Winston was at the Admiralty. Kathleen Drogheda could report on the intense anxiety of Sir Edward Grey at the Foreign Office, where her husband served as an under-secretary. Government and Opposition men were approaching each other. 'In the event, are you prepared . . .' 'What will the Irish do?'

Maxine's total identification with these last days of peace in England made her as one with the whole anxious public of the island. What America was thinking she neither thought nor cared. She was English in passion at this moment, feeling for Winston in his long nights in the Admiralty, consulting with all her women friends—'How can we help?' Only the thought that Tony could not be back for another six weeks turned her thoughts away from the immediate scene. In the noble, clear-cut days that existed before two world wars her anxiety for him was that if war came Tony might get stuck. 'He'd go mad if he couldn't get into khaki at once.'

Tony was involved in a curious side issue of international passions. Tony and Norman Brookes in the Davis Cup semi-finals were matched against the German team, playing in Pittsburgh before a passionately pro-German crowd. On July 31 the Australasians became the unpopular winners in a match that was over so soon that the committee organized an exhibition match the following day to give the people their

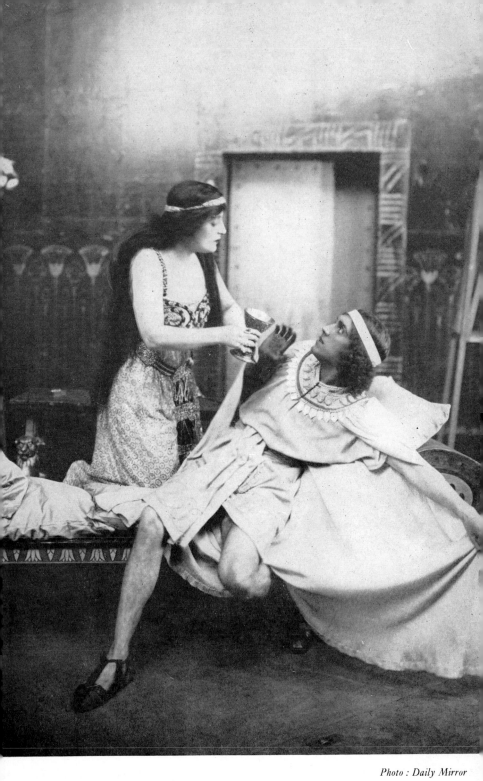

MAXINE TEMPTING GEORGE RELPH IN *JOSEPH AND HIS BRETHREN*

MAXINE LOADING THE BARGE

Photo : Alfieri

SIR ARCHIBALD
SINCLAIR AND
WINSTON CHURCHILL

MAXINE AND LADY DROGHEDA EMERGING FROM A DUGOUT

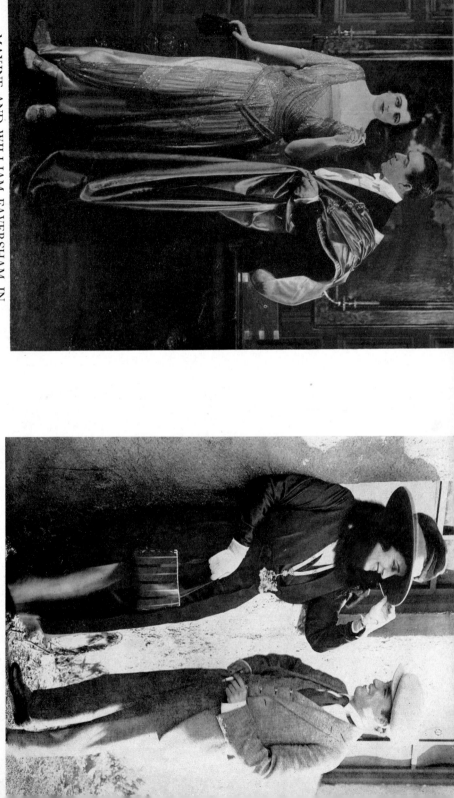

MAXINE AND WILLIAM FAVERSHAM IN *LORD AND LADY ALGY*

MAXINE WITH CHARLIE CHAPLIN

money's worth. Already Austria and Serbia were at war; already Germany and Russia had entered to support their committed sides. Feeling was running high, and the anti-British attitude of the crowd so incensed Tony and Norman that their victory was particularly crushing. The exhibition match just seemed an added torture to go through. It took place on August 1, another savage win for the Australasians; after the semblance of civilities had been exchanged over the net, as boos from the audience were ignored, the players suddenly found themselves rushed out of sight by members of the committee. The news had come through during the game that Germany had launched her attack on the West and had overrun Luxembourg. The Germans dashed to find passage to get back to the Fatherland. Britain was not yet committed; Tony and Norman were trapped by their own victory; they still had to go on to Forest Hills in New York for the semi-finals against the British which, when won, would bring them to the finals against the Americans. Before the long, hard-fought match against Maurice Evans ('Red') McLoughlin and R. Norris Williams was over the news had come that England was at war. As a last act of peacetime, the Australasians were determined to bring the Davis Cup back. They succeeded, and for the four years that cancelled championship tennis the Cup remained in Australia. They scrambled back as best they could, hilarious when they learned that their German opponents had been intercepted by a British destroyer and interned for the duration of the war.

Maxine spent the Bank Holiday week-end, when all England waited to know whether Britain would answer the appeals of the King of the Belgians, in the grip of national feeling. How could a friend of Winston's have felt any other way? Her most unwarlike brother-in-law, Forbes-Robertson, was racked with a similar agony. At Slaybrook, a rented house in Sandling, Kent, where he and Gertrude had returned for the summer with the children, he walked restlessly to and fro, to and fro, muttering, 'Asquith mustn't let them down.'

The solemn Tuesday of August 4 came, and Sir Edward Grey, the Foreign Minister, informed the House of Commons in long, measured terms of the reasons for war and listed all the attempts to prevent it. The last opposition crumbled.

Grey grieved, sitting sunk in his office; the small Monarch in his beard and Admiral's uniform came onto the balcony of Buckingham Palace to greet with sorrow a crowd roaring with excitement. There were tears shed that night, but the sound that swept all else before it in those days when wars seemed gallant were the cheers and cheers and cheers of people who thought it was the right and only thing.

Maxine left Hartsbourne immediately to harry and hound her friends to get her into active work. The Forbes-Robertson children watched the cavalry clattering nobly by for embarkation to France. Tony arrived back and went straight into the Royal Marines. It would all be over in a few weeks.

14

THE BARGE

NEARLY the whole of Belgium had fallen. The Allied Forces had indeed stopped the galloping German advance at the First Battle of the Marne, but had to abandon all hope of a quick and glorious victory. In lowlying, watery country the opposing armies dug themselves into trenches.

Maxine was at Hartsbourne, an empty, autumnal place; the guests were gone, and leaves were off the branches. It had been a shock to learn that an American, citizen of a country not at war, had no real place in the life of mobilized England. She felt as if she had been a mere peacetime luxury, enjoyed while the fun lasted, now unemployable. Her English friends had been faced with few choices; most of them had been snapped up into whatever war service their capacities suggested, and any who were still idly available made poor company. Her chosen friends, men of action, were the men the country needed. Of course she offered Hartsbourne immediately for any purpose it could serve—hospital, home for Belgian refugees. If someone accepted her offer it would be an easy matter to organize. Her desire for personal activity, however, was passionate.

She had hoped to find a place in the early plans of the Duchess of Sutherland, who wanted a fleet of ambulances. Soon it was obvious that professionals must take over. Maxine's donation of a fully equipped vehicle was gratefully accepted, but her own person was not necessary. She had, however, managed to obtain permission to visit France, convinced that once she got there she would find her place. She had friends in power who could grant her this favour and knew that Maxine was a sensible, courageous woman who would not make an unnecessary nuisance of herself.

She was able to get to Calais in October for the first time. The confusion of commands was hard to sort out. It was necessary to know which Allied group commanded which territory so she would know from whom to obtain a pass to see the people she wanted. The Duchess of Sutherland, operating a hospital at La Panne, and Tony Wilding, in charge of seventy armoured cars stationed near Marls-les-Bains, could both advise her. Just to remain at the Grand Hotel at Calais could also be useful; people flowed in and out there, and her ability to listen would gain her some understanding of the situation.

Of course, Maxine found a personal project almost at once. She went to Calais with that intention, and seldom had any plan of hers failed to materialize. In the great locked struggle of armies her idea might sound trivial, but Maxine recognized at once that a woman was largely unwelcome and therefore must find some modest thing she could offer (which only a woman could offer) in this male world of warfare. She saw that one small section of the civilian population was nobody's major concern, so she made it hers. These were people left in the thin slice of unoccupied Belgian territory who resisted evacuation (sometimes in hiding) in an obstinate peasant desire to stay where they belonged. It is possible that some buried Maine memory made Maxine know that her own people might behave precisely in this manner; an old recluse uncle in the woods would prefer to stay on his land even if it was ravaged. She learned there were pockets of people huddled in odd spots between the coast and the last remaining town of Belgium, Poperinghe. The Yser River wound through this country with canals that crossed it at many points, and all along were small villages, many half demolished by shells, where a tiny civilian population clung. Burgomasters came to plead for supplies for their people from government centres at Adinkirk and Dunkirk, but the requirements of the armies must be served first. When she said that she wanted to organize a means of getting supplies to these people—an entirely civilian operation for which she would personally raise the money—she was laughed at. The idea that any Allied commander would allow an American woman to go popping about roads that were under military control was ludicrous. 'Dear Maxine . . . she imagines herself driving about freely in her De Dion, with Gwatkin at the wheel.'

Thus she thought of a barge, the traditional means of transport of the Lowlands. Armoured cars and marching armies were not using the waterways. A floating supply depot could get near these tiny villages; it could even spy out a lonely farm inhabited by half-starved people; and surely it would not disrupt the action of war. In time, reluctantly, some people began to see the practicality of the idea, and challenged her further with the inevitable final phrase, 'But I don't see how it could be managed.'

Maxine figured out the series of steps necessary. She would get a large sum of her own money from America and with it she would buy or charter a barge; she had seen some lying idle in the docks at Calais. After this she would make a public appeal in England and America so that a steady supply of food and clothing could be obtained. If some steps could be accomplished, and people saw that she was serious, each obstacle in turn could be overcome.

Back in England she met with warm response. Lord North-cliffe promised to print an appeal in his newspaper; the American Ambassador, Walter Hines Page, agreed to detach some part of American relief supplies for her use; Lord Davenport, Chief of the Port of London Authority, believed space could be found for storage on the Surrey Docks before shipment across the Channel; Winston Churchill at the Admiralty assured her that freighters which took materials to France could be used for her purposes. The idea had taken form.

Meanwhile, Tom Chadbourne in New York had reluctantly sold out some stock for her. He arranged, too, since he could never stand against Maxine's commands, that Brown Brothers Bank would open a special account in the name of 'The Belgian Relief Barge'. British funds could be handled through Gertrude's bank.

Maxine returned to Calais, and there in the docks she found the barge *Julia*, a solid, serviceable hulk of three hundred tons and a hundred and fifty feet length. The owner felt himself lucky indeed to be able to sell her. Maxine's almost architectural knowledge of remodelling houses made it quite clear to her how the *Julia* could be converted to serve as a big storage unit with living quarters for herself and helpers, but the problem of finding workmen to do the job seemed insurmountable. There was not a workman in France who was not mobilized into the Army. Somehow she browbeat someone to give her a detachment of soldiers to put on the job.

Her appeal was printed in American and British newspapers—'This little corner where history is being made, where the work of the war is going on, is being overlooked' —with lists of the articles most needed: salt pork, bully beef, tinned butter, potatoes, rice, jams, chocolate, candles, matches, warm clothes, and shoes of all shapes and sizes.

The matter of personnel was important indeed. She meant to supervise the whole thing herself, but needed a team. There was no doubt about her maid, Fanny Vandystaedt . . . she was Belgian and burned to come, militantly ready. Two men could also be used who had found no place elsewhere— her butler Doulton, middle-aged and too portly to be called up; Gwatkin the chauffeur, an over-age Army sergeant. There was a woman she had seen at Red Cross headquarters, competent but not young, longing to serve, Miss Close, experienced in professional relief work, who was an ideal acquisition. There would be a Belgian skipper who knew the waterways, of course, and in time other local helpers might be found. Finally Maxine felt she needed a personal friend, someone with whom she could share the events of the day, but as she considered her Hartsbourne group she saw that most were in the thick of work or useless. Then an inspiration came: Kathleen Drogheda, the headstrong aviatrix, wife of the Earl of Drogheda at the Foreign Office, was a dynamo of energy. She had an almost giddy manner which deceived many, for it cloaked organizational competence, an adventurous spirit, and willingness to get down to scrub a floor. Kathleen joyously accepted. At some point the last member of the crew walked on board and sat down: Dinah, a Belgian barge-dog which saw a barge readying for departure and adopted it. The timing of Dinah's arrival supplied me with a nickname;

I was born the day after Christmas while Maxine was preparing final arrangements for France. When she came to see
her sister's new baby, Gertrude told her I would be christened
Diana. My aunt made two comments: 'You'll always call her
Dinah' and 'She looks Japanese'.

The year 1915 dawned with the Western war front little
changed since entrenched attrition had been adopted, and
early in January Maxine left for Calais prepared to begin
her operation. She had handfuls of permits and passes, but
she knew that many more were required. She had made great
progress toward an organization that could be presented as
workable. Now she was ready to perform her usual super-
visor's job when construction was going on to harry the workmen on the *Julia* till every last detail was in place. Miss Close
was her constant companion; Fanny, Doulton, and Gwatkin
were all in attendance now, with Kathleen on call when they
could actually move on board. She used the Grand Hotel in
Calais as operational headquarters. Word of Maxine's project
had begun to spread through the Allied commands. There
were friends from peacetime scattered all about, but most
helpful of all was Tony, because he had made her known to
his commanding officer, Commander Sansom of the Royal
Navy, for whom he operated the fleet of armoured cars. From
this source came the precious commodity, transportation.
Commander Sansom lent Maxine a car and driver, so that
when necessary she could visit officials stationed at various
places. The Belgian Premier, Charles de Broqueville, provided a precious blue pass which got her into Belgian territory.
She was many steps nearer her objective.

On the day she received her pass, January 13, 1915, which
meant a trip to Dunkirk, the city was bombed. German
Taubes flew over, causing wild excitement, but those were
not days of mass raids, and only one house was demolished.
It was Maxine's first direct experience of the killing side of
war. She had seen troops marching bedraggled and weary
from duty in the trenches, and others marching out to replace
them, she had heard gunfire; she had seen flashes in the sky;
she saw the wounded brought in off hospital trains, and civilian
victims of war were everywhere. But here was a death-dealing
weapon doing the job. Thoughts of who would or would not

survive this slaughter were uppermost in her mind that day
(often, amidst officialdom, inconvenience, and endless attention to detail, she could push the ultimate fear from her
mind). She did not know, however, till much later that on
that very day her father Captain Dermot was lying still and
waxen in the parlour of the Oakland house, his face in death
like that of Roman emperor, and beside him among the
mourners sat a visitor to Oakland who was there by chance
only—his own son-in-law, Sir Johnston Forbes-Robertson,
booked to play *The Light That Failed* at Oakland's Mac-
Donough Theatre in the evening, in the course of his farewell
tour of the West. The father of Jessie and the brother-in-law
of Dettie had talked proudly the day before of the war work
she was doing. (And I am happy that Captain Tom knew
just before his death that he had another granddaughter.)

The barge *Julia* was ready on the last day of January, but
blew her boilers; repairs were made; Kathleen had arrived to
complete the party, and there remained nothing further to
do but check with civilian and military headquarters for
Belgian territory to see that passes for them all were in order.
Maxine's own status was largely cleared, helped by the
American flag that flew from the *Julia's* stern, a protector
against the outraged orders of both Sir John French and Lord
Kitchener that any woman seen running about the front lines
should be stopped. They drove in a Belgian staff car (stopped
eleven times by sentries on the twenty-five-mile run between
Dunkirk and Adinkirk), left cards on the Belgian War Minister
at Dunkirk, missed the civil governor at Adinkirk, traced
him to La Panne in a villa next door to Albert, King of the
Belgians, and at last were face to face with the civilian who
must be their official commander in Belgian relief work. The
governor of the province of West Flanders had undoubtedly
sighed when he heard from the War Ministry that he should
take care of these ladies come to help his people—well-inten-
tioned, good-willed no doubt, but how could foreigners cope
with the situation of starving, scattered peasantry that he had
on his hands. They sat formally in a ring and Maxine began
in determined French ('dressmaker's French', as Blossom
described it) to outline the plan; Miss Close took over fluently.
By degrees the governor realized that all eventualities had

been thought of; a barge was waiting in Calais loaded with
food and clothes, skippered by a Belgian who knew the waterways, flying an American flag, and these ladies, one so beautiful, one so slim and animated, one so kind (who, thank God,
spoke French) had every military pass from every command it
was possible to obtain. All had been disorder and improvisation for six months of war, but here were three ladies who
wanted nothing of him except to say 'yes'. He was near tears.
He said, 'It's the best and most individual scheme yet presented.' He issued them an all-embracing document to all
burgomasters and thrust upon them the only detailed map of
the canal system he possessed. The conference was full of
emotion, broken up by the noisy entrance of the governor's
young son, in uniform and fresh from the trenches, who
rushed in and covered his father's face with kisses.

The departure eastward toward the Belgian frontier began
at one p.m. on Sunday, February 7, 1915. Maxine and her
assistants were towed out of Calais by a steam tug at five
kilometres an hour, and had on board an escort of a lieutenant
and three Belgian soldiers. Young Lieutenant Rotzart found
this a most amusing military operation, and an opportunity
to practice his English. One of the soldiers was a chef; once
Maxine's purpose was understood by Belgian authorities, they
poured favours upon her.

During the first two weeks they learned techniques of
operation from a side canal in Dunkirk, not yet across the
Belgian border. Soon a wagon arrived daily from Marls-les-
Bains, which they loaded with food and clothing, and used for
short trips over the frontier as Maxine learned from Belgian
authorities where nearby distressed areas lay. Supplies started
to arrive and grew into an onslaught—far too much for the
barge to take. Maxine acquired a second barge, but it was
requisitioned, so she found a school building for temporary
storage. Kathleen smartly borrowed wagons from one command after another; she developed a brilliant talent for
scrounging. Miss Close, in one wagon, delivered a load to the
Poperinghe burgomaster. At a typhoid hospital for women and
children, the two Belgian countesses in charge had run so
short of food for their three hundred patients that they had
knelt solemnly in prayer, just before Maxine and Kathleen

16

clattered in with a loaded camion. The work at this stage had
the character of improvisation; the arrival and quantity of
supplies was uncertain, the system of communication between
the *Julia* and the burgomasters not yet smooth. One factor
was clear; a permanent motor truck would have to be part of
the *Julia*'s equipment, and with such impressive passes there
was no need to operate by water only. It took a month or
more to learn whether the *Julia* should be stationary or mobile
(she moved on to Firminy canal, then farther inland near
Poperinghe). When Maxine obtained a permanent truck, the
Julia became the supply centre and the truck the liaison
between supplies arriving at Dunkirk, storage on the *Julia*,
and distribution in the countryside. By March, two months
from the inception of the work, the entire province of West
Flanders, comprising the towns of Ypres, Furnes, and Poperinghe and some sixty villages, knew of the barge, and of the
big Army truck which came blundering up to the local *mairie*
to unload food and clothing. The secret refugees, the ones
afraid to report their presence for fear of evacuation, learned
of her too; Maxine's principle was never to inquire of anyone's identity but to give at once because everyone was in
need. If she had a special mission it seemed to be to do the
unofficial work of a woman, the things the men had no time
for. And she performed it in her characteristically masculine
way.

A feeling for Maxine developed that was close to worship.
Harassed local officials met a clear, concise mind that un-
ravelled a problem quickly. They met a person willing to take
prompt, fearless action. Things they did not dare do she
undertook; when a shell fell near the anchored barge—shatter-
ing the mobile bakery that now made a daily output of loaves
from American grain—a child's hand was blown off; the
child could have bled to death, overlooked in the confusion.
Maxine commandeered the truck and drove to the British
military hospital at Poperinghe, which was closed to civilians;
there she had friends, who tended the child as a favour to
her. A burgomaster came to report that he found a house
recently shelled in which all adults were killed, leaving seven
untended children under eight years old; simultaneously
another burgomaster was trying to persuade her to give work

to two distraught mothers whose children had been killed; Maxine deftly put the two problems together and set the women to work caring for the children in a nearby farmhouse she kept supplied from the *Julia*. The actions were small and individual, but each was a contribution toward the mitigation of suffering. Maxine became an object of fascinated interest; in the wet and cold she never even sniffled; in contagion from contaminated water she never got a sore throat. The women noted that when they came for clothes Maxine examined them quickly for size, then told Fanny what she wanted and where to find it, and her accuracy never failed; if there was a slight defect at waist or shoulder, she would show them how to adjust it. They were dealing with a woman who believed she could tell M. Worth of Paris how to achieve perfect fit.

The whole operation of the barge *Julia* lasted from February 1915 to May 1916, during which time she fed and clothed approximately three hundred and fifty thousand people. Her personal outlay of money was large; when the work was over, absorbed into official war relief, she felt obliged to resume acting to earn enough to restore the investments she believed necessary to keep her a rich woman.

She received a decoration from Albert, King of the Belgians (and saw to it that he rewarded Kathleen with a sapphire ring). He pinned upon her very ample breast the medal of a Knight of the Order of the Crown (*Chevalier de l'ordre de la Couronne*, or *Ridder van de Orde de Kron*) and felt her wince.

'Oh, Madame, I'm afraid you're wounded,' said the embarrassed monarch.

'But not by the enemy, Sire,' she replied.

*

It seemed impossible that the luxurious Maxine Elliott could survive in sopping, tragic Flanders fields. The woman who demanded central heating, made scenes if cupboards were not the right size, harried chefs and butlers, and tortured her sister if she was incorrectly dressed, did not fit into this ravaged land. 'But the emergency of war changes people,' some may have said. They would have been wrong in Maxine's case; she had not changed at all. To do the work that she tirelessly fulfilled she created for herself a pattern of living that had elements of high comedy for the entire Allied command in this section of Flanders. The *Julia* was a miniature Hartsbourne.

When Kathleen Drogheda first arrived from England she came prepared to sleep on the floor, never get fully washed, and eat bully beef out of cans. She was amazed when she stepped on board and found comfortable cabins with beds, bedspreads, curtains, ventilation, heating from individual oil stoves, baths and lavatories, and a main sitting room with a card table already set up. Even the smell of cigarettes and perfume and some mysterious thing that Fanny burned to remove cooking smells was the smell of Hartsbourne. To complete the picture, the flow of visitors began; to be sure, the men wore khaki instead of tennis flannels or dinner jackets and the women were in nurses' uniforms or land-girl puttees and trench coats instead of Paris creations, but the world was the same. The Duke and Duchess of Sutherland dropped in for tea; the Duke of Westminster hailed them from the bank; Tony Wilding came and went; Lady Sarah Wilson, Hugo Rumbold, Lord Wodehouse, Lord Leigh, Lord de la Warr, Lady Dorothy Fielding . . . French and Belgian counts and barons soon found their way to the *Julia*, assured of a game of bridge or baccarat and an excellent meal cooked by the Belgian chef, while the tone of the conversation was lazy social gossip about who had seen whom where. Maxine, who had acquired the nickname 'Queen of Harts' at Hartsbourne, was here called 'Lord High Admiral of the Barges' and caused much hilarity with her mixture of devoted worker and impossibly spoiled socialite. In the harbour of Adkinkirk she waved a commanding hand at Admiral Eyres's gunboat and asked him for a tow. He went raging to the American consul and then the British consul, telling them to remove that insolent woman, and was met with roars of laughter; he found himself placed next to the offender at the table of the 'uncrowned King of Belgium', Colonel Tom Bridges, head of the British Mission to Belgium, and afterward became one of the constant visitors at the barge. Kathleen picked up similar friends from peacetime life; at an officers' buffet table in Poperinghe she found someone who had played tennis at her husband's Irish seat, Moore Abbey; she found the motor-boat racer and great surgeon, Morton Smart; she discovered the winner of the high jump at Olympia's yearly horse show, a Belgian colonel, and another colonel who judged the contests. The life of high society survived here on board the *Julia*—in the same tone of voice of pleasure-seeking peacetime—but all concerned were doing the work of the war with devotion. If Maxine helped destitute Belgians, she also helped the high command by prodigiously amusing them and giving them a moment in the day when they seemed to live in a different era. She even kept a guest book.

The sacrifice of their special identities that people are willing to make in wartime was apparently not asked of Maxine. She did, however, lose what was perhaps the original reason for her action. On May 9, 1915, during a new Allied offensive (the second battle of Ypres), Captain Tony Wilding was killed by a shell that fell on a dugout where he was sleeping. He had visited the barge the day before; some unexplained argument had taken place between him and Maxine, and they parted in ill temper.

No one knew what Maxine went through when Tony was killed. Kathleen Drogheda had already returned to England; only Fanny and Miss Close were with her at the time. Perhaps even in the intimate quarters of the barge Maxine was able to conceal from them the depth of her feelings, or their loyalty kept them silent later. Tony's death took from her the one simple, trusty, devoted man of her life, the knight who served and admired her without demand and from whom she could gain nothing in the worldly sense. He was close to the story-book man she had described years ago to her schoolmate Ed Gould in Rockland, ready to perform deeds of daring for his lady, the human realization of a girlhood dream of romance, who died in the full bloom of good looks and vigour, a gallant soldier, only thirty-two, remaining ever young and undefeated by the passage of years. Many friends believed the essential light in Maxine went out with Tony's death. The fact that she seldom spoke of him in later years and continued to manage her life tells nothing of her inner feelings. To collapse and be pitied was not Maxine's way, but she did remain at

the barge through the rest of 1915 into the muddy, chill early
months of 1916 before she was willing to emerge and resume
life under public scrutiny. Death was all around her, an
experience she shared with the Belgian people in which her
personal loss could be sunk during that period of mourning
which lasted for a year.

When Maxine returned to London in May 1916 she went
to Constance Collier, whose spiritualistic and mystic beliefs
she usually mocked, and asked her if she would take her to a
medium. She wanted to find out if it was possible to get
through to Tony in the other world to make up their quarrel.
If she received any satisfaction, it has not been revealed.

15

AUNTIE DETTIE

———

FOUR YEARS of hard work—1917 to 1920—restored Maxine's fortunes to the comfortable million minimum in capital that she regarded as solvency. She made two films for Samuel Goldwyn, for which he paid her a hundred thousand dollars in cash and stock—*Fighting Odds* and *The Eternal Magdalene*, the latter directed by Arthur Hopkins. She loathed the experience and loathed herself on camera. She recognized that her type was passing and the winsome, touching girls, such as Mary Pickford and the Gish sisters, had come into fashion. For two years, cashing in on the theatre-going public's sentiment for old favourites, she toured with another veteran star, William Faversham, in a revival of *Lord and Lady Algy* by R. C. Carton. The weary train rides were back, but she passed them pleasantly enough with Favvy and his wife, Julie Opp, both excellent bridge players. Many aspects of post-war American life frankly appalled her; she hated the excessive use of steam heat, and sometimes members of her company found her sleeping in the fresh air on the platform of the caboose, a large mound of mink. 'If our train had taken a sharp swerve,' Franklyn Fox remarked, 'I thought we might lose our star.' She repudiated any idea of using her war service for publicity purposes: 'I'm not going to make copy out of the most sacred thing in my life.' Seeing that worship of youth had seized the day, she dyed her hair and had her face lifted; she hated the result.

The world she had known was passing. Perhaps she had even a moment of regret when she heard of Nat Goodwin's death in January 1919. He had made a triumphant return to popularity in *Why Marry?*, a Pulitzer Prize play. Two wives had succeeded Maxine, and Nat was contemplating taking a sixth when sickness overcame him in Philadelphia and he was obliged to leave the cast. He died in the Claridge Hotel in New York at the age of sixty-one. His memorial service, which Maxine did not attend, was arranged by his brother Lambs.

Maxine tried one more play on Broadway, *Trimmed in Scarlet* by William Hurlbut, a tale of a lady who returns from Europe with a flamboyant past. It was only mildly received, and she refused to nurse it through a tour, so she withdrew on February 14, 1920, two weeks after the opening. That was the end of her career on the stage. Management of Maxine Elliott's Theatre and backing plays performed by others would interest and stimulate her for a year or two without taking the toll of nervous energy that personal appearances had. She removed her make-up for the last time with vast relief.

From that moment on, Maxine saw little reason to struggle against growing weight. She had been heavy already when she left the barge, a woman of forty-eight, but with professional work still ahead of her she had drastically reduced. Only when her doctor threatened her did she consent to pare down, and at Doctor Dengler's Sanitorium at Baden Baden she submitted herself for a few weeks to control by others— the doctor with his diet and walks, his nurses with their massage and steam baths. The moment she left Dengler's she returned to the diet she liked, heavily sauced meat, vegetables cooked in cream, a hearty tea at five o'clock, when chocolate cake was her preference amidst the rich paste sandwiches and hot buttered toast. Eating was unquestionably a comfort, and she allowed herself that indulgence, along with chain smoking, hosts of friends, and bridge playing, which reached the pitch of a mania. These were unquestionably unhappy years.

She reopened Hartsbourne, but tired of it and sold it in 1923; she moved to London, and her energy revived briefly in the remodelling of 20 Abbey Road, a large mansion in Maida Vale with tennis courts at the back. Here she was nearer the bridge-playing world, and she let it absorb her completely. She became a member of a bridge club and stayed there often till five in the morning. Many an old friend whose game did not come up to the standard she wanted found

Maxine hardly visible any more. In time she recognized what
had happened—professional bridge players had taken the
place of brilliant conversationalists—and was lured to Paris,
where the professional and party-going world of Elsa Maxwell,
the Cole Porters, Noël Coward, the Faucigny-Lucinges, and
Constance Toulmin briefly revived her sense of fun. Often,
though, she would not permit an evening of songs and piano
to take its course but injected a bridge game into it. She
went fondly to see a special favourite, Lord Lathom, an early
backer of Noël Coward, when he was dying in a Davos
sanatorium; there she swept Elsa Maxwell, Clifton Webb, and
Noël Coward into a bridge game at the bedside, which went
on until Noël, seeing Ned Lathom's pale, exhausted face,
broke into her obsession and bundled her out. Talk that
lasted too long seemed to weary her intolerably, so she preferred the automatic movement of hands upon the card table.
She briefly enjoyed creating her Paris flat in a co-operative
building at Avenue St. Honoré-d'Eylau. But once it was
finished, she no longer wanted to live there, and she turned
her eyes to the south of France.

*

It was at this time that I became aware of her; the weary,
heavy-hearted woman was the only Maxine Elliott I knew.
Often my mother said, 'Oh, if you'd only seen the old Dettie
. . . the sparkle, the gaiety . . .' Once Mother came joyously
back from dining with her at Abbey Road, where Gene
Tunney was the guest of honour; Tom Chadbourne had told
Tunney to look Maxine up when he went to London in 1928
as world heavyweight champion, and Maxine's delight in the
'man of the hour', especially a man of sport, had brought
back all her animation, Mother reported. Maxine had used
all her old techniques of charm and command on Mr. Tunney
(she even provided American coffee for him), so he found
himself standing up to demonstrate for the entertainment of
her guests how he defeated Jack Dempsey. He had come to
London to find 'that other half of an Irishman', George
Bernard Shaw, and thought he had put boxing behind him,
but Maxine conned him into re-living the big fight once more.
It was especially difficult for us to imagine the woman she

had once been; a child cannot recognize ravaged beauty, and
in Maxine's conversation the sparkle Mother spoke of was
missing. Heaviness was the prevailing impression she gave,
heaviness of body, movement, and spirit; I remember sighs
of Auntie Dettie's, deeper and heavier than any I have ever
heard.

My sister Blossom could remember her before the war and
was struck by the change in her when she came to reopen
Hartsbourne in 1920. Visits to Hartsbourne were hard on
Blossom, a young girl ready for fun, because Maxine spent
Monday to Friday almost entirely alone (sometimes with a
woman friend—Lady Portarlington, Kathleen Drogheda,
Muriel Wilson, Olive Winn), and invitations that sounded
delightful she refused out of hand. 'We don't want to go up
to London to the theatre tonight, do we?' The words were
put in the form of a question, but were in fact a statement of
what was to be. Week-end guests were not really welcome
before Saturday lunch, and were dismissed on Sunday night.
Bridge playing absorbed the time after dinner, and Blossom's
company was frequently whoever was dummy. (In self-
defence Blossom never learned to play bridge, and neither did
the rest of us.) Once a real dancing party took place; there
were Lady Diana Cooper, Ali Mackintosh, Kay Norton, Mona
Dunn, Harry Dalmeny (Lord Rosebery's son), and many
more, and they rolled up the rug and danced to the gramo-
phone. 'Oh, what a bore,' sighed Maxine when they had gone.
'Never again . . .' But she did, in fact, have a proper ball when
she and Frieda Dudley-Ward were co-hostesses at Hartsbourne for the two princes, H.R.H. the Prince of Wales (the
Duke of Windsor) and H.R.H. the Duke of York (George VI);
then Blossom saw first-hand the brilliant thoroughness with
which Maxine trained the servants to manage a party with
royalty present and saw that the detectives were properly
cared for.

The dreaded clothes fittings took up endless time. Blossom
stood till she grew pale and unsteady, but relentlessly Auntie
Dettie sighed and grunted in annoyance at the efforts of the
sewing woman, who knelt on the floor beside Blossom's hem
or waistline. Once it endured so long that Blossom did in
fact faint outright; a flash of something like fear crossed

Maxine's face, and she said like a little girl, 'Don't tell your
mother.' And the clothes which took such a toll were so
disappointing to a young girl. Maxine loved a bargain; she
loved to make over; a dress of Winnie Portarlington's cut to
Blossom's figure was far more satisfying to her than a new
creation straight from the shop, which she could have afforded
many times over.

She took Blossom with her on visits to St. Moritz or to
Cannes, and spent much of the time in hotel rooms playing
cards with a friend while Blossom hung about. Some of it
Blossom loved; if properly chaperoned she could go and enjoy
the fun, Maxine happy to remain peacefully playing cards,
but the heaviness of spirit in her aunt was a worrying and
pervading thing. Blossom longed to please and have everything easy and cheerful, but found instead that she was the
cause of a discontented groan because once more her costume,
her hair, her face had failed to produce the effect Maxine
required. Blossom was being compared with that impossible
idealized version that Maxine had of her family.

Maxine's yearning for the emotion of family was expressed
always in her plan-making and directing. She could not show
it any other way. Somewhere the communication was impaired; love refused to come out in a simple, easy flow. She
loved us, so she made plans, often with hurt to follow. When
she decided to leave Hartsbourne she was a lone woman
about to inhabit a very large London house, and her practical
nature said that the obvious thing was for Forbie and Gertrude
to give up 22 Bedford Square and move in with her, with all
their children. Rather than two London houses there would
be one, and she believed herself so much more capable of
running a house than Gertrude (which was true) that here
lay a perfect solution. There would be a suite, as at Hartsbourne; Forbie should have his own study, the children
(Chloe and I) should have nurseries, and Blossom should have
a sitting room where she could entertain 'young friends'.
('Imagine me daring to,' said Blossom.) Gertrude was still
acting and Jean was just beginning to, and late supper could
be provided for them by Maxine's staff after the performance.
It would have been a perfectly sensible idea if it had not
demanded that a man give up his male identity and hand it

to her as general of the tribe. She calmly went ahead with her plans. Nervously Blossom tried to say that she really did not think her parents . . . The sentence was difficult to finish because Auntie Dettie's mind went straight on to the next physical detail. Gertrude, in a panic at having to face a new situation wherein either 'Little Dettie' or Johnston would be distressed, only brushed over the question, and then had the luck to be leaving immediately for a long tour of Australia and New Zealand, taking Jean with her.

At last Johnston discovered what was about to be done to his peaceful retirement. He never welcomed being forced to cope with a situation, but terror at her implacable will sped him to his desk at Bedford Square. On October 25, 1922, he wrote her.

My dear One,

I fear you are under the impression that we are all to live together with you in your new house, and that you, in the most handsome fashion, are planning to that end. Now with the best intentions in the world on both sides, this scheme will never work. There are a hundred insurmountable obstacles which with all the good will there is cannot be surmounted. As regards myself and the family, here are my roots, and here we must remain. Nothing would induce me to break up the home which I have kept together now for near upon fifty years. I have spoken to Blossom on the subject and she is entirely in agreement with me and I have written Gertrude to confirm what I said to her before she sailed when I heard of the scheme for the first time. I had the impression she had told you how I stand in the matter, or I should have written you long ago. Well, my dear One, this is a painful letter and very hateful to me in the writing.

Your ever affectionate

Johnston

It is hard to imagine what kind of hurt this letter brought Maxine. Outwardly she shrugged and said, 'Forbie is being tiresome,' and gave Gertrude much misery on her return. 'Those girls will never develop in the right way if they stick in Bedford Square all the time. . . . I could do so much for them.' She did not say she was hurt, she merely scolded. Gertrude knew better; she said 'She will be so hurt' to us always when we had delayed writing a thank-you note. To us this

seemed out of character. We did not, of course, know the
woman whose star-making play had been called *Her Own
Way*, who had set her defences high and deep. She refused
to admit that we did not really want the life she offered; she
merely said we were too young, too silly, too much under
the influence of our nurse to know what was good for us.
She ignored the implications of Gertrude's flight from her
authority long before. Inside her she had never relinquished
Gertrude, and merely tried to add on Forbie and their
children too.

Obstinately she refused to learn, and when Blossom became
engaged Maxine began busily creating an apartment in her
house for the bride and groom. Once more there was agonized
debate and the plea, 'But we want a house of our own.' She
turned to the theatrical career of Jean, which flowered immediately into something shimmering and magical (a great
Hedda Gabler, Viola, an incandescent Juliet, an unearthly
performance in *Berkeley Square*, and a Peter Pan that was
the realized dream of its creator, James M. Barrie); but Jean
shied away in terror at her attempts to manage or dress her.
Maxine could tragically destroy the joy of a triumphant first
night by coming to the dressing room to say, 'That light in
the second act makes your nose too big. . . . I want to refit
that pink dress. It's ghastly.' She had no intention of being
cruel; she merely stated with unadorned directness what she
thought best for her loved ones. With a warmth that Jean did
not know Maxine wrote to Louis Levy, at that time a partner
in Tom Chadbourne's firm, 'This is literally my first breathing
spell . . . rehearsals go on daily [*Dancing Mothers*, 1925, in
which both Gertrude and Jean appeared], and the moment
they are over the eternal fussing over clothes and photographs
and the million necessary evils connected with a stage production. . . . It is a marvellous cast and Jean is playing like an
angel—you must keep your fingers crossed for her opening. . . .'

All of Johnston's sense of privacy and Gertrude's shyness
met in Jean and her resistance to Maxine was implacable.
Maxine recognized this niece, possessed of genius, as less
malleable than all other members of the family ('malleable'
was a pet word of Maxine's), and when Jean became engaged

to Hamish Hamilton did not urge on them a suite in her own house. She offered them outright a charming house in Grove End Road as a wedding-present and it was Jamie Hamilton's painful duty when he hardly knew Maxine to inform her that her gift could not be accepted.

Chloe, our painter sister, met her with the least distress of any of us; her bland Bloomsbury calm seemed to look straight through Auntie Dettie's directives, so elusive, so impervious to command that she slipped rapidly through her aunt's fingers and was left in peace to paint. 'She mustn't be allowed to come into the drawing room in her smock,' said Maxine to Gertrude, who had to shoulder the blame for Chloe's defection. In those years I was still a schoolgirl— 'That child is getting enormous, she must be taken to Dengler's.' She visited me at Heathfield School, and in the conventionality of my age I found her make-up, mink, and diamonds an embarrassment in front of my friends, but I remember that I sat on the edge of the lacrosse field with her, passionately explaining the intricacies of the game, and she listened kindly.

We were all she had left that approached an emotional meaning to her life, and we could not fulfil her needs. She never gave up working on us, but we were poor material for the hands of Maxine Elliott, being the children of Johnston Forbes-Robertson and Gertrude Elliott. The suffering of my mother must have been considerable; she longed to please 'the Little Thing', but she had no desire for any of us to become smart, worldly figures; if we had she would have been most ill at ease. Nieces are often the obvious outlet for the energies of a childless aunt, who can offer them fun, relaxation of discipline, and a warm, comfortable affection. Aunt Maxine could never be that cosy. I do not think we gave her pleasure as people, but somewhere in her imagination we gave her enjoyment.

Beyond family feelings a single woman moving from her late forties into her late fifties has other means of outlet, although they may not be easy years for a woman. For Maxine Elliott, who had moved from action to action, a missile of a life guided by herself, the moment of halt was hard indeed. She refused the solace of art; when Constance Collier urged her to come and enjoy a picture gallery with her, she said, 'How could I possibly be interested in something I haven't done myself?' The life of the spirit and the life of the emotions had both been so smartly brought to order long ago that they could not be revived. She was trapped in a body that got always more cumbersome. It had once been her asset; it was now a big, hungry nuisance. I was frightened of her then and often resented her, but now I look through the crowds of friends and worry over what she thought about at night, and want to weep. . . . A vision comes of the three-quarter-size bed, with wicker back and foot and scrolled woodwork, pink coverlets, a reading lamp. There is Auntie Dettie, one very small foot protruding from the bedclothes; her face is creamed (and the eyes are so beautiful without make-up); a sturdy, pink hairnet encloses her hair. She is contentedly and sound asleep, emitting little clicking snores, looking rather like a young baby; a detective story has slid from her hands onto the floor beside two tiny slippers.

16

THE CHÂTEAU DE L'HORIZON

PURPOSE, happiness, and beauty returned to Maxine in the last decade of her life. They stemmed from a new house, a place as positive as Hartsbourne, which gave her a passionate interest and her own setting. Here she sat down and let people come to her. In fact, anyone who suggested going anywhere else was accused immediately of being a 'gadabout'.

She tired of cities at about her sixtieth birthday, and turned toward the Riviera for a place to settle. She tried renting the Samuel Lewisohn villa, Corne d'Or, which she shared one summer with Cuckoo, Mrs. Gordon Leith, and this determined her to have her own place. Charlotte Boissevain drove her up and down the coast in search for the right house. Failing to find one, Maxine decided to build. Charlotte brought her two architects, a young Anglo-American team who had just finished a first job remodelling part of Mr. Somerset Maugham's Villa Mauresque. Barry Dierks, the American of the pair, was the creative architect (his partner, Colonel Eric Sawyer, the Englishman, ran the business side). Dierks was a man of special intuition. His designs were precisely what Maxine wanted, a 'great' house, greater in fact than Hartsbourne had been in its conception, but with Maxine's particular feeling for casualness. The ideas of comfort which Maxine had already developed to a science were brought to perfection. At first there was a clash between aesthetics and practicality ('Oh, you men, you're always worrying about beauty,' she told Barry), but Dierks's gifts were such that he welded the two into one, with the willingness many architects lack to create the house that is wanted by the person who will live in it.

The project was started in 1930 and finished in 1932. In the background lay the great scar of the 1929 Wall Street crash. Maxine had lost money, not because she gambled on margin, but because all values fell; her income, however, was enough to start on a project which is supposed to have cost three hundred thousand dollars before it was finished. When others lost money, Maxine had a way of making it in the most infuriating fashion, and did so precisely at that moment.

The site for the house seemed an impossibility. There was a narrow strip of land lying between the combined routes of railroad and motor road and the ocean. The width was not more than fifty feet, and on the ocean side there was a sheer drop over vicious rocks. Maxine insisted on being on the sea, and she wanted to be very near Cannes; the site combined both advantages. The project had the enjoyable look of something that could not be done, so she set about doing it. Her friends cried, 'But you can't swim off those rocks'—'Maxine darling, there's no beach'—'How will you ever get to your property?' Imperiously the railroad schedules between Marseille and the Italian border were disrupted and a bridge was thrown across the tracks. The rocks were blasted and levelled, and on their top was poised a swimming pool that had a water chute down which you simply slid to the sea. Into the narrow space between the swimming pool and the bank of the railroad bed a long, low villa was welded into the rock as if part of it, and behind, to insulate the whole property from the noise of passing trains, a huge wall. House, wall, and swimming pool gleamed brilliant white. It seemed like a great Arab fort or even a seraglio.

Maxine's experience with building in the past told her that you had to be on the spot or nothing got finished, so she moved into the small cottage which already stood on the property. Once there, she needed a chauffeur and a small easy car. The days of the White Incomparable were passed, and so were the days of Gwatkin in his uniform. She acquired a standard Citröen, and Dierks and Sawyer suggested she might like to interview a man who had worked for them, Jules Fagioli, driver, mechanic, stone mason, electrician, and gardener. Jules, a sturdy young Provençal with bright blue eyes

17

and a warm grin, presented himself at the Carlton, where Maxine was living until she could move.

'*Jules, vous voulez travailler pour moi?*' she asked in broadest English pronunciation.

'*Oui, Madame,*' said Jules in broadest Provençal.

'*Alors, travaillez,*' she said, and a gleam of humour and understanding passed between them. Thus, with Madame Fanny Vandystaedt from the barge *Julia* and Jules Fagioli, Maxine had acquired for the last years of her life two people whose idea of work and attitude toward people were in perfect tune with her own, now that her needs were relaxing and softening. Fanny and Jules were not 'perfect servants'; they were characters, they were good people.

Maxine was busy and happy; her tiny feet carried the heavy frame around tirelessly; she went threading in and out of the unfinished shell with Dierks and Sawyer, supervising and inspecting. The words the partners came to dread most were 'It won't do. Rip it out.' Painstakingly Eric Sawyer would point out the extra cost of more material and more working hours, but she insisted it must be right. Earnestly Barry Dierks implored her to see that he had designed the long windows of the salon in precise proportion to its height and length, but she insisted they were too narrow and she must have light. When the work was completed and the furniture moved in she suddenly knew Barry had been right, and without comment commanded the curtains to be drawn a couple of inches forward over the sides to create the exact width Barry had wanted. She took over the department of comfort with the result that future clients of Barry Dierks benefited by the tricks he learned, for which he always gave Maxine full credit.

There came the day when the exact width of the water chute had to be decided. The partners had an anxious consultation with Madame Fanny, then borrowed her dressmaker's tape measure. They walked with Maxine around the edge of the pool and stood on the high platform looking down on the rocks below, where a swarm of workmen were putting final touches on the cement bottom of the chute. Suddenly Barry leaned forward, pointing, and asked Maxine to observe something below. She bent over with him. Behind her, Eric shot open the tape measure and took the width of her buttocks. They did not know whether she would use the chute herself, but in case she might they wanted to be sure there should be no grazing of the owner's hips and thighs on the cement sides. Now the work could go on.

The first party at the Château was given in the summer of 1931 around the pool. The house was unfinished but the kitchen worked, so fifty people were fed. All summer long hordes streamed over to swim while the workmen sat poised on scaffolding, serenading the parties below with loud bursts of Provençal song. Maxine led conducted tours of inspection which exhausted her visitors with hours of standing as she showed them just how the big central staircase was going to rise out of the hall, just where the flower room would be. It was all of passionate interest to her, and she was loving the worry and fuss and confusion of work in progress.

In January 1932 the house was sufficiently ready for her to have Gertrude and Forbie. Forbie had been ill with bronchial pneumonia, and it was thought the Riviera sunshine would restore him, now very frail, aged seventy-nine. Maxine took it as a personal insult when bad weather closed in—day after day of penetrating, driving wind and rain, with Dad obviously longing for his comfortable London fireside, disturbed by the constant click-click-click of the backgammon board (the new craze). He fell ill again with exposure to cold passageways. Maxine visited him daily in his room on the ground floor (once more a 'Forbes-Robertson suite' had been created), but, though the passage of years had quieted much of their warfare, they had little to say to each other. Maxine had wanted so much to offer her beautiful house on the sunny coast to cure her brother-in-law, but in the eternal pattern of misconceptions of each other's needs the visit was not quite a success. It was the chatty visits of the local physician, Doctor Brés, that cheered and rallied him.

Others who were not her family found the Château de l'Horizon all they desired. A new version of 'the great days of Hartsbourne' began once more. Here Winston Churchill, who had faded out during the years when Maxine was tied to the bridge table, was delighted to come yearly with his paints and whatever book he was working on. People flowed

from up and down the coast; letters poured in from London
—'Darling Maxine, when would it be convenient . . .' Her
house was the showplace of the coast, and everyone wanted
to be invited. Droves came for swimming, droves for lunch;
there were always dinner parties for small numbers, and
always at least six or eight people staying in the house. Maxine
went out of the house less and less; she liked people to come
to her, and it was a feat to get her to dine anywhere but at
her own table. Jimmy Sheean, my husband, suggested that in
her vast observation of protocol in the past, and the experience
of many occasions when she was lowest-ranking person
present, she now only really enjoyed sitting at the head of her
own table.

The Château de l'Horizon was run on much the same lines
as Hartsbourne. The comfort of the bedrooms was supreme.
Each bedroom had a private balcony overlooking the Bay of
Cannes. Each bathroom was shaped like a slice of cake, the
narrowest end toward the sea, with the window opening onto
the guest's private balcony. (Maxine gave the idea to a hotel
manager in New York twenty years earlier but he had failed
to use it.) There was an enormous salon opening onto the
terrace that led down to the pool; there were a dining room, a
small card room, and a library. The furniture was exactly the
same as at Hartsbourne and Abbey Road, causing Barry
Dierks to burst into tears when he first saw it being unloaded
in the driveway; but he recovered and suddenly rejoiced—
'This is her personal world, and if my house can't contain
heavy upholstery, tasselled lamps, and silver-framed photographs it hasn't succeeded.' Housekeeping was now in the
hands of Madame Fanny; there was a tiny little man with an
enormous moustache called Michel, the chef, who promptly
learned Madame Elliott's taste for corn bread, vegetables
cooked in cream, and chocolate cake; there was a white-haired
Italian, Domenico, the butler who seemed to run wherever he
went, and his assistant, Alexis, a local boy, whose wife Ger-
maine was an upstairs maid with two other helpers. On the
outside Jules ruled supreme, keeping the strip of lawn under
the Forbes-Robertsons' windows watered, the rock garden
growing, doing all chauffeuring and repairs, keeping the great
pumps of the swimming pool in smooth working order so that

a cascade tumbled into the pool and kept the water flowing down the chute.

Breakfast was given to house guests on their own private balconies (and gossip said the appearance on balconies of others than the occupants was frequent). Lunch was beside the pool. There was one indoor meal, served in the shaded cool library in mid-afternoon. It had a secret character, the hearty tea with cakes and hot buttered scones that Maxine often had alone while everyone else was still at siesta. Dinner was on the terrace above the swimming pool immediately outside the drawing room.

Over this terrace towered two large trees. From them the last love of Maxine's life usually made his dramatic entrance: Kiki, the lemur, who brought dread to the hearts of many guests and caused Maxine untold delight. He came at the end of a long line of pets; Sport and Flossie, the Boston bulls; Inky, a terrier; Dinah, the Belgian barge dog; Peter, a hunting Pekinese; Bill, a very stupid Dalmatian; and many more. Christopher, a crisply white English fox-terrier was the first animal at the Château. He shared the honours with a curious break from the dog world: Maxine had been given at an Easter party a tiny yellow chicken, which grew into a large white rooster which supervised the building of the Château, always revealing where he had been by the colour of paint on his tail feathers. He was called 'Feet', because he walked firmly about on two outsize claws and reminded Maxine of Effie Barker, my one and only friend from school days. Effie was a magnificent girl who fitted none of the specifications for 'the right friends at school', being neither titled, socially important, nor interested in adornment; she was a horse-woman, a farmer, and a Red Cross worker, whose irreverent brothers had given her the nickname 'Feet'. Maxine could sometimes be very surprising. I was afraid she would bitterly disapprove of Effie as a countrywoman and 'unsmart', but she adored her. She complimented Effie in the best way she knew by calling her striding chicken after her. 'Feet' started to drink the paint, and died.

At last came Kiki. He was hooded, with a little bright, pointed face that looked out from the snug-fitting cap of close, grey-brown fur; he was small, light and agile, his long arms

swinging him merrily through the branches and landing him
plop on the dining-room table amidst screams. Eleanor Loder,
Maxine's neighbour up the Californie Hill of Cannes, begged
gently and sweetly that Kiki should be shut up when she came
because she was genuinely afraid. Maxine was fond of Eleanor
and seemed willing. But when Kiki appeared, Maxine's comment was, 'How can I help it if my monkey is clever enough
to escape?' If protests were loud, Maxine was brutal. When
Elsie de Wolfe (Lady Mendl) said either she or the monkey
stayed away, Maxine said it would not be Kiki. A Portuguese
lady cried that her royal sovereign had died of monkey bite
and it was no good saying Kiki's teeth were clean because the
same had been said of the king-killer. 'Maybe your King's
blood was too blue. You don't have to worry, my dear,' said
Maxine. Effie Barker's brother Gilbert brought violets when
he came calling and was dismayed when Kiki destroyed the
bunch before Maxine even appeared; he found, however, that
his gift was a greater success than he had expected, because
Maxine was charmed to find the petals strewn all over the
carpet. If Kiki dropped pellets on the dining-room table and
guests recoiled, Maxine laughed; if Kiki bit them, she said,
'Domenico, bring the iodine.' Only when Kiki had inflicted
so many wounds on her that her hands and ankles were continually running sores did she consent to have his needle-like
canines sawed down. The newspapers said that Maxine had
her pet monkey's teeth pulled when he bit her; on the con-
trary, she merely made it a little safer for him to go on
nibbling.

It almost seems as if Maxine were mocking humanity a
little in her passion for Kiki. His naughtiness, the discom-
fiture he inflicted, filled her with chuckling amusement. Perhaps the antics of all human beings by now seemed to her
monkey-like, and Kiki did everything better and with greater
dash than people.

Kiki represented also the moment of her total grandeur.
You liked her monkey or you got out. She kowtowed to
nobody. People could come to her house and receive the
amusement she had to offer—her pool, her good food, her
monkey, and her friends, including certain women who caused
eyebrows to rise but who amused Maxine, somewhat as Kiki

did. She would do everything her own way now. Imperturbably she sat in the middle of a row when a French baron and a French marquis screamed with rage because she had got the seating wrong at her table. Maxine had not got it wrong; she knew all about protocol and acted with intent. She put Sir Robert Vansittart on her right and Winston Churchill, a guest in her house with no rank, on her left. She knew precisely what she meant by this gesture. She no longer fussed to know anyone new, no matter how grand they might be; when Mr. Churchill asked her to invite the Windsors to dinner she acquiesced a little unwillingly, indicating that she felt the abdication had been an untidy way of doing things ('We did it better in my day'), and when the guest list for the dinner party was under consideration he suggested Lord Derby. 'I forget, Maxine, do you know Harry Derby?' Maxine's answer was simply, 'No.' Lord Derby was the most distinguished resident of the Riviera, but Maxine did not bother to use this opportunity to meet him. She knew how to do everything and did it if she chose. She received the Windsors with the most perfect protocol; she sent Jimmy Sheean to the car to conduct them in; she posted Mr. Churchill to greet them and bring them to their hostess, with myself and Mr. Lloyd George lined up behind her. The ceremonial of the evening was faultless, followed by the eager talk and laughter of a vivid group. I looked across the table and saw Maxine's attentive smiling face, a glimpse of Hartsbourne's hostess. The air of grandeur she carried when she wished to was stupendous; at another house I saw an entire roomful of guests rise to their feet, including the Duke of Windsor and Mr. Churchill, when she came to the door to indicate that it was time she took her house party home. She was dressed in white, all diamonds flashing, her hair pure white. That was when I fully recognized the stories of her beauty.

This grandeur was particularly apparent when Mr. Churchill was her guest. She knew perfectly well that he, though out of office, towered above the familiars of the Château who came and went. He was the only person I saw permitted to be late for meals, and the only one who could leave the Château to paint at Saint Paul de Vence all day without being scolded as a 'gadabout'. Climbers who came to see the house

were lazily tolerated by Maxine most of the time, but none
were allowed to come and gawk at Churchill. He was a link
with 'the great days at Hartsbourne', a reminder that she
carried within her the knowledge of better times. There was
no longer Curzon to raise his haughty head and listen abstractedly, while Forbie, presenting his little Blossom, recited the
honours and offices of the man who stood before him, and
then lower his haughty head in a series of nods, saying, 'Perfectly correct, perfectly correct.' There was no more Rosebery
to yawn with boredom or flash with wit; no 'F.E.' to match
against Winston; no Arthur Balfour with a languid leg draped
over the chair arm, nor the old Prime Minister himself, Mr.
Asquith ('Always looked like a high-class butler,' said Maxine).
Winston and herself remembered days when many of the
people who adorned her pool could not have entered any of
the houses they knew in common. At the dinner party for
the Windsors Winston remarked to Maxine in an undertone,
'What a lot of *ci-devants* we are here tonight,' and she
smiled without rancour, proud to belong to a period that
was past.

Even before the Duke of Windsor abdicated, while he was
still Edward VIII, his royalness did not prevent her from
grumbling miserably when he requested the Château de
l'Horizon for a summer holiday, knowing she was obliged to
acquiesce. She wanted to stay in her home, and there was
nothing further to add to her history by having a king as
tenant. But she would do it right if she had to do it at all,
so the house was prepared impeccably, and then came word
that it was considered unwise for him to spend his holiday
in such a public place as the Riviera (Mrs. Simpson was of
the party). She happily sent back his cheque, and I remember
the appraising and contemptuous 'humph' with which she
examined the eighteenth-century silver snuff box he sent her
in apology for changed plans. Perhaps she had memories of
more kingly presents; there had been rumours of an all-gold
dinner service King Edward VII gave her, but no one I know
ever remembers seeing it. At all events, she was unimpressed,
happy to settle back beside her pool and forget her royal
tenant.

She was more vitally amused now by accomplishment or

THE CHÂTEAU DE L'HORIZON

MAXINE IN THE POOL

MAXINE WITH KIKI

DIANA
FORBES-ROBERTSON

THE ROCKS OF
THE CHÂTEAU
DE L'HORIZON
FROM A PAINTING
BY SIR WINSTON
CHURCHILL

MAXINE'S LAST VISIT TO NEW YORK

entertainment, reverting to an earlier self. With the whole social world won she was free to enjoy what she really wished to enjoy. She was like an eager fan when Douglas Fairbanks Senior came over. She loved it when Johnny Weissmuller came to the Château and dived from the top terrace, over the dining terrace into the pool, and she plagued her nephew-in-law Jamie Hamilton, an Olympics sportsman, till he rose at dawn to practise his diving, preferring to spatter out his brains without an audience if he failed. She went with me one day into Cannes to see the film *Stage Door*, with Katharine Hepburn and Ginger Rogers, and cried her eyes out. At the end she said to me, 'Let's stay and see it all through again,' and we did. She was charmed with gadgets and small new nonsenses—the epitome of the very rich who have to find pleasures in things beyond those that only money can buy. She loved the silly and useless or the practical and cheap. On her last visit to New York in 1937 she had discovered S. Klein, the bargain store, and would buy ten dresses at a time there, then send Fanny back with the discards. She found Childs Restaurant as well, and would not eat anywhere else.

In the feeling of renewed life that the new house gave her, she even decided that her serviceable little car was not beyond her power; if the highly tense Gertrude had learned to drive, so could she. She did it firmly and boldly, and it was best for the rest of the traffic to look sharp. She made a right turn with a generous swing to the left first, and ignored squealing brakes and ringing curses. If she could be urged away from the pool it was more likely that she would consent to go and sit in the open-air dance halls of Juan-les-Pins than corset and bejewel herself for a dinner party. She liked watching the boys and girls jiggling round, and it required no effort on her part. If, however, you were one of the younger members of her party and failed to do your proper share of jiggling, she prodded you out on to the crammed dance floor without mercy. Oddities amused her in a detached way, though no human being was as funny to her as Kiki; I went out with her one evening under the guidance of David Herbert, who showed the 'seamy side' in a sailor's dance hall where one woman in a fit of jealousy kicked another in the seat of her very short shorts. Maxine raised her lorgnette on a pearl strand and laughed heartily.

The last time I stayed at the Château was when the Spanish Loyalists were being fast defeated in the Spanish Civil War. Mr. Churchill was sunk in gloom, recognizing that the Fascist supporters of Franco were sure to spell danger for England. Maxine, deeply Conservative, who decried Mr. Roosevelt in the terms of the class she adopted—'The madman in the White House'—remained unshocked when Mr. Churchill said to Jimmy and me, knowing our passionate feeling about the Spanish Republic, 'We're all in the same lobby now.' Others cried, 'Winston! You're not capable of backing those terrible Reds?' and it was Maxine, looking back to the days before 1914, who nodded quietly when he said, 'I'd make an ally of the devil himself if it would save England.' Her head seemed to lift in memory to the brave days before World War I. She was sad, too, because she knew all about war, but practical as well. When Blossom's second husband, Miles, suggested to her that the Rolls-Royce expansion into aircraft engines was making the company an excellent investment, she shook her head. 'I think war is coming. Assets in England will be frozen the moment it comes. I would have to keep my money in America.' Her money, yes, but not herself. When war did come in September 1939, no amount of persuading would remove Maxine from the Château.

She had the first serious breakdown in health six months before the war began. She had become grossly fat (she weighed about two hundred and thirty pounds), but went right on eating, ignoring doctors who warned her that her body had an excess of salt deposit and the sugar balance was out of line. A mild stroke came—unconsciousness and slow rallying—but left no paralysis. Friends rushed into the salon of the Château, winter residents such as Charlotte Boissevain, Princess Julia Ottoboni, Madame Louise Edvina, and sat in hushed waiting while Doctor Brés was upstairs. Into their midst strode Elsie Mendl in shorts, wimple, and coolie hat. 'I told Maxine, I've told her a thousand times. She should diet like me'—she struck herself on her flat tummy—'and exercise the way I do'—another triumphant blow. She began to demonstrate to the death watch what she did to keep herself trim; she bent, stretched, and finally turned upside down and stood on her head. 'Oh, God,' prayed Charlotte Boissevain, 'just let Maxine live so I can describe this scene to her.' Maxine did live, and as she began to receive company she forced Charlotte whenever present 'to perform Elsie', including hand stands. At last Charlotte protested, 'Oh, Maxine darling, please not today. I'm not decent underneath.' Maxine sent for Fanny, and said when she came, 'Fetch Madame Boissevain a pair of underdrawers.'

She was supposed now to remain forever on a rigidly bland diet. She laughed at the idea. Elsa Maxwell came to lunch and watched appalled as Maxine tucked into a full-course meal. She said, 'If you go on eating that way, Maxine, you're going to kill yourself.' 'Can you suggest a better way to die?' said Maxine. She went out to tea on the Carlton Terrace with Eleanor and Eric Loder, who solicitously inquired what she was allowed to eat. 'I'll have that,' said Maxine, pointing to a large slice of rich chocolate cake. 'Oh, darling, surely the doctor said no cake.' Like a naughty child she flashed back, 'But he didn't say no chocolate cake.'

The last group of guests arrived in August 1939, and was there when news of war came. Three of the guests—Michael Renshaw, Sir Charles Birkin, and Sir Michael Duff—were Englishmen of fighting age; there was a scurry of packing, accompanied by the mistral, which banged shutters, blew tissue paper about the house, and mingled its mourning with the weeping of French maids whose husbands had been called up at once. Mickie Renshaw went into Maxine's bedroom to say good-bye. They gave each other cheerful, untrue promises to meet again soon. 'I won't urge you to write, Mickie,' she said. 'I know how frantic everyone gets going to war . . .' He did receive letters from her; she wrote, 'My one faithful correspondent is Winston, but then of course he has more time than you younger ones . . .' She did not live to see him become Prime Minister.

An even later leaf to go scurrying past on the way back to England was Noël Coward, who dashed over by boat from Cannes to say good-bye. He was distressed at how thin she had become, her eyes enormous, her hair pure white. The tears that sprang to his eyes came partly from the certainty that he would not see her again and partly from emotion at her beauty, which he had been too young to see in its prime. Fat had left the classic features, her eyes had regained their original proportion to the face, and she now had an ethereal look which had never been there before. The studied expression of hauteur that belonged with the period of her triumphant youth had been entirely discarded for gentleness. 'I'm a cat with nine lives, Noël,' she said, 'but I think this is the ninth.' They also told each other lies and kissed good-bye. Noël tore down the stairs, everything blurred as he thought of the bed-ridden woman upstairs, and dashed to his boat. He turned to take a conscious last look at the Château, and there was Maxine on her balcony, in white nightgown and flowing white hair, defying Fanny and doctors to wave a white handkerchief. 'Like Isolde on her tower,' said Noël, and with his tears there was laughter: 'Who said she wasn't an actress?'

After a few weeks of war the mayor of Vallauris came to call upon Maxine. He was the acting mayor only, replacing *le maire mobilisé*. He had a sad tale to tell; some of the women and children of Vallauris were in dire straits, suffering because their men had been promptly jailed as subversive elements dangerous to the war effort, for Vallauris was predominantly Communist. 'Ridiculous,' said Maxine. 'The innocent always suffer.' She promised to think out what help she could give. The acting mayor walked through the rich halls of the Château and shrugged his shoulders, doubting that the rich American would be good for much. As he drove up to the *mairie*, about thirty-five minutes away, a Citröen slid in behind him and Jules jumped out and handed him an envelope. It was the first cheque from Madame Elliott, for five thousand francs. After that the flow continued: five thousand, seven thousand, two thousand, five thousand . . .

Giving money in time of emergency was not enough for Maxine. In 1914 she had said, 'I gave the Allies my money for war-relief work but I told them if they took my money they must take me too. Like offering a peach on the point of a bayonet.' Though she could not leave her bed, she organized a group of sewing women through Fanny, and had her entire wardrobe cut up to make clothes for the needy children; she put women to work on layettes for the newborn babies; she got another team to make up packages for the various posts of the Chasseurs Alpins, containing knitted Balaclava helmets, soap, razors, and tobacco. Jules's unit, sitting cold and idle in the hills, was given a football to keep the men in trim and warmed with exercise; the unit stationed at St. Paul de Vence had no radio and received one immediately; as for the unit billeted at the Château itself, they got a bottle of wine per man per meal and a feast at Christmas. She began to learn the individual problems of the men and their wives; letters poured in on cheap exercise-book paper in cramped hand-writing—mothers were thanking her for blankets, for baby bonnets, for shoes. She became a godmother again—to two hundred Provençal children, young Communists, who joy-fully celebrated Christmas around the tree she had put up in the Vallauris cinema, with a special gift for each child at its foot. She lay in bed, looking out at the Mediterranean, and directed the operation, happy and busy, her counterpane strewn with letters.

On March 5, 1940, Fanny helped her out of bed to go to the bathroom. A minute later a small grunt and a bumping sound came through the half-open bathroom door. Fanny rushed in and found Maxine lying dead on the soft white rug.

The first friend to come was Barry Dierks. He had loved her dearly; he had always cheeked her and knew this had caused her to love him in return. He was weeping when he arrived, but was moved to choked reverence when he saw a single Chasseur Alpin, one of her own unit, standing guard outside her door, his head bowed over his musket in the position of the guard of honour that watches the catafalque of a monarch. He went in and saw her, small and white, lying on her pink bed, and knelt beside her.

Blossom and Miles got special Home Office permission to fly out to the funeral. Winston Churchill knew that George Keppel was obstinately hanging on at the Riviera, refusing to leave for home, and telegraphed him to be his representative. The mayor of Cannes, the mayor of Vallauris, the British consul John Taylor, and such friends as were left gathered in the salon of the Château. Her coffin lay in the middle of the room piled with flowers, and around it stood the guard of honour of children, all dressed in Maxine's own cut-down clothes. She was buried in the Protestant Cemetery of Cannes, and her Chasseurs played the Last Post over her grave and fired a volley. Later Blossom was asked to take Maxine's place in a ceremonial which presented the Poste Château de l'Horizon with the fanion that Maxine had just had made for them. Posthumously she became *marraine* of the regiment.

Blossom hurried back to England, bringing the papers found in Maxine's desk and her jewellery. She went immediately to see Mother, who had been widowed by the death of Dad three years before, and was living in St. Margaret's Bay, Kent.

'I ordered the stone,' said Blossom. 'I think it's just what you wanted. It's a plain granite headstone and simply says, "Maxine Elliott" and the dates, "Born 1873, died 1940".'

'Oh, dear, oh, dear,' said Gertrude, clicking her nails against her teeth.

'Isn't that right?' Blossom asked.

'It's just that naughty little Dettie was never quite truthful about her age. It ought to be 1869.'

Even Gertrude was a year off.

*

An adjustment of five years in the face of eternity makes little difference. She invented her name; she invented her dates. They had become far more true of her than the truth itself. It was her desire to be Maxine Elliott who died at sixty-seven. To refuse her this, her own way as always, after death would have been an impertinence. In fact, no one would have dreamed of disobeying her. The invaluable letters of Lord Curzon, Winston Churchill, and Lord Rosebery were dutifully destroyed because Maxine left instructions that they should be. Fanny thought out what Miss Elliott would have wanted when the German occupation of the Château came, and fled for the hills with Jules, taking only the silver and the pictures painted by Mr. Churchill. Barry Dierks, deeply involved in the French resistance, used the Château de l'Horizon as one place of rendezvous under the very noses first of the German Army, then of the Gestapo. Jules marched straight back into the house after the Germans had scurried out as the Allies landed, and perhaps it was the spirit of

Maxine—the confident, lucky spirit that said if you dared, all would be well—that enabled him to come out alive without stepping on a land mine that lay within an inch of his foot.

She had left an estate of a million dollars, divided among her family. None of us lived in the Château after her death. It was her house, and I don't believe any of us would have dared give an order in it. Maxine Elliott's Theatre was torn down in 1959 after Mother had already sold her share back to the Shuberts. The Paris flat that Maxine had given me was occupied by White Russian princely squatters during the war, and I could never get it back again; I felt guilty towards her that I had not been cleverer. Recently I found the package of letters that had come from her desk. The letters of thanks from the people of Vallauris poured out; accountings from the mayor of Vallauris; a letter from myself. I read it with fear, but it was all right. It expressed warmth and affection and contained some foolish drawings to amuse her. At last the warmth and affection, dutifully performed at the time, can be truly felt. I might even, if she were alive today, be able to ask her directly if I had come anywhere near the truth about her life. Her reply would probably be a look from those unfathomable, quizzical eyes and her favourite phrase, 'More fools know Tom Fool than Tom Fool knows.'

INDEX OF PERSONS